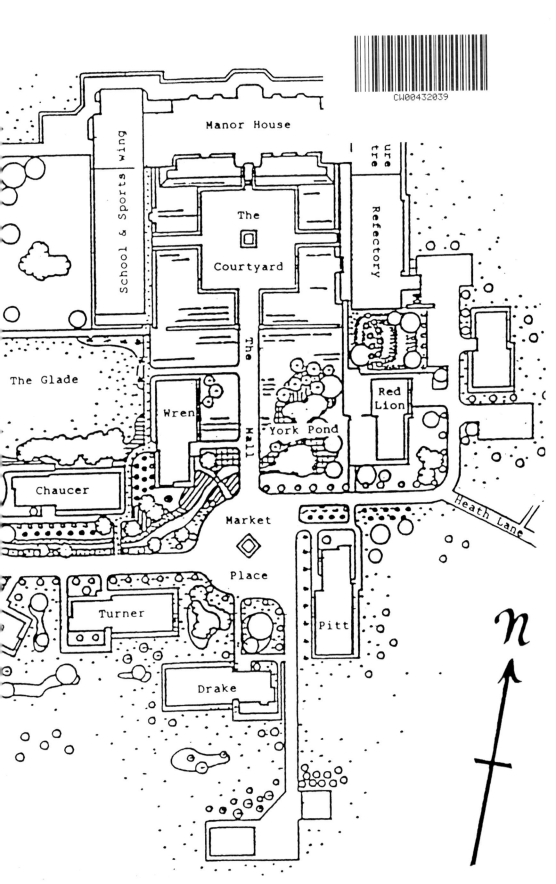

Westbury Meets East

The Butler Did It

(IN JAPAN AND THEREABOUTS)

Peter Westbury

The Pentland Press
Edinburgh – Cambridge – Durham – USA

First published in 2001 by
The Pentland Press Ltd
1 Hutton Close
South Church
Bishop Auckland
Durham

www.pentlandpress.co.uk
sales@pentlandpress.co.uk
manuscripts@pentlandpress.co.uk

ISBN 1-85821-919-1

Typeset in Bell 11 on 13 by
Carnegie Publishing
Carnegie House
Chatsworth Road
Lancaster
www.carnegiepub.co.uk

Printed and bound by
Cromwell Press Ltd
Trowbridge, Wilts

For Donald and Rebecca

Author's Note

To respect their privacy, the names of almost all the characters who populate this book have been changed (as have some of the place-names). One person who merits no such privacy is Sheila Hatch for whose word-processing skills much gratitude is due, though her patience also deserves mention.

There are many others, too, on that far side, whose immense kindness and hospitality can never be repaid. Only a small number of them feature in the book but they are all remembered with gratitude and affection.

Please note the author's claim that only 99.5 per cent of the narrative is true. This declaration allows for half of one per cent to be a matter for conjecture (and no two readers' conclusions are likely to prove identical). It is also a device that enables his mother to continue wearing those powerfully lensed rose-coloured spectacles, dismissing the rude bits as fiction.

In any case, only 99.5 per cent of the rude bits actually happened.

Wiltshire,
January 2001

Peter Westbury

Author's Note

Contents

Westbury Meets East

Prologue

23rd June 1997. Three years ago today I was met at Tokyo's Narita airport by Ben Symons, a Canadian who had recruited me in London to head up the team of native English-speakers to manage an ambitious and exciting Japanese venture, a village built in English architectural styles designed to function partly as a boarding-school and partly as a Five-star hotel with its own Manor House, pub, tea-rooms and so forth.

O N   T H E   *shinkansen* headed north-north-east through Honshu to the southern edge of Fukushima prefecture, Ben, who had lived in Japan for six years and would be in charge of the curriculum planning for the education department, briefed me that every *gaijin* I encountered would be ready with free help and advice on culture shock but that it was his experience that every foreigner working here had to find their 'own' Japan and that mine would be further complicated by the artificiality of our 'English' working environment.

These extracts from my diary pages, my bulletins and character sketches, my compilations and travelogues are an attempt to describe three years of events and encounters, the fun, the frustration, the endearing, the illogical, the generous and the disenchanting. And how I came to wake up this morning under a strange roof, on a *futon*-covered *tatami* floor, next to a pair of slender brown legs.

But I am jumping ahead.

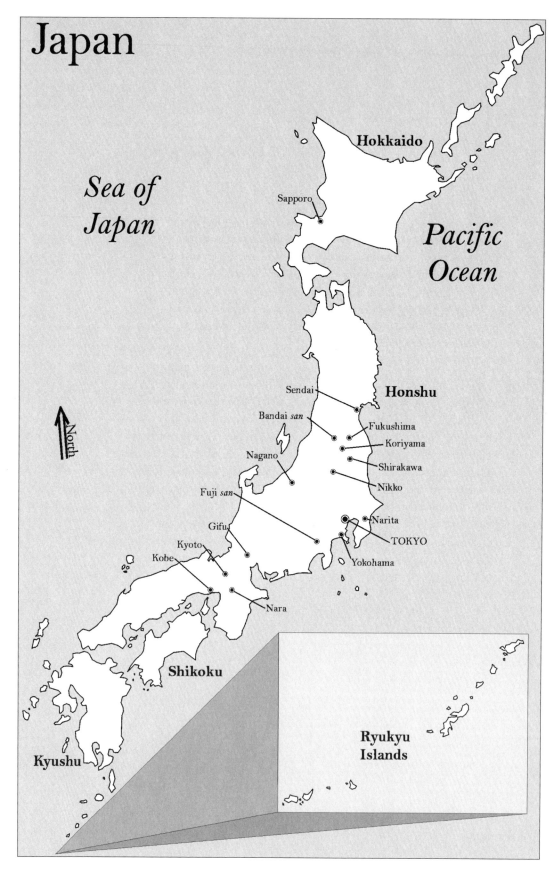

Diary:
Year One
July 1994 to June 1995

Through the Door Marked Wigwam

17th July 1994

TODAY IS MY VERY FIRST DAY OFF (well actually I am on call) since I started work in this extraordinary place 23 days ago and I'm sitting in my *apato* (flat) at my bureau, sipping apricot tea from Mr Luff's Wallingford emporium and trying to summarize my thoughts and first impressions of this artificial concoction of a village, built in a variety of historical British architectural styles from Wealden to Victorian but anachronistically incorporating the very latest in Japanese technology. I was told my lack of Japanese language was not going to place me at a disadvantage but I can already see that communication will be a major problem. I should have picked up on this during the Air France flight out from Charles de Gaulle, Paris when I sat next to a young French-speaking Japanese with whom I could converse. When I asked him to write down his name and address, though, he drew lots of little intricate pictures. More of these hieroglyphics (*kanji*) surrounded me in the Arrivals Hall at Narita where, the flight having arrived 40 minutes early, this bowler-hatted, rolled umbrella-wielding traveller felt both apprehensive and conspicuous while waiting for a friendly western face to appear.

Eventually, Ben Symons, who is in charge of the educational curriculum here, did arrive and escorted me via the Keisei Skyliner rail service to central Tokyo (Ueno station) and thence by 'bullet train' to Shin-Shirakawa where we were met by leather-faced Hamanaka *san*, the chauffeur/caretaker who by virtue of his age does very much as he pleases and seems to run the place. He is also a painfully slow driver, taking 45 minutes to reach Bridewell Heath, a journey time for which 30 minutes is easily achievable and 18 minutes the record, albeit in a Mazda RX7! So now, for anyone determined enough to struggle to this amazing outpost 1,000 metres up a mountain

Westbury Meets East

in Fukushima-*ken*, there you have the prescribed route, roughly 3 hours from the airport if you're lucky with the connections. With a non-stop talker like Ben sitting next to you it passes very quickly. He was generous with his advice and, I'm pretty confident, will prove a useful ally but it was also clear that I was being indoctrinated into the politics of this new work arena, just short of being brain-washed.

The subject of a large part of that conversation was the Director-General, Mikada *san*, and it was he who officially welcomed me, in over-perfect, well-rehearsed, phrases full of bluster and distinctly over-the-top. In fact his name, his manner, everything about him, says 'Gilbert & Sullivan'. Here is a Lord High Everything-Else, the Great Panjandrum, head-hunted from Mitsubishi Corporation. His style is decidedly theatrical/military; he carries a swagger cane. His patter is borrowed from movies of the thirties and forties and he treats this project like a battle campaign, finding analogies in European history to endorse his tactics for the way forward. All of which would be very impressive were it not distractingly punctuated by the random body noises escaping from a faulty anal sphincter of which he seems totally unaware. Much of one's concentration is therefore focused on avoiding eye contact with one's colleagues, judging the moment when it is safe to laugh with him, not at him, thereby releasing the build-up of tension. The President, Sako *san*, far quieter in manner and with no English at all, was also, unexpectedly, present. [This was to prove the pattern for the future, his unannounced arrivals almost certainly deliberate, but then this is very much his bat and ball.] I wondered what their initial impression was of the weary jet-lagged me: not the ramrod-backed Sir John Gielgud (*Arthur*) nor the controlled Sir Anthony Hopkins (*Remains of the Day*); not, I hope, Stephen Fry's pompous Jeeves. We shall see. Some play-acting seems inevitable . . .

It was the mother of Sako *san* who had the brilliant idea for this incredible hill-top phenomenon. Her original concept was for a training-centre to be built in Japan, modelled on a British boarding-school, designed with cultural and recreational courses in mind and not solely for language tuition. Young Japanese students who could not afford the air fare to Europe would then be able to experience the 'culture shock' of visiting a foreign

Peter Westbury

This page and following pages: Bridewell Heath Village, views and interiors.

'country' within their own just two hours from the centre of Tokyo. She and her husband set up the Sako Foundation to administer a university and a language school but she died before the third part of her plan could be realized. It was their son who took inspiration from her dream and then expanded the notion, commissioning a team of British architects to produce a design for a whole village. That was a 6-year process followed by 18 months of construction. In Hereford and Worcester, ten enormous half-timbered frame houses were built by a local specialist. These were dismantled, the parts numbered and coded, packed and shipped to Japan. A Japanese construction company with experience in preparing earthquake-proof foundations was entrusted with the re-erection of the buildings – a Pub, a Craft House/tea-rooms, four Guest Houses and four Student 'Dormitory' Houses – under British supervision. In addition, there is a mock Manor House complete with battlements and flagstaff, a huge Refectory and Kitchen wing, Lecture Theatre, indoor pool and gymnasium. Tennis courts and a croquet lawn make up the outdoor sports facilities.

None of the preliminary drawings that I had been shown at interview had prepared me for this amazing achievement. To criticize the unrealistic scale of the buildings and their newness is to be nit-picking and ungracious. They will never be authentic in spite of the colossal expense and expertise involved but, as I said to one of the TV reporters, 'Come back in a few years when the ivy has grown over us and earthquakes have given character to the roof trusses and we shall have begun to resemble the real thing.' Authenticity is not helped by the installation of much sophisticated Japanese technology, quite unbelievable, some of it, as well as operationally complicated and the instruction booklets still in *kanji*. Buttons, switches and sensors control everything from the pump that gets the stream going to the window-openers, from the heated loo-seats to the urinal jets and I have requested an interpreter to translate all the gadgetry in my apartment never mind the office.

Engaged to head up the English-speaking staff at Bridewell Heath, it was thought an advantage for me to arrive ahead of the others to familiarize myself with my new surroundings and so forth. The

Year One: July 1994 to June 1995

'and so forth' part has been very much more to their advantage than to mine as, early on the scene, I have provided another pair of hands for the unloading and unpacking of truck-load upon truck-load of late deliveries of furniture and light fittings from America. In parenthesis, I console myself that they are an expensive pair of hands as I am now on the pay roll. The American suppliers landed the contract because, coupled with the fact that they had the copyright on reproducing many of the specified furniture styles, they gave every assurance that they would deliver on time. The British contenders played fair with delivery quotations and lost. So it was that literally within hours of Opening Day, the vast expanse of the Refectory floor still resembled an indoor dry ski school with great drifts of white polystyrene packing material up to sill height. Each building is being furnished and accessorized to match the individual historic period. Estimates of the inclusive cost of this project (Phase One!) are in the region of $22 million. The extravagance is such that 'tax loss' springs to the cynical mind.

Here on a hastily arranged 90-day visa, I learned a few days ago that my Work Visa application has been successful. I'm in. For me it's the door marked wigwam [入口], entry. Mind you, I have first to go through the door marked cactus [出口], exit, on my way to Korea, the nearest neighbour to Japan where I may have the visa stamped before I can return through the door marked wigwam to be legally employed here for up to one year. That is, if I survive the probation period. [For several days on end I seriously began to doubt whether I should be pleased about the visa approval. Still in culture shock, frustrated through lack of proper communications, unable to get my systems in place, no decisions without interminable meetings, tentatively feeling my way with the gang from Tokyo Office (the hierarchy who say they want the place run in British style . . . but not really); I was half way into my resignation letter before I started to think more positively.] At that stage, they provide me with foreigners' protection plan insurance cover against earthquakes and similar previously unmentioned accidental but customary natural hazards. Which reminds me: yesterday I surprised my first snake in the wild (more accurate to say it surprised me), about a metre long, greeny bronze, a poisonous variety.

A typical day should start with my alarm clock at 5 a.m. But cock crow or cuckoo song or the barking of Hamanaka *san*'s dogs outside the apartment immediately below mine take turns to wake me at irregular intervals considerably earlier than this. The dogs are disturbed by the hitherto unadvertized presence of brown bears in the surrounding woodland. To be fair, there is a warning notice (but in *kanji*) that when translated reveals that two bears were sighted and shot here last autumn. Neither snakes nor bears will feature in our promotional literature.

I meet the first of the 'work holiday' staff going on duty at 6 a.m. to open the water spa for the benefit of any early morning swimmers; then the Food Services personnel come on to set up for guests' breakfast in the Refectory. This is an area that seats up to 132 which seems to be an error of calculation since we have accommodation to sleep 182. There is a rostrum at one end for speeches and so on, a Minstrels' Gallery and a VIP balcony for special guests to dine and wine in splendour – by which I mean off Minton bone china and out of solid silver goblets. The first receptionist goes to the Entrance Hall for an 8 a.m. start and the House swings into action. As well as containing the Operations Centre, a large windowless office positioned out of sight of the guests, and other rooms with desks for the senior Japanese officers with inappropriately grand-sounding job-titles, there are an Armoury, a Trophy Room (both erroneously named as they contain neither), the 'Royal' bed-chambers (both lavishly over-furnished suites described as representing private rooms at Windsor Castle or Buckingham Palace), a magnificent Library designed to look like the interior of a reading-room in a St James' gentlemen's Club and containing 1,600 antique books, a Snooker Room with bar and three Thurston tables, a Chapel with four stained glass panels, plus a grand staircase leading past more stained glass and carved panels to the Upper Hall and Portrait Gallery. All this is in my charge.

We are now in the throes of three successive Opening Days being held on three consecutive Saturdays with a ceremony at noon, partially of my own devising. Each group is of the mistaken belief that they are first over the threshold and we shall say nothing to correct that illusion. Even the first group will not be strictly the first ones in as we have already held a reception for all the contractors. Heavily influenced by America, the Japanese are very strong on razzmatazz, very un-British: tape-cutting, cheerleaders, that sort of thing. I sought to present a more dignified approach and, after the silver band had stopped playing, offered a short welcome address (in English, of course) and a ceremonial rapping upon the Tudor-arched double doors of the portal at the top of the stone steps. The doors would be opened, the flag raised and

Peter Westbury

the invited guests led by Jack in his kilt and with unsheathed sabre through the Hall and up the staircase to the Champagne buffet. This all received approval but was *additional* to the aforementioned razzmatazz and a whole string of speeches. As my part required me to be in position from noon onwards and as cloudless skies produced temperatures in excess of 30 degrees, I wasn't sure whether I was going to melt before I passed out or vice versa. In my three-piece wool-worsted morning suit with gloves I was cooked. The gloves were to disguise the improvised knuckle-duster I used to knock on the door, giving the required resonance which my enthusiastic rapping during practice failed to produce. I still have the bruises. The Japanese insistence on rehearsals timed by stopwatch counted for very little on the day because we are becoming resigned to the fact that it seems to be in their nature to want to make eleventh hour and fifty-ninth minute alterations to the agreed schedule. I sometimes think the behind-the-scene panics would inspire the Fawlty Towers writers but, so far, from the guests' viewpoint at any rate, everything appears to have run smoothly.

We have had a number of VIPs to dine, mostly foreign academics or business associates of the President, so far, plus our first week-long seminar for students (mature ones). Most of my problems arise from the place being open sooner than we are ready. The contractors handed over the keys and BANG we were expected to be up and running. That was on the first of July. We are still receiving daily the backlog of delivery shortages and breakage replacements and because we are short-staffed (just 13 Australian 'work holiday' boys and girls – very willing, mostly, but very raw and laid back about everything) we are diverted from setting up our procedures to unload vehicles and break open packing-cases and, ten to one, report more damages. I have been lucky to get to bed by midnight. It can only get better.

By contrast, on this my first day 'off', I took an early morning swim and *jacuzzi* and a walk through the woodland comprising acers, cedars, sweet chestnuts, wild irises and lace-cap hydrangeas, to where I came upon a Celtic cross, brand spanking new, imported by Mikada *san* from England! They are trying. I wrote letters most of the morning and then went to the 'Red Lion', our pub, for staff brunch. Tonight we have planned a barbecue for all staff – we do need to build bridges with the Japanese after some frustrated outbursts over the last few days.

There are several events looming in the coming months

Westbury Meets East

View westwards from Bridewell Heath at sunset.

including Press Release Day which has the Japanese in a flap. I do wish they'd let us handle it but I suppose this place is very much their 'baby' and they've been nursing it along for 6 years or more. They are almost as pre-occupied with the weather as a topic as we English. This mountain location enjoys, if that's the right word, a micro-climate; at this altitude we have not suffered so badly during this humid season though it has been bad enough, showering and changing shirts three times a day and the ironing does pile up. We have had reports of 40 degrees Celsius in Tokyo and humidity exceeding 80%. The publican, first in the queue for the visa-stamping trip to Korea, has returned from Seoul reporting 110%! I hope that changes before my own visit next month. For one week we were shrouded in hill mist which really gave the village a spooky atmosphere. But on bright days the cloud formations are unlike anything I've seen before and from the roof of the Manor House you can see mountain scenery for almost 360 degrees and the sunsets have been dramatic. My favourite view, though, is to the north over an irregular shaped lake. Could be Scotland, if you squint a bit; but Scotland's a very long way away.

View northwards from Bridewell Heath across Lake Hatori: high summer, low water. Could be Scotland 'if you squint a bit'.

❀ ❀ ❀

5th September 1994

I am hurtling through Tochigi and Saitama on the 'bullet train' (only it's not called that in Japan; it's the *shinkansen*), southbound from Shin-Shirakawa to Ueno, Tokyo where I change to another train for Narita airport.

No – I'm not on my way home! I am on a delayed visit to Seoul where an embassy official will stamp my visa allowing me to stay in Japan for up to one year. Tinkly music is a prelude to recorded announcements advising passengers of the identity of the next station. I'd like to meet the lady responsible for the English version; she sounds delightful; I wonder if she irons shirts.

The last time I travelled this section of the JR system was also the first. I had Chef for company and we had been invited to Tokyo to attend a luncheon buffet function at the Imperial Hotel where the Group that included the Japanese firm of architects contracted to supervise the building of BH was celebrating its centenary. Even Chef's customary Gallic arrogance dissolved and he admitted it was an impressive affair.

I had never witnessed such large-scale catering and the presentation was superb, the service excellent. It was intended that we should see the tops in Japanese hospitality and style. The tables, the staff, everything was immaculate. Every kind of cuisine was displayed and, in spite of the heat, massive ice-carvings. The only surprise was that we had to ask especially for vodka to accompany the caviar. Playing chamber music was a miniature orchestra (well, everybody's on the short side here!) and I couldn't believe my ears when the room filled with the *Andante* from Mozart's Piano Concerto No. 21 – I was convinced it had been specially requested. How presumptuous!

We had been escorted by Ayako Matsunaga, Sako *san*'s extremely personal assistant, a powerful lady who has been really helpful acting as a go-between, translating messages from myself to our mutual boss. This has, to some extent, alienated Mikada *san* who refers to her as Madame Pompadour, so I shall have to be careful. She next took us down to the waiting chauffeur-driven limousine to be whisked off to our associated Language Institute and also the University from both of which we are due to expect students in great numbers from mid-September to late December.

I think we made all the right noises. In any case we were treated to a nine-course supper in a French-style restaurant

Westbury Meets East

One of many 'opening' ceremonies conducted from the Manor House steps — the Mike, the Meatball and the Union Jack.

later, at which point Chef was just beginning to realize the nature of the exercise. Anyway, from there we progressed to the Ginza, a blend of Mayfair and Montmartre; Ayako introduced us to some bars and it got very late ...

The diary of events through July and August has blurred somewhat into a series of deadlines and panics. In the end we had several 'Opening Days' — it became a set-piece. On each occasion, at noon precisely, I would find myself looking down on the crowd assembled around the life-size bronze statue of a seated William Shakespeare in the courtyard below the Manor House steps, perspiring profusely (me, not Shakespeare) in my tails, giving the welcome speech and then rapping three times upon the door as signal for the porters to open up. The Japanese staff insisted that I used a microphone and I was temporarily flattered that the audience might want to hear what I was saying, but not at all: it was only to amplify the sound of my 'knuckles' on the wood. The throng would follow me up the staircase, past Jack Rouse (my second in command, a Geordie and a hoot) in highland costume with his sabre at the 'Present arms' trying hard to avoid eye contact (it's all such a farce) and onwards to the Bollinger. Thus we survived two Gala Openings, an Organ Recital, Press Day, an Open Day for local dignitaries, Contractors' Day and Alumni Day, though at this remove I could not distinguish one from the other nor swear that I have the order right. We worked long hours but enjoyed a lot of job satisfaction to help counteract the tiredness and frustration with our Japanese colleagues.

Peter Westbury

Visits from the media have also taken up a lot of my time. I 'went out' live in a local TV interview which was an unforgettable 'first' for me. The interviewer was a very dishy young lady with her own show and a young audience. I would have expected her to have been accustomed to the pressure of the job but she seemed more nervous than I and so we spent a lot of time hamming it up between rehearsals which helped her to relax. Her director seemed pleased with the result and I have subsequently featured in a 30-second commercial for the same channel. We also recorded a promotional video due to be broadcast on the 15th September.

I've just transferred to the Skyliner service out to the airport, retracing the journey Ben and I made when, jet-lagged, I arrived in Japan. I feel quite pleased with myself for finding my way because it is quite definitely a challenge everytime you emerge on to the street, your eyes peeled for helpful directions among all the hieroglyphics. Anyway I made it with three minutes to spare.

Narita Airport Departure Lounge and there's forty minutes to boarding, enough time to jot down a few observations on rail travel. The Japanese are very uncomfortable unless there is a system to govern their behaviour. It doesn't even need to be a good system for it is not in their nature to question the *status quo*. The fact that they are familiar with it is enough and in the case of the procedure of making a railway journey the system is actually brilliant, based as it is on the perfectly justified assumption that every train will not only arrive precisely on time but at exactly the same stopping point on the platform. On main line railways, platforms are marked with colour-coded lines and numbers so that waiting passengers know where to queue in orderly fashion. Those with reserved seats can read their car number off the ticket. On the *shinkansen* and certain other express services, you will have received two tickets for each journey; one is a receipt for paying the flat rate and the other for the surcharge levied for the superior service. You can check the number of cars, which varies from 8 to 16 on most lines, from the ever-changing timetable display signs, each train identifiable by name and number, e.g. *AOBA* 123, alternating with its *kanji* version and it is then possible to work out where to stand to board the appropriate car whose (usual) two entrances will line up exactly with the numbers painted near the platform's edge. Reserved seats guarantee you a seat in your choice of smoking or non-smoking compartment, usually placed in the central section of the train. Unreserved seats

Westbury Meets East

are often at the front and/or rear of the train but your ticket does not guarantee you a seat. It is therefore more important for holders of these tickets to arrive early and wait where the door-ways to the unreserved cars will arrive. The non-smoking cars will arrive opposite the internationally recognizable signs on the platform pillars. Once you've got the hang of it, it's brilliant. Unfortunately, there remain certain pitfalls and it is not unknown for Japanese travellers to struggle. It is worth knowing, for example, that some platforms receive both 'Up' and 'Down' services! Knowing the departure time alone to identify your platform number is not sufficient; the complexity of networks means that there may well be another line operating to a very different destination but with the identical departure time. With less traffic than on the line you actually need, that departure may be advertised on a display board that sends you in a totally wrong direction! Only earthquakes disrupt the precision-run timetable. By checking your due arrival time against your wristwatch from time to time, you should ensure that you alight at the correct destination. Most stations display their name in both *kanji* and *romaji* (Roman alphabet) but 'a certain gentleman's law' says that the *romaji* sign will never line up with your train window.

One of our teaching staff went off on a jaunt recently to Nagoya. On his return journey he discovered he was mistakenly travelling west. He changed trains at the earliest opportunity and half an hour later found himself heading even further west.

I do most seriously recommend the carrying of a compass and memorizing the *kanji* for 'north', 'south', 'east' and 'west' (*kita, minami, higashi* and *nishi* respectively in *romaji*).

Travelling around locally is not so difficult as my contract provides for access to a vehicle and I can choose from the BH pool. Mostly I drive the Mitsubishi '*Pajero*' (a 4WD Range Rover style of car) but when I'm just driving around on site I use the '*Toppo*'. This is more of a cartoonist's idea of a car and great fun to drive. It has a little recessed shelf in its domed roof that is the perfect shape for my bowler hat. These two vehicles plus two Mitsubishi '*Chareiyos*' and a 25-seater bus (all in distinctive BH livery – Lincoln Green with coats of arms on the front near and off side doors) plus an ancient hand-me-down 'Lancer' and a clapped-out flat bed truck make up the BH fleet. Add in the '*Cima*' for ferrying VIPs and you have the complete picture. We are expecting delivery of a bull-dozer, a 'JCB' type grab which is sure to come in bright green or pink or purple, and a snow plough. We are preparing a large

Peter Westbury

H for the croquet lawn in case supplies have to be helicoptered in come the winter.

I was stopped by the police at a road-check late at night recently in sleazy Koriyama and I'm going to have to do something about a driving licence. They are not at all convinced by my British one which I have to agree is unimpressive and has no corroborative photograph. The President's son, an absolute plonker who has some high-ranking job description on our staff, was with me at the time but he is not particularly Japanese-looking – more Filipino, I'd say – and he preferred to pretend not to understand the policemen who eventually waved us on. In theory, driving here is on the left [but see Westbury's Alternative Guide to Japan – 'All Over the Road']. This came as a surprise considering, once again, the strong American influence upon the country but then this is to ignore the Anglo-Japanese *entente* dating from the mid-Victorian era.

The mountain roads are great fun with their hairpin bends; I may alter that opinion when the snows come.

At 30,000 feet in this United Airlines DC10 minding my own business, whose voice should come through the headphones but that of Pat O'Shaunessy with his Men of Shamrock – dear old Peter Sellers and his 'mind me harp' number. Quite surreal in these surroundings. You'd have thought the airline would have provided some Seoul music.

Seoul approach. A group of high-rise very flat flats resemble giant tombstones in the sunlight. Once inside the airport buildings you could be anywhere in the world. The limousine bus service delivered me into the city centre just in time for me to miss the Embassy opening hours so I shall have to go back when they re-open tomorrow. The streets are really crowded and there's a massive security cordon around the US Embassy. I'll take a wander after supper; if Seoul is remotely like Tokyo there should be a real buzz in the evening and I'm told the shops are open round the clock. Prices in Japan are so horrendous that I've changed some *yen* into *won* in the hope of buying some off-duty but smartish trousers. I must have lost a stone in two and a half months and with it has gone half a collar size. So, white shirts, too. And I badly need a haircut.

After shopping that evening, I found a jazz club called 'Elle' in a basement, phonetically close to the truth and then decided boringly but prudently to return to the hotel. Jack, on the visa trail the week before, had fallen in with a Korean TV crew and in to a fountain . . .

Westbury Meets East

Body and Seoul

6th September 1994

MY BUSINESS AT THE Japanese Embassy completed, I set about my quest for a haircut and finished up having two! The first one was so good that I went back afterwards and had another one. It did say 'BARBER SHOP' on the outside of the establishment; perhaps something was lost in translation (or gained more likely). The team consisted of the barber and his two female assistants, the one a slim attractive 19-year old, the second a much older broken-toothed pithecanthropoid. I had prepared two silhouette drawings of my head: one with the stepped effect at the nape (which I hate and had marked with an X) and the other with the preferred tapered finish (marked with a tick). Nods all round.

So far so good. Now I did get the haircut but if I explain that it all began with the young girl washing my feet!... This was followed by a manicure, the clipping of nostril hairs and the removal of ear wax; a thorough tune and de-coke by blissfully gentle caring hands. She then adjusted the chair to the reclining position and turned out the light, placing a hot towel over my face. Soft, relaxing music. The massage that followed, starting with my feet became gradually more interesting and varied as it progressed northwards. Finally, the hot towel was removed and I opened my eyes to see the grinning face of the hag with bad teeth! At some stage they had switched! The barber then took over, contriving, against the odds, to disguise my thinning patch so that by the time he'd done I appeared to have more hair on top than when I came in.

For this I was disproportionately grateful because it all collapsed later. The experience cost me 40,000 *won* – just a little more than a tenner each for the hour and a half that it had taken – not bad at all when some ladies of my past acquaintance spend all that and more for a hairdo alone. Recalling the expressions on their faces when I called back later for the 'same again' . . . absolutely priceless!

Peter Westbury

Evening. Deprived, back on the mountain, of much that I used to enjoy by way of music, theatre and the arts, I was thrilled to have obtained a ticket for this evening's concert by the Seoul Philharmonic. I was to hear that Seoul music, after all. It has been a great treat, Beethoven's Violin Concerto plus Holst's 'Planets', an accidental choice on my part identified only at the time of performance since the programme and all the advertising posters were incomprehensible. The intermission was filled by a very funny man on the stage showing abstract looking slides of planets with an uproarious commentary. He had the audience convulsed. Without understanding a word he was saying, I found myself laughing out loud at his sounds and gestures alone! What a wonderful gift.

27th September 1994

After a few fraught weeks since the Seoul trip, I'm sitting today in my little sectioned off office wondering what on earth can happen next. The 'phone rings and it is one of my Reception staff who we released from duty so that she could meet her parents in Hong Kong for a few days. She is calling from Immigration, Narita, where they are giving her a hard time. She has made the mistake of leaving Japan without first obtaining a re-entry visa and has spent the day negotiating for a temporary visa which will only give her 12 days in which to restore the *status quo*. She's from Australia and the only way she will be able to continue working in Japan to complete her contract with us will be for her to fly to Melbourne and re-apply for a new work-holiday visa! It's unlikely she'll want to spend that sort of money on the return fare and I see little prospect of replacing her, which will leave us short-staffed in an already very stretched situation with students now pouring through the place at the rate of 120 or so for 3 days twice a week! BH has really come to life and for the purpose for which it was intended.

Outnumbering the boys by four to one, the girls, unexpectedly tall, many of them, with amazing continuous legs, are a grievous distraction to my male Australian staff (and others!) who cannot believe their luck. The teachers, who had been complaining of being under-occupied, as well as my hospitality staff (who had been complaining of the teachers being under-occupied), are now drooping from over-work and lack of sleep. The senior Japanese staff seem surprised that segregating the students by sex into separate so-called 'dormitory' accommodation has proved so ineffectual. Even the fact that it is entirely comprised of twin-bedded rooms has done nothing to deter the enthusiastic nocturnal traffic between the houses after 'lights out' although it has, arguably, reduced the actual size of the orgies. With the students' all-night partying, the resident house-masters and house-mistresses, whose private rooms, they will confirm, are by no means sound-proof, look every bit as haggard in the morning as the participants who have been having a high old time.

Part of my own role is to be involved in the syllabus, teaching, with only a modicum of success, western-style etiquette and table manners and voted the single most boring lesson in the entire curriculum, against some pretty stiff competition, I might add. To be perfectly fair, though, I cannot, in the circumstances, take sole blame for the level of somnolence which is by no means exclusive to my classes. It is totally predictable that the boys will fall asleep and in so doing become the butt of my humour. The girls seem more receptive or, at any rate, more polite. I am also involved at meal times in the Refectory, especially in the evenings when, before supper is served, I lead the short procession of teachers – Ben, his wife Amanda, Harold, Angus, Susan and Liz – through the long tables of standing students to the High Table and to say grace. If this is what we are here for, to reproduce the tradition and daily routine of a British boarding-school, then this is what they will get.

'You and I need to talk.' It's the publican. What is it about the man that makes me inwardly groan? Is it the chip on each shoulder or the pole-axing combination of tobacco-smoke and cheap aftershave that precedes his appearance by several seconds; or is it the fact that there is not a single occupation at which he is not an experienced expert? He reminds me of a brother-in-law I once had. 'What is it, Fred?' It seems one of his staff has been appointed to teach the students how to play snooker. When helping the girls he is allowing his hands to wander. 'I think you should say sunnink to the bloke.' Thanks, Fred. Nothing in the Butlers' Course Manual on how to deal with *that*!

Peter Westbury

The Director-General puts his head round the door to complain of shortness of breath and tightness round his heart. He has been punishing himself lately with liberal doses of Laphroaig and cigarettes, a clear case of stress. Will he survive? Late one evening, he and I were last leaving the 'Red Lion' and fell into step on our mutual way to the Residence where we are next-door neighbours. With Mikada *san* on trumpet and myself on drums (or it may have been the other way round), we simulated military marching music all the way home, errant notes from his anal sphincter contributing to the volume if not the actual tempo and a surprisingly high proportion of them in tune. Hardly a bum note, one might say. [You were ahead of me, yes?] Other instruments of the band were improvised at whim. I think this is the procedure known these days as bonding. I don't think we were seen.

He is an extremely colourful character, whatever Ben says about his harrumphing, highly anglicized and mostly disrespectful of his Japanese colleagues whom he accuses of having no pedigree, he having an aristocratic background himself. At every opportunity he refers to the national flag as 'The Meatball'. For each event or mishap that occurs here he finds a parallel in European military history. Our vehicles are 'panzer cars', his own a 'cable wagon'. I do not argue with those who say he offers no direction only bombast but I find myself liking him because he is trying so hard to play the part even if it turns out to be the Duke of Plaza-Toro. We have fixed appointments for him with the heart specialist in downtown Shirakawa and we shall have to await the verdict. Not that I would want his office in preference to my little cubby-hole. The President's is much more to my taste.

A disapproving cut-glass voice answers the 'phone; 'Yes?'

'Is it convenient to speak to Pamela Farquhar?'

'Who wants her?'

'My name is Westbury – I'm the Butler Administrator at Bridewell Heath.'

[Still hostile.] 'Speaking.'

'I believe you and I have booked the same soprano for a recital next month and therefore share the same concern in that the Japanese Consulate in London is making it very difficult for her to obtain a visa?!'

'Yes, the poor love was on the 'phone in tears only an hour ago.'

'Well, she gave me your telephone number and I thought

Westbury Meets East

you'd like to know that I've just been speaking to our Embassy here and the Minister has promised to speak to the Consul in London direct and supply a letter to help smooth the way through Immigration, etc . . .'

[Now gushing.] '. . . etc . . . etc. Well, Peter, Thank you so much, it's been lovely talking to you. Do speak to Daphne if you're interested in booking the *Così fan tutte* and, by the way, I should drop the 'Butler' bit and just use 'Administrator' – sounds so much better, don't you think?!'

'"Butler" has served me very well so far, thank you Madame.'

Little madame!

Since returning from Korea I've been to New Zealand and back on the recruiting trip to replace the Aussies who the Japanese directors have found too laid back. Everything went according to plan, very largely due to the terrific co-operation from the Department of Hotel & Restaurant Studies at Auckland's Institute of Technology who could not have been more help-ful nor more hospitable. I am hopeful of welcoming 17 Kiwis to Bridewell Heath in December provided the Board agrees with my proposals. More meetings, I suppose, followed by a last-minute decision.

It was a real bonus to be able to visit my married daughter while in NZ and to be introduced to the BYO system whereby you buy the wine of your preference (at off-licence prices) and take it to the restaurant of your choice, a pretty sure-fire formula.

I was thinking, on the flight back to Narita, what a relief it is when the air stewardesses (although they are all flight atten-dants now – that is, if they're not Cabin Service Directors) have safely removed the debris that forms by far the largest com-ponent on any airline picnic tray. But you know very well that, sooner or later, due to the law of averages, you will be the victim of turbulence. [I have a question: is turbulence the oppo-site of flatulence?!] So. It happened.

The almost untouched gin-and-tonic that had been on the fold-out table next to mine, suddenly became airborne, helped by the idiot in the next seat, and my shirt absorbed most of it. Totally drenched was I and to much hilarity from the near vicinity. Why is it the human reflex (if that's not too generous an appraisal of the jerk sitting next to me) to raise the liquid

Peter Westbury

high in the air to avoid spillage, when actually lowering the glass to the floor would render it harmless and at the same time cut out the entertainment value.

Back in the *apato*, nothing had changed. More shirts to add to the pile. Nothing exciting in the post. At the beginning of the month I wrote to three hot-air balloonists on the BBAC list in the hope of getting back into the sport. Each was fairly local to Fukushima. I'll just have to give them longer.

19th October 1994

For any *gaijin* coming to work in Japan – an introduction to banking, beginning with a useful tip: try to have your wages paid to you directly in cash. At Bridewell Heath, senior staff salaries are paid into personal accounts at the local branch of the Fukushima bank in Shirakawa. Getting at your money is not an easy matter nor one for the meek in spirit. While the intention may be to be helpful, banks (in common with manufacturers of cars and electrical appliances) favour *kawaii* (cute – a word one hears a lot) cartoon characters to illustrate instruction leaflets and brochures. Accordingly, when you go to draw money from an ATM, there are small children and animals romping on the screen to guide you through the stages, as if coping with the hieroglyphics was not challenge enough. Notes in Japan come in the following denominations: 1,000, 5,000 and 10,000 *yen*. You don't get much for 1,000 *yen* so it seems easiest to plan withdrawals in multiples of 10,000 *yen*. Punch in the sum you've decided, but hit the wrong instruction button and you finish up with, for example, thirty 1,000 *yen* notes instead of three 10,000 *yen* notes. You should have hit the button marked with a gothic 'h'. In theory you could feed the thirty notes back into the machine and start again but don't let's go into that here. In case you thought differently, this service is not open 24 hours but only for a few hours extra to weekday banking hours in the early evening and for part of the weekend, a recent facility. When you try to transfer funds out of Japan there is also a real conspiracy to make this difficult. The concept of the 'Standing Order' is either not known or they simply do not want to grasp it. [Perhaps it is too difficult to interpret in a cartoon sequence.] So each month, or however frequently you require, you must

Westbury Meets East

make a visit in person to the branch, complete a form, wait while it is checked and then hope that the exchange rate has been set for the day. Whenever you time your visit ... the exchange rate will be decided in 'about an hour from now'. Add together the time in the bank to the travelling time up and down the mountain and it is easy for the procedure to take half your day off. A telegraphic transfer currently works out at £38.00 a throw in bank charges. A cheque-book facility is totally unknown and as *gaijin* we are not entitled to a Bank Credit Card. I shall never criticize English banks again.

21st October 1994

Today I was informed, by a grown male colleague with moist eyes and a lump in his throat, that promenaders at the Albert Hall have just celebrated the 100th anniversary of the Last Night at the Proms. I do have to agree – that 'Land of Hope and Glory' really gets to you ... more than ever when you're abroad. Back in July for our Gala Opening Concert in front of invited guests we presented a performance by Carlo Curley, the world famous organist. During his rendering of 'Pomp & Circumstance' I had to leave the Hall for fear of losing my composure. [With him, incidentally, he brought a funny little chap to tune the organ; I labelled them 'Shorty and Curley'.]

The media continue to be drawn to this anomalous village and a Channel 4 freelance crew have been nosing around with their cameras. Apparently they were here a year ago during construction and I understand they expect to transmit the total compilation in the UK some time in November. The Beeb, too, is sending a team next week to interview the Director-General and myself. Another group calling themselves Planet 24 have also threatened to give us some coverage on one channel or another back home. Journalists appear out of the half-timbers, as it were, and the working day is constantly interrupted by these very agreeable diversions but which leave one catching up with routine matters late at night. However, I did manage to escape for a whole day earlier this week on a most beautiful autumn day. I drove up into the Ura-Bandai, a National Park named after the mountain that erupted in 1888, transforming the local terrain, burying whole villages and damming local rivers to create numerous lakes and ponds. A group of

Peter Westbury

these known as Goshikinuma (Five coloured lakes, really no bigger than ponds) are usually tourist-ridden but my timing must have been lucky.

Away from this popular beauty spot and after an hour's hill-climbing, I reached the top of a mountain and unexpectedly came upon a lake. And I had this tranquil scene all to myself. Pleased I had packed a picnic lunch in my daysack, I settled to devour my victuals in the sunshine, remembering to keep my eyes peeled for bears – there had been some warning pictures on the trail's edge. No harm befell me except that, forgetting my manners and eating with enthusiasm, I managed to trap half of my inner left cheek between my upper and lower molars; and then did the very same thing again within a few seconds. 'Loyfe, y'know, can be a bit loyke that!'

We have a hefty looking winter schedule ahead. The soprano/harp recital next week heralds the first festive programme. We were hopeful that the President would approve our proposals for a truly traditional English Christmas. Unfortunately he liked the plans so much that it will be Christmas Day on *five* consecutive weekends throughout December. Some of these, as well as the de Rothschild concert will be edge to edge with the 'business as usual' student invasions by the hundred plus.

We shall be on our knees!

26th October 1994

It's 9.30 p.m. and I should be ironing shirts but instead I'm unwinding with the help of a G and T and *The Boyfriend* soundtrack which always lifts my spirits. It has been an amazing week and it's only Wednesday. I've lost count of the number of radio microphones that have been threaded up my waistcoat as a result of the media onslaught. They've all been tripping over each other, cameras and lighting cables everywhere, TV and radio and newspaper journalists desperately trying to out-slant one another in original angles on this phenomenon called Bridewell Heath and, as for the butler, he's too good a target to miss. So, whether it's the BBC or Nationwide Asahi TV or Transatlantic Radio or the *Daily Telegraph*, they all want part of the action. As the Japanese have a problem with saying 'No, I regret that won't be possible' they say 'Yes, of course, I'm sure he'll be pleased to' and I am reduced to a very fixed grin. It would be misleading to give the impression that I'm not enjoying it all but it has been stressful to an extent (I've never had to handle anything like this before) and I also worry about the power of these people to put words into your mouth and to edit the material to suit their own prejudice. I suppose it can be regarded as fortunate that they never seem able to get your name right. I've only seen one piece of accurate reporting so far – by Yoko Mizui for the *Yomiuri Shinbun.* [It is perhaps worth quoting from this article, dated 5th September 1994, the words of our President: 'People say that this facility is too luxurious for students – they tell me I could make money if we operated the place as a resort facility. But I have no intention of making money from Bridewell Heath. This place may never see a profit but I don't mind. I just want to educate students so that they can become as much as possible internationally-minded people.' Taking six billion *yen* to build, a fifth of which came from the Fukushima government to help boost the local economy, somebody is surely going to want to see a return on the investment.] The three minutes coverage on BBC1 Breakfast TV was condensed from one and a half days of shooting. The one playing the part of the haggard old man so realistically... was me! Those few seconds were repeated on BBC World Service so I got to see myself and rather wished I hadn't. They left the good bits out – no sign of 'Hello to Mum and Dad in Shepton Mallet!'

'Pure Hi-de-Hi'

The press cuttings file is growing fast. Some of the photos are pure 'Hi-de-Hi'!

27th October 1994

Mayhem! A call from Auckland to report a hitch in the work-holiday visa application process for the 17 New Zealanders. It will be catastrophic if they fail. The non-arrival of the wine order, a find from Pauillac with 'de Rothschild' on the label to coincide with Saturday's performance by Charlotte de Rothschild, pales into insignificance by comparison. Crises line up here for my attention, one after the other, pole position constantly changing. If this development with the New Zealanders is unresolvable I might as well pack my bags . . . as soon as they release me from the sanatorium.

31st October 1994

We have been justifiably basking in the after-glow of Saturday's concert (the wine did arrive – that morning). Total credit *should* go to the charming and talented Charlotte de Rothschild whose programme was delightful. Accompanied by the harpist, David Watkins, he of the divine waistcoats, she treated the audience of mainly *glitterati* from Tokyo to a selection of music linked with her family history and gave me my first experience in compèring and stage management. But we didn't finish until 2 a.m. Four hours later saw me up for the guests' breakfast service from 7 o'clock and I've just crept home at 8 p.m. for an early night, only to lie awake worrying about the New Zealanders! I am slowly beginning to think of this as my home. Very occasionally, I wonder how my little garden in Wiltshire is doing but I don't get homesick. I do miss the Saturday *Telegraph* though I'm sure it would last me all month instead of only to Wednesday. I've run out of Frank Cooper's Thick-Cut Oxford Marmalade and cannot locate a source – which is a bore. On a brighter note, the consignment of apricot tea from Mr Luff has arrived safely and that should last me a while. The Japanese can keep their green tea; it's a bit like the water drained from boiling Brussels sprouts. It's mainly the people I miss: family, of course, but also my hot-air ballooning chums in Berkshire (still no response to my enquiries here) and other friends who were just a short telephone call away. I'd like to be able to discuss my house-

Westbury Meets East

plants with someone to find out what I'm doing wrong. Maybe I should start talking to the plants. Perhaps I have! This flat is comfortable enough but I've not yet mastered the techno-logical idiosyncrasies. Things start and stop of their own will; there are whirrings and switchings that occur at random through the night and, for all I know, during the daytime, too. On the food front, I've been leading a campaign for more European style meals in the staff dining-room but the Japanese cook continues to serve greasy, sloppy, inedible, unappetising dishes, loved by the Japanese staff but utterly unpalatable to we English; the Aussies will eat anything! I've even started to cook for myself again – yes, it's been that bad. But I haven't the appetite today. Yesterday I had to dismiss a member of staff and there is a distinct tension about the place. Those I work with closely have been very supportive but even though my action was totally justified, I find I haven't the stomach for it. And still no-one to iron my rotten shirts.

Mid-November 1994

Peter Westbury

The Refectory. 118 students stand in rows flanking the long tables as I look down from the rostrum, the teachers behind me, stage right. Tape sound fades. Sliders to 'off'. MIC4 up to strength 7. 'Bless us, O Lord, and these Thy gifts which, from Thy bounty we are about to receive. May the Lord make us truly thankful. Amen.' 'Amen.' The students, some of them, complete the grace before meals and I usher the teachers to be served from the buffet tables. It is another supper for students in the Master's Hall at BH but this particular group has given us a lot of satisfaction, their command of English being such that they've responded wonderfully to our attempts at humour and seem to have appreciated what we've been trying to achieve. My table manners class this morning was a joy – the timing, their response – pure West End! I exaggerate, of course, but it did give me a real kick and underlined what Harold meant when he spoke about the acting element in a teacher's role. The television cameras were here again and zoomed in on my 'how-to-eat-green-peas' sequence. I was required to re-enact this later in a tête-à-tête with the presenter at a candle-lit table on the Royal Balcony. I find myself saying 'Isn't this romantic?' with a camera pointed at my forkful of peas while trying not to be distracted by the zit on the nose of the otherwise very dishy presenter. 'You're such a good actor,' she proclaims. I bet she says that to all the butlers. So it looks as though I may have come all the way to Japan to achieve a cult following from all those Japanese (not many!) desirous of eating green peas correctly. My place at last in the hall of fame. And still no lady to iron my shirts.

Next, to Tokyo with Amanda and Ayako to spend the half-million *yen* budget on Christmas decorations. Even with the 40% negotiated discount, we spent it all! I learned a new Japanese verb, 'to *takkybin*'. This means 'to use a personal courier truck service' and is most efficient.

Expensive, too, like everything else here so I took the opportunity to send back some private purchases to BH, too. The main business completed, we had taken the chance to visit the Kinokunya International Food Store and I discovered the availability of Marmite, Rioja, Monbazillac and horseradish sauce. I was so euphoric at seeing the familiar labels (mascarpone, too) that the prices were ignored. Until later. The tiny Marmite jar was a fiver; the wine a tenner; the wee bottle of sauce . . . £5.00! But I am stocked up with some treats for the winter months!

Westbury Meets East

A Blessing in Disguise

AND WINTER HAS ARRIVED. We took delivery this week of our snow-moving vehicles. It is in keeping with Shinto tradition to conduct something of a ceremony on such occasions and Hamanaka *san* set up a clothed trestle table to serve as a makeshift altar. On this he placed a squash, an apple, a cabbage, two enormous long white *daikon* (radishes), a bowl of salt and two litres of *sake* – meaningful symbols that clashed with the fresh paintwork. At short notice (a full five minutes – longer than usual), I was asked to say a prayer while the salt was sprinkled and the corrosive *sake* splashed over the re-conditioned machinery. With straightest of faces and relying heavily on the Japanese inability to detect any irony and the English staff's co-operation in suppressing their mirth, I declaimed my improvised petition: 'Snow to slush and ice to water, we are gathered here in thanksgiving before this snow plough and this snow blower and to rejoice at their delivery. We ask a blessing on these additions to the arsenal of Bridewell Heath in our fight against adversity and the elements. We call upon St Christopher, the patron saint of travellers, to protect those who will drive and service them. Grant us all the strength to endure the approaching winter months but, above all, we intercede for clement weather in the futile but humble hope that these machines may not actually see action at all. Amen.' The Director-General, who would keep referring to me as 'Reverend', then explained at some length about St Christopher in Japanese. After what seemed an interminable duration, we finally got to drink what was left of the *sake*! Which was actually quite a lot for a very small congregation, so I have to admit it is not now clear what became of the vegetables! It is just possible they got puréed in the blower!

Reverting to the recent Tokyo expedition, Amanda's husband, Ben, joined her in chaperoning me around for some of the time and we enjoyed some excellent meals together if you close your

Peter Westbury

The snow-blower
and other beasts

mind to the cost. We went pseudo-Italian for lunch but stumbled upon a Brasserie Flo for dinner! Yes, part and parcel of the same group that owns the London chain so, if you've enjoyed the ambience and good food in Richmond, Islington, Hampstead, Kensington, Fulham, Marylebone or St Martin's Lane . . . you may be sure of the same friendly service the next time you're passing through Tokyo! A memorable meal in very chic surroundings was not all that expensive but we had, perhaps, been on the 'careful' side. [Unlike Jack who, later, pushed the boat out somewhat when he dated one of the TV presenters and wined and dined her at the same place: £232.00 for the two of them. I think we're paying him too much.]

Let me describe the phenomenon known as *karaoke*, a well-established Japanese invention that has enjoyed a measure of popularity in the pubs of university towns in the United Kingdom. It is still all the rage here, certainly in provincial Japan but then there is little else. It rhymes with 'jokey' (rather appropriately) and means 'empty orchestra' (rather inappropriately). You pay your money and you take your choice from titles listed in fat directories. Backing sound is then provided from a machine and the vocals are contributed by amateur performers of widely varying talent, from passing fair to really quite unendurable. Your reluctance to participate will only heighten the degree of persuasion from others in the group. Memory lapse is not an acceptable excuse: the lyrics are actually there in front of you, whizzing across the TV monitors and, sometimes, actually keeping pace with the accompanying background music. Dissuasion, while frequently contemplated by the suffering listeners once the song is under way, is politely never voiced. The younger members of my family will be aghast when they learn that I have become something of an *aficionado*. Well, out of character or not, I am rapidly gaining a local reputation for my rendering of 'Love Me Tender', thanks to voice-enhancing technology, which, up until my debut a few months ago in Shirakawa's downtown night-spot 'Knights & Queens' (!), was the only English language choice in the repertoire. Now that I have convinced them of a demand for a selection of English song-titles . . . I am spoiled for choice. 'Yesterday', 'White Christmas' and 'Somewhere Over The Rainbow' all tantalizingly beckon. Now, culture this is not; but in this neck of the woods there are no pubs or cinemas or concert halls to escape to and for this extrovert introvert it

Peter Westbury

has been almost therapeutic to descend from the mountain and hit the fleshpots of Shirakawa, get in a few songs not to mention the odd beverage . . . and shoot back up again.

The 'will they, won't they' saga of the New Zealanders continues. I refuse to be panicked by my Japanese colleagues. It is their own kind in the Japanese Consulate in Auckland who are being difficult. Here is a neat little true story told me when I was in Auckland. Over the stretch of water dividing the city from its southern suburbs there is a road bridge which was designed by Japanese engineers. When it proved inadequate for the amount of commuter traffic, it seemed natural for the local transport authorities to ask the original designers for a solution. The Japanese answer was to devise and produce two additional lanes to be attached, one on each side of the bridge. Here is the punch-line: it has become known as the 'Nippon Clip-on'!

These Japanese place-names present a bit of a challenge when it comes to composing Limericks but in keeping with a Yuletide tradition in my family here, with apologies, are a few:

A butler in Shin Shirakawa
Found the *sake* incredibly sawa
So, he added some sugar
And then, silly booga,
Got more and more drunk by the awa.

A serious drinker in Sendai
Reflected one day to his friend, 'I
Say, look here old chap,
This *sake*'s pure crap
And does nought for my *modus bibendi*.'

A mortician from old Koriyama
Ran short of his liquid embalmer.
He enlisted balm aid
From a flighty barmaid
Whose spirit averted a drama.

Westbury Meets East

From *karaoke* to a bit of a challenge

7th January 1995

Woken by another earthquake this morning.

Seismologists measure these on something called the Richter scale which is, by itself, pretty meaningless to the layman – just a set of numbers 1 to ?? indicating the strength of the tremors, at the epicentre, I suppose. This morning's was strength 5, enough to make the international press. The bed shook and the bedroom door was swinging as I peered out from under the bedclothes. I've adopted a rule-of-thumb method of measuring an earthquake myself by whether it was the bread-board that fell over or the ironing-board (which any half-alert reader of these pages so far will know is almost always in the upright operational position). Today was one of the rare occasions when the ironing-board was folded away. The bread-board scores 2 or 3; when the ironing-board goes over it's a biggy. The end walls of my apartment are already, due to the sloped ceiling design, irregular quadrilaterals. When the rooms are distorted during an earthquake they assume a surrealistic quality. You would only have to add a melted Salvador Dali watch and quickly take a Polaroid snap and you'd have a work of art. The rubbery image soon returns to normal but while it is happening the experience is truly mind-bending, there is no word more apt. As we were finishing up in the Manor House one evening around 10 o'clock, my translator Masumi and I, feeling what we thought was a tremor, ran out into the Reception Hall. Her face took on a western appearance fleetingly as her eyes opened wide at the sight of the chandeliers swinging around. You have to laugh. And there cannot be many snooker-players who can blame seismic activity for a deterioration in their game! There can be even fewer players who, like myself, can attribute an improvement in their game to an earthquake . . . but only very temporarily!

If we 'wind the film back' to mid-December I can reveal that after a brandy-fuelled journey through the night in a specially chartered 36-seater bus with Jack Rouse and Sako Junior, the President's son, to 'help', we successfully met 15 Kiwis off their flight into Narita. They all got through Immigration, no thanks to the obstructive handling of their visa applications by the Japanese Legation in Auckland, and we whisked them and what looked like all their worldly possessions back to Bridewell Heath without incident. Two days later I started their

Peter Westbury

orientation and training programme and I was able to tell them (truthfully) that they were an even better-looking bunch than I remembered: six chaps and nine girls, a bright crew, willing and able and a great improvement over the departed Aussies (some of whom were up to all sorts of scam – like posting 'souvenirs' home, for example). These New Zealanders have a sense of humour and an initiative which is making a heap of difference to my workload already. I feel I can safely delegate and while every other 'officer' is taking a break during this first half of January, I have been taking the opportunity to get to know them better.

Talking of 'officers', here are the semi-coded faxes that passed between myself and Mikada *san* in nautical signal mode, during the NZ recruiting trip on which I had been accompanied by Jack Rouse:

12 OCT 94 TO BH DIRECTOR-GENERAL COO FORTY YACHTS SIGHTED IN BASIN STOP FIFTEEN ON PARADE TODAY STOP MANY WELL-RIGGED STOP REVIEWING NEXT FLOTILLA TOMORROW STOP REAR OF FLEET FRIDAY STOP FORECAST OPTIMISTIC BUT BEFORE WEIGH ANCHOR WILL SIGNAL INTERIM REPORT STOP WEATHER COOL OVERCAST STOP OFFICER ROUSE RESTLESS HAVE PLACED HIM IN LEG-IRONS SIR ONLY WAY STOP HIM JUMPING SHIP STOP WITH YOUR PERMISSION PROPOSE ALL SHORE LEAVE CANCELLED AND WHAT WAS THAT ABOUT HIGHEST YARDARM IN BRIDEWELL HEATH NAVY QUESTION CAPTAIN WESTBURY

Reply from Mikada *san*.

13 OCT 94 TO CAPTAIN WESTBURY RN DSO HMNZS 'AUCKLAND' DELIGHTEDLY ACKNOWLEDGE INITIAL RECCE REPORT WHICH UNDOUBTEDLY PLEASES THEIR LORDSHIPS STOP AUTHORIZING YOUNG OFFICERS OF ALL AGES TO ENGAGE TARGETS AT WILL AFTER SUNSET UNDER PRIVATEERING COMMISSIONS PROVIDED NO SCRATCH ON HULLS STOP GODSPEED C IN C PACIFIC

14 OCT 94 TO C IN C PACIFIC OPERATION 'SEARCHLIGHT' CONTINUES STOP ARMADA GROUPED TO

Westbury Meets East

SET SAIL FOR SEA OF JAPAN SUBJECT TO ADMIRALS INSPECTION OF SHIPS PAPERS STOP DETERIORATION IN WEATHER BUT MORALE GOOD STOP REGRET TO ADVISE MINOR WHARF-SIDE SKIRMISH WITH NATIVES RENDERING BOTH FLAG OFFICERS TEMPORARILY AWOL STOP RECOMMENDING LENIENCY AS NO NOTICEABLE SCRATCH ON HULLS STOP GENEVA CONVENTION RULES NO KEELHAULING FLOGGING ETC CLEMENCY RESPECTFULLY REQUESTED STOP CAPTAIN WESTBURY

From which it should be possible to detect that our Director-General, too, has a sense of humour. [In fact the only humourless character in these parts lately has been one of the English journalists, scruffy to boot, who completely failed to see beyond our professional facade to the essential tongue-in-cheekness that we need to adopt to survive!] The latest health report on the indefatigable Mikada *san* is that he has to keep taking the medication. As the 'medication' (prescribed by himself) continues to include the smoking of cigarettes and liberal doses of Laphroaig, I anticipate relapses of his condition which is contradicted by his absolute 'strong as an ox' appearance. He continues to maintain a wicked line in humour and some near-perfect English that, without beating the bushes around, completely creases me sometimes.

A Christmas Story 1994

Christmas-time is mercifully behind us. The snow lay on the ground, deep and crisp and terribly uneven and will remain so until Hamanaka *san* masters the snow plough with which he is chewing up the kerbstones. From home I received a mega avalanche of cards, faxes and surprise packages including one emotional depth charge – an audio cassette from my children to which they'd added recordings of their childhood voices. The strangest gift was something called 'Chewable Balance' given to me by a Japanese colleague firmly believing it to be . . . Whoops, there goes another earthquake! Did the Japanese offend the Almighty such a great deal or is it *me* He's after? . . . firmly believing it to be an English-originated speciality. Raspberry-flavoured, it has (I quote from the label) 'newly entered Japan. It is always easy to take the nutritious supplements which have been appeared in the new market under the technical agreement with Synpharma Int. UK. The calcium is

Peter Westbury

existing for 99% of our body in hard organization like bones and teeth and it is much concerned to maintain our health.' Aren't we all? 'What do I do with it?' I asked the colleague. 'You chew it', he replied [ask a silly question . . .], 'It will be very good for your stressful job.' Recognition at last and so much more useful than a medal.

Our series of traditional English 'Christmas' weekends, while not disastrous, were certainly a compromise due mainly to lack of co-operation from the direction of the Kitchen. The Christmas Eve programme was a success, surviving the attempts by Chef to sabotage it. Originally the dinner had been planned as plated courses but the number of guests grew and grew to the point where the only way to cope was to implement buffet-style. Now turkey with all the trimmings looks great on the individual plate. It's a bit of a tall order, though, to create an attractive and impressive buffet display solely with the ingredients ordered and prepared for plate service. All you are doing is presenting more of the same: turkey, ham, vegetables, turkey, ham, etc. Chef was no help, determined as he was to disassociate himself from this English menu. We did our best with bowls of nuts and fruit, smoked salmon and salads but it was a struggle and, on top of everything else, Chef refused to carve, remaining well in the background. [His lack of co-operation has been his undoing; but that is another story.] His Christmas puddings, knocked up with bad grace at the last minute (would you believe?!), were the wrong colour, texture and flavour but the Japanese knew no different and it was decided to proceed with our little ceremony. The Refectory was darkened in anticipation and I led a procession of four waiters, each bearing a silver tray with two flaming puddings, or so I believed, through the tables in a large figure-of-eight finishing at the central buffet table for slicing. The only trouble was that, owing to Chef's meanness with the brandy, the flames had died out within seconds of our leaving the kitchen, not immediately obvious to me puffed up in front. Desperate to rescue the situation and to produce the intended climax, I had somehow to re-ignite the puddings. We quickly heated some more brandy in a metal container and I returned to the expectant diners, still sitting patiently in the dark. Their stoicism was rewarded by a spectacular, albeit impromptu, flame- throwing act as I accidentally set fire to the brandy container itself, pouring liquid fire on to each pudding with a pyrotechnic flourish inspired by fear!

Westbury Meets East

What had previously evaporated so very quickly in the first abortive attempt, stubbornly refused to burn out and I had to resort to throwing the still blazing container out into a snow-drift through the dish-washers' window. I can still hear the applause but I have no plans to repeat the performance.

Later, we dismantled the buffet to make space for musical entertainment in-the-round. Four very talented young players had been booked to play seasonal Baroque, Renaissance and Tudor pieces using 'early musick' instruments: the *ciambala* (like a harpsichord), *viola da gamba* (like a cello) and various woodwind contrivances that produced sounds similar to the recorder, *sopranino*, cornet, etc.; plus a soprano voice. I had pointed out that we were presented with the perfect opportunity to use the Minstrels' Gallery, high above the Refectory stage, for its intended purpose and it was agreed that a recorder solo would be played from up there. In true Japanese (or should I say Bridewell Heath?) style there had been no time to rehearse this manoeuvre so it was with a certain misgiving that I found myself as the only person available when the time came to operate the spotlight (which I must remember to add to my *curriculum vitae* alongside 'car park attendant'). So with some trepidation, at the end of item 3 in the second half as planned, I lit the musician as he made his exit at ground level and killed the spot. I then trained the lamp on the gallery entrance above, switched it back on and waited. And waited. Good grief, I showed him the way – surely he can't have got lost? I realized later that, before emerging to play his solo German Nightingale bit, he had paused to regain his breath after the climb up the back stairs. Finally he appeared. I tracked him across to the centre, timing his walk. Perfect. He plays his piece; I dare not let go of the apparatus lest I spoil the effect. An eternity passes while the blood drains from my arms. Then, a pause. Followed by applause from below. I track back to the gallery exit and kill the light as he exits. Now, re-train the spot on the point of re-entry underneath and switch back on. And wait. What's he doing now?! After what seems forever, the door finally opens. Applause. For a very confused small boy returning from the loo!! Magic moment!

A favourite set-piece in the early evening was when guests and staff gathered for the singing of carols around the foot of the staircase in the Entrance Hall next to the decorated tree, the log fire crackling. With a mulled wine lubricant, it came close to *karaoke*. The 'Story of Christmas' in the chapel was more surprisingly well-received, my English script adapted from

Peter Westbury

The story of
Christmas in the
chapel.

St Luke alternating with Mikada *san*'s version in Japanese, there
being just enough similarity in key words like 'Mary' and
'Bethlehem' in each for me to get the cues right. Several guests
came to thank me afterwards most unexpectedly. 'Did you learn
to speak like that at Butler School?' I ask you!

Completing this twelve-month contract has now become a
challenge. It has been possible to save money here because
we're working all God's hours. The Japanese, because of their
work ethic, see nothing strange in this: they live to work, not
work to live. But I do miss those civilizing elements that give
a quality to life – the arts mainly – and to which, due to distance and cost, I have no access. As for extending, I cannot
imagine another winter here, shovelling one's way to work . . .

Westbury Meets East

■ **Eight Japanese aged between 45 and 95 have choked to death and 10 have been taken to hospital in the past two days in Tokyo after eating traditional New Year glutinous rice cakes. The *mochi* rice cakes, served in *ozouni* soup, are eaten in the belief that they bring longevity.** AFP, Tokyo

△ **Making rice cakes**

Left: Invited to help pound the rice to make *mochi* in a nearby village.

Top: Newspaper cutting (reproduced from the the *Daily Telegraph* of 3 January 1998)

Above: Cartoon illustration.

New Year's Eve with no guests (unaccountably) became a tad riotous. After a smart, formal dinner in the Refectory in grand style, all the staff adjourned to the pub for a 'Bad Taste' party and hair was seen to be let down. Haggis was served. In retaliation, the Japanese served us a traditional dish called *mochi*, made from pounded rice, which actually grows in the mouth and kills by choking several elderly people every January. The exact number is announced in the national TV news programme gaining them a posthumous fame of sorts. They probably place wagers on what the number will be; the Japanese are a gambling race.

5th February 1995

By taking a light-hearted view of earthquakes in recent correspondence, I had hoped to allay the fears of family and friends. But the gods are not mocked and within a week of writing my jokey piece, the Hanshin *temblor* had taken over 5,000 lives and

Shim-kyo footbridge at Nikko.

injured many, many thousands more. We were well away from the epi-centre in western Honshu but, since the television set had by then been installed in the staff canteen, there was no escaping the incessant bulletins showing the aftermath, the damage and the search for victims. Mealtimes, no cause for celebration at the best of times, became particularly subdued until eventually we became pre-occupied once more with our own parochial problems and the vicissitudes of winter at Bridewell Heath.

The planned cultural excursion for *gaijin* staff to the Tosho-*gu* shrine at Nikko came under threat when a white-faced Ontoku *san* returned late with the bus one evening. He had been forced by an on-coming truck to take a hairpin wide. The metal safety barrier had saved him from the edge but had had the effect of a giant tin-opener on the off-side of the bus whose intestines were clearly visible through gashes in the wheel-arch panels. He has handed in his notice. There is no guarantee that his replacement will prove to be any better; to some extent, luck (usually bad luck) plays a part on these tortuous mountain roads in winter and nobody really wants the job. This time, though, I believe we have taken the precaution of seeing whether the new man knows how to change gear. After nearly four months of riding the clutch pedal, the centre plate was completely knackered and nobody seemed dismayed when Ontoku *san* literally bowed out. The panels were beaten out and riveted back temporarily (in anticipation of further problems, I suspect; the 'accident report' season is far from over yet) just in time for the Nikko trip and the staff of 15 New Zealanders plus teachers and

myself enjoyed a day out together on one of the few days without a fresh fall of snow. The mountains looked spectacular and inviting and the shrines looked, well, like shrines really. Quite a few of them, too, so we had a lot of practice at shoe removal and re-tying of laces – an exercise I can recommend to any westerner planning seminars and struggling for new ideas for foreign staff bonding courses.

Entrance to the Tosho-gu shrine.

How Chef Cooked His Goose

THIS EPISODE HAS NOTHING WHATEVER to do with Christmas fare as, in spite of repeated requests, we never did get to eat goose. Chef had been his uncooperative best over the Yuletide menus and with growing discontent at his performance in every direction (with the possible exception of the girls we later discovered he was inviting up to his apartment from Koriyama) I was asked by the Director-General to write an assessment to submit to the President. I had hardly completed this when I received the news that *Chareiyo* No. 1 had been reported seen 10 kilometres away at the side of the road, its bonnet divided by a cedar tree. There was no sign of any occupant but in the back there was a strange bicycle, probably stolen. Chef had been in the habit of unofficially appropriating this vehicle, never completing the requisite paperwork and now he'd compounded the cheek by writing the thing off, or so it appeared. Telephone calls to the local hospitals failed to locate him.

We finally ran him to ground at 1 p.m., sleeping it off in his very own BH apartment. The accident had occurred at 6 a.m. and he'd done nothing about reporting it, a legal offence in itself quite apart from the discourtesy. He and the girl with him were lucky to have escaped uninjured but his arrogance was damaging. His failure to apologize incensed the Japanese and his demise became absolutely certain. Under Noda *san*, the *sous*-chef (7th Dan, massive chap built like a *Sumo* wrestler), the Kitchen has been running much more smoothly and a much more positive attitude now prevails when I request English dishes to be included on the menus.

The sacked Chef limped away last week, his French pride dented, still doubtless mystified as to where he went wrong. Mikada *san*, with his sense of the historical, likened it all to Agincourt, though his final summary to me in private was 'We are running an educational establishment, not a *bordello!*' I still

Peter Westbury

find him a bit of a hoot – most of his conversation is flavoured with B-movie dialogue; and he rang me the other day and called me 'Darling'! He has style (and a wife, thank goodness!) but I'm going to have to watch him . . .

A replacement chef is due to arrive from the contract company later this week but not, alas, from their London branch.

Clothes Encounters with Sumo

S o FAR, I have failed to grasp the subtleties of a sport that unbalances the Japanese (there is a clue) but which I have had difficulty treating seriously while finding it the perfect accompaniment to ironing. I refer, of course, to *Sumo* wrestling, a deceptively simple sport, 90% ritual and 10% action, a phenomenon that is obligingly there whenever one sets up the ironing-board and turns on the television set. I have to acknowledge that I have only seen it on the television screen, it being regarded as hardly the done thing to erect one's ironing-board on the terraces of a public stadium.

The same-iness of each bout, together with the frequency of slow-motion action replays from many angles, ensures that one will miss no part of each confrontation however much attention one is paying to a sleeve-head or a trouser crease. Look up and the seemingly identical opponents are still crouched in ritual squat or spraying water around or hurling salt or sipping from a miniature saucepan or spreading their side quills lest they inadvertently spike their meaty thighs. Built to stop a *shinkansen*, the unsmiling wrestlers overlap their low-slung bright red or blue or black or purple padded cummerbunds joined front and back through the goodies area by a matching ribbon that divides the impressive botty cheeks that serve to cushion many a loss of balance. And one should never assume that the big *buddha* is going to win – the short quick guy is often the victor. The score-board in *kanji* resembles any illustrated page from a price list for motor-cycle exhaust systems.

The object of the contest, for it is not, in spite of appearances, a pantomime, is to topple the other chap very politely but convincingly from the raised circular *dohyo* (rope-edged mat) while an over-dressed *gyoji* (referee) straight out of *The Wizard of Oz* does his best to get in the way. Over and over again.

Sumo ritual also involves a watering-can, a besom, a curved pole like a stringless long-bow, much bowing and a total lack

Peter Westbury

of tongue-in-cheek. The disembodied voice of the TV commentator treats the whole thing in a very remote matter-of-fact tone with long pauses. The fact that you never see him lends credence to my theory that he's actually working from home with most of his mind focused like mine on some attention-seeking shirts!

Limerick Competition Results. Munching away on my *genmai* flakes this morning (similar to corn flakes but made from rice, so . . . um, more like crispy blotting-paper), I devoted half a minute to judging all the entries (yes, surprisingly plural) for the 'Tokyo' Limerick Competition that I set back in December. My task was made very simple, not by virtue of the poor quality (which was outstanding) but by the fact that many were unprintable, the one featuring Pinocchio achieving maximum points in the 'Rude' category – shame it didn't scan but then most of them didn't. Everybody deserved a place and so did their contributions! The winning entry – and the writer may prefer to remain anonymous as it wasn't all that brilliant – was:

> Should you ever try eating in Tokyo,
> The prices will slay you, no jokey-oh;
> A steak and two veg.
> Cost an arm and a leg
> And you stagger home totally brokey-o!

1st March 1995. Notice I would like to see in Oyama *san*'s Music Shop Window in downtown Shirakawa:

> **'YAMAHA Automatic Piano Recital'**
> **'Chopsticks'.**

18th March 1995

Complimentary tickets and the Company's willingness to pay the railway fare have obliged me to brave the world of hieroglyphics once more and find my way to Makuhari *Messe* to attend Foodex '95, the International Food & Beverage Exhibition. Writing these notes, I'm now on the platform of Tokyo Central Station for the second leg of the return journey.

Westbury Meets East

Mobile 'phones are less in evidence here and the reason is obvious. The noise is *shinjiraranai* (unbelievable), an adjective I find myself using quite a lot. It is as though a child has gone berserk with the bing-bong machine as announcers vie with each other for attention with over-lapping information; the alarms which are sounded as pre-departure signals have the strength of air-raid sirens. But the Japanese wait in their orderly queues, obediently standing inside the coloured marker tapes on the concrete floor, unperturbed, many of them plugged into their Walkmans. My train comes in and is cleaned; half the population of Tokyo pours inside. The train then pulls out disconcertingly in the opposite direction to that expected. In Japan, everything works in the opposite direction to that expected: light switches, door locks and, of course, the printed word. But once you are on the *shinkansen* you are safe in the dual language world of travel. On the subway trains, too, there are reassuring illuminated maps inside the carriages which actually pinpoint with a light the stage of your journey and some of the stations are even shown in *romaji*. On the JR Keiyo line, however, from Tokyo to Makuhari, the maps are in *kanji*. So are the fare lists and as the tickets are only issued by machine, your average inexperienced *gaijin* (foreigner) is somewhat disadvantaged. The trick is to buy a ticket for the minimum fare and then pay the difference at the fare adjustment window at your destination. Simple.

Having successfully reached the exhibition, I was reluctant to leave the security of the giant womb-like halls containing all my needs including the chance of conversation in a choice of English, French or Spanish with some of the visiting exhibitors from Europe and America. I made what I hope will be some useful contacts, mainly in the beverage sector. But, after six hours of this, I tired of the Champagne and smoked salmon samples and made my way back towards the city centre. The pollution-diluted sun's rays struggled to highlight the dockside cranes along Tokyo Bay and the unmistakable silhouette of the Disneyland rides as I anxiously peered out from the train trying to identify the stops. Nothing but *kanji* at every station until, as in a bad dream, a station with no name at all . . . and everybody piled out. The end of the line!

Peter Westbury

An unexpected find. Mikada *san* (who is bearing an increasing resemblance to Mr Toad), in his determination to impress an art buff and leading authority on calligraphy soon to visit Bridewell Heath, toadily bought the man's book and discovered within its pages several reproductions of Pre-Raphaelite paintings. To his surprise, some of these formed part of the Loder Collection which had been acquired by the Koriyama Museum of Art not an hour's drive from here. Knowing of my own interest, an outing was planned (I got to drive the *Cima*, probably the most expensive car I've ever driven, the pleasure somewhat blunted by the treacherously icy road conditions); a cornucopia awaited us. A litany of familiar names, as intoned inimitably by my dear old art master, echoed in my head from those History of Art classes. 'Sir Edward Burne-Jones [his 'Flora' here, in her deep magenta robe and rich blue veil, plus 38 circular miniatures]; Dante Gabriel Rossetti [his 'Sleep of Arthur']; etchings and wood engravings by John Linnell, Edward Calvert, Samuel Palmer, William Blake, James Abbott McNeill Whistler et al.' What a find! And works by Constable, Reynolds, Gainsborough, Joseph Mallord William Turner all housed in a stylish modern museum on the outskirts of one of the sleaziest cities in provincial Japan. [*Yakuza* money? One cannot help speculating.] Not much else on display worth a mention save the hammered iron and glass sculpture of Junshiro Sato (d. 1988), reminiscent of the work of Hampstead sculptor Robert Adams in the sixties.

Nine months into my contracted year and I'm enjoying a rare day off. Further north in the Bandai region, the depth of snow on the mountain tracks still rules out trekking but here, in Ten'eimura, I have just re-traced my 10-inch deep footsteps in some of the most glorious mountain scenery I am likely to encounter anywhere. A gin-clear day with a gentle breeze tickling the bamboo leaves and cedar branches, it's a perfect day for hot-air ballooning but the terrain too rugged even if I had the team to go with, which I haven't. I'm sitting in a rock-strewn gully in the *Pajero* with the heater on. Higher up where I've been climbing, the melting snow is feeding numerous miniature waterfalls cascading between the boulders.

When I first arrived in Japan, all I could see were the overhead cables and concrete posts. Now, my brain (my what?!) edits these out – leaving only the garish *kanji* signs. But there is no need for editing today. I have taken a turning at random through a small village and out along a track, past some notices

Walk in the snowy mountains of Ten'eimura

in *kanji* and some of those international signs for falling rocks until the real fallen rocks prevented me from driving any further so I reversed and parked. I am in the middle of nowhere and the scenery is breathtaking. Not having seen a soul for hours, my solitude is disturbed when along the track comes a chap foraging among the loose rocks. I ask to see his spoils. A simple fellow, he shows me a plastic shopper full of tiny lettuce-like plants – they will be in tonight's *tempura*, a dish of deep-fried débris that might have included anything from the seemingly ever-present green bean to a chrysanthemum flower, depending on the season.

Next day I had Masumi *san* translate for me the *kanji* notices I'd copied down. She professed great difficulty in interpreting the exact meaning; the nearest she could get was: 'Air Pockets, Terrain Unstable'!! It rather explains how I had had the place pretty much to myself! And the other fellow was simple! A true case of 'when ignorance is bliss, 'tis folly to be wise.'

❀ ❀ ❀

Rocked gently awake this morning by another earthquake. Having consulted a geophysical map of Japan recently, I can reveal that we are astride the Nasu volcanic belt and equidistant from two major seismic epi-centres, one a little further south at

Peter Westbury

Mount Nantai and the other east of us in the Pacific. There was no mention of any of this at the job interview.

I appear on the front page of the Japanese equivalent of the *Financial Times* today but cannot think why. We have just heard that the UK's Central Television channel will be screening a film entitled 'Forever England' on the 2nd April. I imagine a transmission on April the 1st would have branded it a hoax, which is what we sometimes feel this place to be. The film was made by the crew whose interviewer closed by disarmingly asking me whether it was true that the butler had to spank the maids, to which I retorted 'Chance would be a fine thing!' – meaning that we don't actually have any here. I expect they've distorted it somehow.

15th April 1995. From a 'winter of discontent' when it was a real struggle to maintain the staff's morale and fill their rostered hours with more fulfilling duties than the daily shovelling of snow, we have emerged into a very busy spring-time of manic activity with everyone on overtime. The nubile young Tokyo students are back, together with the simian males, still fortunately in the ratio four to one, on five-day courses this time, instead of three and, concurrently, an abundance of adult groups requiring hospitality on a different level which has proved to be the predicted nightmare since we have only the one dining area for all and are still seriously under-staffed. Nevertheless we have adjusted the Bridewell Heath motto to read 'No Problem' – at least, that's the polite version – and we are at full stretch living up to it.

I've drawn the short straw and in addition to the etiquette classes I am to teach ballroom dancing which anyone who has danced with me will agree is the biggest joke ever. We do a lot of what I call busking but no hoofing so far. I shall have to pick up a manual when I'm next in Auckland.

In the evenings during the quieter spell, Jack and I were able to go off site together. A real 'Jack the Lad', he has saved enough to buy a second-hand Mazda RX7 which makes our high profile even higher, there being no other foreigners in the neighbourhood. We have set about investigating alternatives to the *karaoke* bars which were wearing a bit thin for entertainment, neither of us too impressed with the other's voice. Very popular with Japanese men, but well camouflaged downtown, are the Filipina clubs. The girls are brought in mainly from

Manila to serve drinks and keep the men company. The best part is not that they are attractive, which most of them are, but that they can speak a certain amount of English and discovering this new social outlet has come at a time when we were beginning to go demented. There is usually a Japanese Mama *san* in charge of the girls who are kept on a very strict rein. Every now and then one of them rebels and runs away to take her chances in Tokyo or another major city. It is the job of the girls to make sure that your glass is always full and that you're having a good time. You can tell how much of a good time you've been having by the size of the bill. Everything is charged as an extra: buckets of ice cubes, snacks, bowls of fruit, even the *oshibori* (hand-towels) I wouldn't wonder. The girls expect to be bought drinks, too, and although these are usually restricted to iced tea or cola or juice, they seem to get through oceans of the stuff and there's no means of checking the amount. The classier places put on a cabaret of sorts, mainly to justify the fact that the girls have described themselves as dancers to obtain their visas. That they have been lying is soon apparent... but nobody seems to mind. The girls sit with the customers in rotation so there is a strong chance you will enjoy the same quite stereo-typed conversation several times in any one club. It pays to remain in one club as there is a cover charge each time you enter. It also works out cheaper (marginally) to go along with the 'bottle- keep' system whereby you take out a mortgage on a bottle of brandy, say, and whatever you don't drink is kept on one side, bearing your name-label, pending your next visit, a major incentive to return especially if you're only a short distance into the current bottle.

In the interests of research we have winkled out a number of these dens of distraction, selflessly consuming an alarming quantity of alcohol, often being the last to leave. Although some Filipinas do finish up married to Japanese husbands, most of them don't actually like them so please imagine the impact of two strange male *gaijin*, one with a ponytail and Tom Selleck moustache and the other eccentrically attired and old enough to be their father, in contrast to the average T-shirted *Nihon-jin* in denim jeans. Added to which, we joke and tease, largely ignoring the rules, avoiding for as long as possible the inevitable invitations to participate in the dreaded *karaoke*. It has not taken long to establish our identities as 'Peter Pan' and 'Captain Hook' leaving a trail of would-be 'Wendys' and tentative 'Tinkerbells' in downtown Shirakawa. And what could be more harmless than an evening's relaxation in the

Peter Westbury

company of pretty girls to pour the drinks and pat your knee with everyone knowing where they stand or, rather, sit. I'm also beginning to pick up rather more Tagalog than I have Japanese.

Almost equally excitingly, Ben and Amanda have found some local restaurants that actually serve European-style food so it has given us another incentive to contrive an alternative working pattern to the seven-day week.

Komine-jo's elegant elevations.

Cables and concrete
posts.

With the exception of two particular locations within its environs, our nearest town, Shirakawa-*shi* (population anything between 20,000 and 40,000 depending on who you ask!), in Fukushima-*ken*, must be one of the ugliest places on earth. It has a geographical significance for Japanese people because of its famous Shirakawa gate which in bygone times marked the boundary between the 'civilized' country to the south and the untamed northern area over-run by merchants and brigands. The two exceptions to the ugliness are, firstly, the exquisite castle Komine-*jo* with the most elegant elevations and of quite family-size proportion. But you wouldn't choose to live there yourself because from the inside looking out you would have this uninterrupted view of the town below, a tangle of aerials and masts and cables and concrete and railway lines. The second picturesque feature of Shirakawa is Nanko Park, said to be the oldest public ornamental park in Japan with its very pretty lake and a Japanese water garden stocked with azaleas and irises and lace-cap hydrangeas just coming into their own at this time of year.

The city has a third redeeming feature and that is the existence of Shin-Shirakawa, the new railway station on the Japan Rail Tohoku line which provides us with the means of escape from time to time. The *shinkansen* service has really put the place on the map and judging from the amount of new construction work, commerce is moving in to take advantage of the good communications. The town already stands astride Route 4, the main north-south trunk road through Honshu and has an access point to the expressway that connects Sendai

Peter Westbury

with Tokyo. With no cinemas, theatres, concert halls or discotheques, local entertainment boils down to one ten-pin bowling alley or video-hire. Convenience stores proliferate but there is just the one department store (with three departments: food, fashion and household goods). There are garden centres and DIY shops but with no garden and an allergy to carpentry and plumbing, they won't get rich on my custom. Obviously catering to a demand, though, are the dry-cleaners; I've never seen so many thriving outlets in one town. The number of restaurants serving splashy food probably has a lot to do with

Top: approach to the shrine at Nanko Park.

Middle: Bonsai stall.

Bottom: Nanko Park lake.

Westbury Meets East

that. So, from my point of view, Shirakawa represents food shops, *karaoke* bars and the eventual way home.

14th May 1995

Her Britannic Majesty's Ambassador to Japan, His Excellency Sir John Boyd and Lady Boyd honoured us with a visit this weekend. Previous invitations to HM the Queen's representative had been thwarted by his overloaded diary, his absence abroad and then ill-health but he finally proved available to present the trophy to the winner of our first 'Ambassador's Cup' Golf Tournament held just two minutes down the road on what is probably one of Japan's most beautifully situated golf courses. As a non-golfer he'd no doubt have preferred to have gone fishing but it left me the privilege of escorting his wife on a mountain trek while the match was being played. A most gracious lady, she seemed very appreciative. On reaching the summit, I produced coffee from my day-sack and served it in Royal Doulton 'Dorchester' pattern bone china (the black and gold), which she thought quite a hoot.

For the banquet for 130 guests that evening I did the toast-master bit. With the re-writing of the Japanese constitution in 1946 when the political power of the Emperor was dismantled, Japanese aristocrats were required to shed their titles. Everybody became '*san*'. Prompted by Mikada *san*, it was thought appropriate to use this occasion to temporarily restore some of these titles to a number of one-time noble men and women on our guest-list. So, in addition to the elaborate mode of address known to be preferred by the Ambassador, I had to rehearse, pre-fixed by 'the former' to be on the safe side, the names of their Highnesses the Prince and Princess Kitashirakawa and a whole string of ex-Lords and Ladies which proved great fun and fortunately went down well with all concerned. I also made a couple of brief addresses during the proceedings, realizing afterwards that I had rather enjoyed it all myself. Mostly I just get on with playing the part but just occasionally the word *chutzpah* springs to mind.

Next weekend we will stage the first wedding in our Chapel which I've had blessed by the Mexican priest I very unexpectedly stumbled upon in the nearest town. He's quite a character – a big hit with the ladies of his congregation – and

Peter Westbury

devotes part of his time undercover, investigating the illegal human traffic between such countries as the Philippines, Korea and South America . . . and Japan! He has also kindly and very ecumenically lent us some Roman vestments for us to use for the obligatory Wedding Photo shoot-out for promotional purposes. All I have to do now is to find someone on the staff willing to pose as rector . . .

With the combined experience of my own weddings and that of one of my step-daughters fairly recently, planning this occasion has been a doddle, mainly a matter of compiling comprehensive checklists. [It hasn't stopped the Japanese from panicking, though, mainly because of the short notice which has, tediously, become the norm.] Ben and Amanda, too, had the recent celebration of their own marriage vows little more than a year ago and they have assisted with the planning. With mischief in mind, I suspect, for she is aware of my marital history and current single status, Amanda extracted a promise from me to give them my views on the state of matrimony:

'Dear Ben and Amanda,

Thank you for yesterday evening's introduction to a *ryokan*, [traditional Japanese inn] but more specially for your company. In a weak moment I agreed to write down my views on marriage and so here they are for what they and it are worth.

Marriage is an unnatural state. Statistics prove that it does not suit the majority and you need to embark on it knowing that fact and wanting it just the same. If you challenge that view by asking why it remains so popular, I suggest that, as an institution, it owes much to lust.

If you want to be exceptional and if it is to work then you must both work at making it work and take nothing nor each other for granted.

Make each other feel special; together you can take on the world. Prepare surprises – give everything. It has to be two-sided. And exclusive. If it fails you are both at fault. I write as one who has failed a number of times but, distilled from experience, I hope these thoughts do not reflect too cynical a view.

If you need luck then I wish it you but I do believe that you make your own. I join Gary Player who is reputed to have called back to an ungracious spectator after sinking a sixty-foot putt: 'And you know what?... the more I practise, the luckier I get!'

Perhaps even I am getting better. My last marriage lasted 20 years! I lost that match to her career – it happens in these days of female emancipation and thirst for independence. Today's relationships may need to adjust accordingly but to marry and at the same time require 'space' and seek independence seems to me a contradiction. This is not a complaint; merely an observation. From someone who has enjoyed a generous amount of undeserved luck.

To the ladies – God bless 'em!

Yours truly,

Peter Westbury

✽ ✽ ✽

I have been to New Zealand and back on my second unofficial recruiting trip, this time to find replacements for those Kiwis leaving in mid-June. The recruiting is 'unofficial' because it contravenes the spirit of the 'Work-holiday Visa' agreement between the two countries (Australia and Canada are also involved in the scheme but not the UK) which was set up to enable young people in the 18 to 26 age group to exchange visits explicitly to extend their cultural knowledge of Japan and not for the purpose of full-time employment. To help the visitors support themselves over the period of six months (extendible), the governments agreed that they may work non-continuously for up to a maximum of two months and for no more than 20 hours in any week. We are offering contracts for the whole 6 months and for a 40-hour week, often exceeded due to overtime. It makes any kind of advertising out of the question, other than word of mouth. It also makes it necessary, for those who are keen enough, to fudge the visa applications by submitting a creative month-by-month itinerary for what will be a completely imaginary tour of Japan. I am not at all comfortable with this but it is the recruiting policy adopted by the company to bring in native English speakers to fill hospitality positions, to interact informally with the students at BH

Peter Westbury

and, in some cases, to actually participate as assistants in the curriculum itself and it is the cheapest way of achieving all this. I see myself very much as the 'fall guy' and would prefer to be able to recruit from hospitality courses in UK colleges. However, the alternative 'Work Visa' conditions require applicants to have a degree or 10 years' experience in a job category that could not be filled by a Japanese. Such candidates would also expect higher salaries . . .

During my presentations in Auckland, I make the position clear but only a very few are deterred. My selection approved, the nail-biting process now begins and we wait to see how successful the visa applications will be. As eight of the existing staff are willing to stay, we also have to weather the procedure at the local Immigration Office for visa extensions which are by no means automatic. Of all the aspects of my job this is by far the most stressful though I have thoroughly enjoyed my role as interviewer of these young enthusiasts. The trip to Auckland (alone this time) has been almost as good as a paid holiday. There is no knowing whether I shall return in September but I have begun to know my way around and to make some charming acquaintances.

19th May 1995

Yesterday was one of those 'Basil Fawlty' days. Short-staffed, I greeted the guests at the front door, checked them in at Reception, ushered them to the dining-room, helped them to choose the wine and served it, waited at table, escorted them later to their rooms, conversed with them in the pub, finally bidding them 'Good night' at 11 p.m. Today, when they came up to the House for a pre-breakfast swim, it was I who booked them into the spa and provided them with shorts and towels at 6.30 a.m.! To be fair they did give a double-take at seeing me yet again. They are breakfasting now; and me? Well I feel as if it's my birthday, which it's not. With the Refectory staff back on duty and all guests accounted for, I've actually taken time off for a swim and a jacuzzi myself, the second time in nearly a year, and I'm sitting at a poolside table having breakfasted off a silver tray, the works, brought to me by Kim and Jack as a surprise 'Thank you' for standing in for them yesterday evening!

Ripping Yarn

25th May 1995

THINGS STARTED TO GO WRONG when I volunteered to collect a family's luggage from their suite in the pouring rain. I took one of the estate cars, drove it down to 'Turner' House and loaded the bags into the rear section. I parked up in front of the Manor House leaving the luggage ready for transfer to the shuttle bus on its return from the first run to the station. My next mistake was to go up to the Library to prepare and set up the place settings on the Board-room table for my Table Manners class the next morning. This usually only takes me about 20 minutes but time enough for me not to be in the main Operations Room when the new chef came to borrow a vehicle and guess which one he took?! The first thing I know about it is from a sheepish looking receptionist in the doorway asking my advice on how she should break the news to the unaware Mr & Mrs Kosuge and their delightful daughters that their personal effects were rapidly gaining distance from where they were thought to be. So mustering the Westbury charm, I did my best to smooth things over – grovel, grovel. I offered them refreshment while they waited for Chef's return. (Still a Frenchie with all the arrogance but fractionally more co-operative.) So, tea? Coffee? No, hot chocolate, please. Certainly. The School for Butlers teaches that 'Nothing is unavailable.' And so began the search for cocoa powder.

Luckily one of the assistant chefs had a personal supply. This took eleven minutes to track down and transform into the desired beverage; I scavenged some home-made biscuits from the Craft House, delivered it all on a silver tray with a flourish and suddenly *they* were ready to apologize to *me*! But, at best, there were still two hours to kill. So, I dropped everything and fielded the offer of a snooker lesson . . . at which they jumped. Upstairs, on the one free table, the President's favourite, I set up the balls and go through the routine, wincing every time the ladies miscue, putting the cloth at risk until

Peter Westbury

– it happens! Riiiip! I can still see it now in slow motion: millions of *yen* and it had to happen sooner or later with all the students passing through but if only I'd emptied the luggage from the estate car!

Our first wedding event went smoothly. The monumental cake did a 'Leaning Tower of Pisa' in this heat but that was after the photographs and nobody seemed to notice what with the flow of sparkling wine. I don't think anyone noticed my accidental spoonerism during the speeches either when I announced the toast to the Glide and Broom. This was ironic, as I had been correcting the Japanese office staff's mispronunciation in the run-up, when references were constantly being made to the 'Bloom' or the 'Gloom'!

I pointed out of the train window a few weeks ago, on a compulsory cherry-blossom viewing expedition to Tokyo with Mikada *san*, to ask the significance of the goldfish-shaped windsocks. 'Oh they're strung up before Golden Week to celebrate Boys' Day. Easy to remember: May 5th – the fifth day of the fifth month. Girls' Day? – that's easy, too. The third day of the third month'. Pause for effect. 'And in between? The fourth day of the fourth month? Transvestites' Day, of course! Hah!' and he explodes with laughter. Oh my Gaad!

9th June 1995

A day of swirling mists, giving a quite spooky atmosphere to the village, has put paid to my planned hike into the surrounding landscape which had been looking so inviting: azaleas, *fuji* (wisteria), weigela (that 'first rate second rate shrub'), hawthorn and elder all in full bloom in the wild. I had been looking forward to testing the elderflower champagne recipe. Oh well. May has been the most delightful month here – as in England as a rule.

June, now, threatens to see the start of the rainy season, the year having come full circle, almost, since my arrival in Japan. In the valley the rice paddies reflect the sky once more and the hawks play at hang-gliders above the trout farms. But up here on the mountain visibility is reduced to 10 metres and I'm apartment-bound.

Westbury Meets East

They want me to stay and the terms are right. 'The devil you know...' applies to both parties and things are slowly improving as both 'sides' make allowances for the two contrasting sets of national characteristics. Their inability to plan ahead is largely explained, I discover, by the fact that there is no future tense for them to use. The job itself, which almost defies description, is providing some unique situations that I'd never have dreamed would have been my good fortune to experience; and with the current exchange rate, it is no hardship being paid in *yen*!

The staff change-over looms: exit 7 New Zealanders to the rear to be replaced by 7 newcomers who, with the 8 incumbents will see us through to mid-November. The extension visas have all been granted and the signs are good that I shall be collecting the initiates from Narita Airport on the 15th.

In the meantime, I have a day of escape to look forward to next week when I am invited to give a lecture to the Guild of International Tailors (Japanese branch) at their Annual Dinner in Gifu City. This will take me on a long haul by *shinkansen*, passing within sight of Mount Fuji. The organizer is arranging for my first-class travel throughout plus overnight accommodation in the Hotel Nagaragawa, the host venue, which sounds very special and has its own *onsen*. I suppose I should give my speech some thought: 50 minutes on 'The Lifestyle of an English Gentleman'.

A bit dry, what?! The worst that can happen is that they won't ask me again. I'm going to try and cheer it up with some 'business' with my hats. As well as my bowler (correctly called a 'Coker') I have with me the straw boater, my linen stripe-banded summer trilby and the 'Rex Harrison' tweed.

The hoped-for balloon flight has still not happened in spite of a meeting here with the Vice-president of the Japan Balloon Federation, no less. Much talk in accordance with the Japanese way but no further forward. I'm pretty sure I could get myself invited to the Saga Balloon Festival which this man organizes, but that's not until 1998! Next month, though, will see me in Siena where I hope to fly with Roberto and, who knows, weather permitting I may be out with the Berkshire team soon afterwards.

Peter Westbury

Diary:
Year Two
July 1995 to June 1996

Flying Visits

4th July 1995

I BEGAN THIS JOURNEY INAUSPICIOUSLY enough sitting on my suitcase in the connecting corridor to the lavatories on the first commuter *shinkansen* of the day with *12 Red Herrings* (J Archer's latest) to distract me from the discomfort. But I'm airborne now and feeling like a prince, attended by the exquisite willowy Malaysian air hostesses. The starboard wing dips and we commence our descent to Kuching Airport for a two-hour transit stop. It is mid-afternoon; volcanic islands and lush mountain forests bask invitingly in the sunshine but we are restricted to waiting in the transit passengers lounge in the grotesque glass and metal buildings that the 28 degrees Celsius idyllic palm-tree setting can do nothing to enhance. This is Sarawak, previously no more to me than an exotic name atop a page in my boyhood stamp album. Perhaps it *is* true: philately *will* get you everywhere . . . eventually. At 35,000 feet once more in this Boeing 747, a turbulent living-dining room bumping around the sky above the world's trouble spots of Karachi, Tehran and Bosnia, it is difficult to feel touched by the announcement from CNN that Mexico City is sinking or by news of the coke war being fought on the ground between Coca Cola, Virgin and Sainsbury's!

Subang airport next and it is early evening and getting dark by the time the taxi-driver has made his leisurely way through the plush villa estate neighbourhood of Belvedere in Kuala Lumpur's suburbs to the outskirts of the city. What resembled floodlit landscaped rock gardens at night were revealed as merely quarries next morning. I stayed at the Grand Central, which was neither.

However, a short walk took me to a decent restaurant and afterwards to a Fitness Centre where I enjoyed a Thai massage in a mattress-lined room where girls bend you into positions you would not believe possible proving, quite unnecessarily, that they are considerably fitter than you.

Westbury Meets East

I have been unable to route myself directly to Florence, so I have had to fly firstly to Stansted involving an overnight stay with Katy which was no hardship at all except that, I don't know whether anyone else in the family has noticed, I'm convinced she stables a horse in her airing cupboard.

Siena from a hot-air balloon has to be one of the enduring mental snapshots of this very self-indulgent holiday but the most exciting experience of all was the private visit to the Villa Cetinale, where Liz is painting, and being invited to stay for lunch with Lord Lambton and Mrs Claire Ward. The original farmhouse was built by the Chigi family in the fifteenth century; they were bankers to popes and English kings. Subsequent occupants added two protruding wings, a double marble staircase, a *limonaia*, a *fattoria* and a chapel. An impressive five-storey hermitage was completed in 1713. Pope Alexander VII spent his youth here and the Emperor Napoleon is believed to have visited in 1811. Much had been vandalized by the time Lord Lambton bought Cetinale in 1977 and much restoration has taken place. The grounds are extensive and littered with the most amazing statuary. Liz is finding it a painter's paradise. What is hard to imagine is the *Palio* taking place here (the horse race which now takes place two or three times a year in Siena), but it did so sixteen times between 1690 and 1710 due to riots in the city.

London, Epsom, Shepton Mallet, Cardiff, Bristol, Cheltenham, Bath and Pangbourne: nothing seems to have changed in a year, the roads as strangled as ever.

2nd August 1995

Nothing much has changed here, either, back in The Land of the Rising Cost of Living where I have just spent £7.00 on a comb. There is no denying, it is a most handsome comb. Were you to see it for yourself, I am confident that you would immediately proclaim 'What a handsome comb!' While the reproduction on the next page falls a long way short of doing it justice – the deep sheen for example, is entirely lost – this illustration is life-sized, from which its very practical design may be appreciated without any risk of exaggeration on my part.

Peter Westbury

And it came in a very smart clear plastic sleeve WITH

INSTRUCTIONS! As you can see, these are in *kanji* so did not influence me at the time of purchase. What did influence me at the time of purchase was the fact that it was the *only* comb in the shop. *But* – a comb with *instructions*: how to use, how to care. And such a satisfactorily round price: 1,000 *yen*. I've yet to determine the significance of the toreador, the large dog with the library book, the man with the cane waiting for a bus or the man with the cutlass all standing around inside the brackets after the price. But *you* can tell, I'm sure, that I'm beginning to master this strange language. I do confess to having had help with the instructions, though. It seems that, with my fine hair, I should only use the left-hand end – roughly 500 *yen*'s worth. WANTED – lady to share comb: English-speaking Japanese preferred, with ironing skills; must have thick hair.

資生堂メンズコーム
（あらどき&仕上げ）

○1つで2つの機能（あらどきと
仕上げ）をもった便利なくし
です。
○耐熱性のよい樹脂でつくられ
ていますので、ドライヤーでの
仕上げにも使えます。

HOW TO USE （ご使用法）
●あらどきするときは歯の間隔
のあらい方を、仕上げのとき
は細かい方をお使いになると
便利です。

HOW TO CARE （お手入れ法）
●洗うときは、ぬるま湯に中性
洗剤をうすく溶かした中で、
軽く振り洗いをします。十分
すすいで水気を拭きとってか
らお使いください。

材質…ポリエステル系樹脂

1,000円・(税抜)

発売元　株式会社 資生堂
東京都中央区銀座7-5-5

49 01872 637942

Comb and Packaging
illustration, with instructions!

Westbury Meets East

Above and opposite: 'Toppo' in the stream.

Westbury Meets East

'. . . there is a small problem'

Closet Encounter

17th August 1995

O F ALL THE KIWI STAFF for whom I must take responsibility for engaging, Abel is the most inappropriately christened. I am only talking phonetically; there *were* times when I *could* have happily murdered him. This 'butter-wouldn't-melt' son of a prominent Auckland figure has proved to be a real liability. His own high profile was established only days after his arrival last November when he overturned our luggage vehicle in spectacular fashion, as the photos in the accident report confirm. When called to the scene ('Mr Westbury, there is a small problem.'), I found it upside down in our stream having taken a lamp-post with it. How he came to be driving at all, since he has no licence, became the subject of an investigation and subsequent crackdown on young foreign staff driving Company vehicles on site. Abel's huge feet had been unable to distinguish brake from accelerator.

His latest misdemeanour, for which I have no photographic evidence, I am relieved to say, has become known as 'the peeing in the wardrobe incident'. Abel and one of our local suppliers had struck up a friendship. The man owns a white goods business and his wife runs a shop selling very expensive porcelain. One night earlier this week, after a binge in the town, Nakajima *san* invited Abel to his home, offering to drive him up to BH next morning in time for breakfast duty. Abel was to occupy the bedroom of the absent son.

After more toasts to internationalization, cultural camaraderie and other high-minded booze-loosened buzz-words, they finally retired, well lubricated. At bladder-relieving time in the early hours, the semi-conscious Abel groped in the dark for the way to the bathroom and it isn't hard to guess the rest. To the dismay of Nakajima's wife, the pool was there when she went to tidy the room mid-morning. That afternoon I was called to a meeting in the Director-General's office where a

Peter Westbury

group of Japanese staff had already assembled. There, too, was Nakajima *san*, having been sent by his wife to register their complaint – she being too embarrassed and distressed by its nature to visit us herself. He told the story while we all kept very straight faces. Abel was sent for. He remembered nothing, of course, and asked whether the Nakajimas kept a dog! The poor translator spluttered but nevertheless relayed the question. There was a pause. Then the dear man smiled and began to laugh and the tension was over. Of course there was no dog and still the matter of an apology to his wife, so Guess Who was elected to go and make it . . . ? Next trip home, my family and friends will all be receiving porcelain souvenirs, lots of them, purchased at the full and undiscounted retail price. And the order for the new store-room freezer, which had been put out to tender, went to Nakajima *san* whose quotation had actually been the highest.

All Over the Road

28th August 1995

I'VE BEEN ASSEMBLING some notes for what might one day be Westbury's 'Alternative Guide' to Japan, starting with a category entitled 'All over the Road'.

1. To put the record straight, the impression may have been created that cars are driven on the left in Japan, the same as in Britain. This is pure rumour and applies to only a small percentage of the large and increasing driving population, usually those in the 'housewife', 'middle-aged' or 'chicken' categories.

2. It is worth remembering that this is the nation that produced *kami-kaze* pilots. They are all over the roads and late at night one can hear the squeal of rubber on tarmac echoing round the hills as the newest generation of car-owners practises handbrake turns on the local mountain roads.

3. When asked why they drive on the wrong side at selected sections of the highways such as hairpin bends and blind corners, the serious standard reply is that it shortens the journey and saves fuel (especially, of course if they finish up dead or in hospital). One rich bitch driver, complete with yappy dog accessory, knocked one of my staff from his mountain-bike as she took a bend fast and wide, shouted at him for scratching her paintwork, adjusted her hat in her driving-mirror converted to a looking-glass and raced off before he recovered sufficiently to think about the need to take note of her number. Bruised and bleeding, he received a sympathetic hearing from the police but they were unable to trace her. By the way, it is the location of the accident that controls the choice of hospital and the police station to which you should report, neither of which will necessarily be the nearest to the accident nor the most convenient for subsequent and very time-consuming visits.

Peter Westbury

4. Have no truck with lorries. Lorries, as a Noel Coward character might have said, are 'very big'. Except flat-bed trucks, which are 'very small'. If the flat-bed truck in front of you moves out to the right without signalling, you may be one-hundred per cent certain that it is about to turn left – NOW! The lorry-drivers do not use the slow lane on hills. Well, actually that's only half true. They do use half of the slow lane. Do not try slip-streaming up the inside because you will not be able to read the signs in *kanji* that are telling you you're running out of road and the other lorry that was following you has meanwhile closed the gap.

5. As a speed deterrent, at the side of the trunk roads, there are realistic looking police patrol car silhouettes complete with flashing roof lights, very convincing at first, especially at night-time. Just as you get used to these fakes and start to ignore them, one of them accelerates after you.

6. So certain are they of the average Japanese driver's inability to avoid bumping into road works barriers, the highway authorities employ elaborately uniformed young ladies to swing long illuminated batons to motion cars away from the hazard. At first, I thought they must be robots . . . until one smiled back. A useful invention at temporary traffic lights is the countdown display panel which shows digitally the number of seconds you have left to light a cigarette, go find the map you left in the boot or take a quick nap before the light changes (to blue) in your favour.

Uniformed lady traffic controller.

7. The Japanese nation as a whole has poor eyesight. Opticians and panel-beaters are among the highest earners.

8. While drivers are mostly aggressive, pedestrians, on the other hand, are wisely timid and totally unused to being given any consideration. Perhaps out of shock at such a courtesy, even from a foreigner, a whole crocodile of school-children reached the opposite kerb where I had signalled them to cross, turned as one and bowed to me. It ain't all bad.

9. One of the frequent distractions to drivers of both sexes is the fact that, totally without modesty, male Japanese drivers are prone to blatant peeing at the side of the road. Well, not actually prone, you understand.

10. Most city car parks will charge you 100 square-framed spectacles for 30 walking lampshades. As you are now aware, the way in is the square with the wigwam; the way out is the square with the cactus.

25th September 1995

With September the landscape changes as the rice crop ripens from lime green to a wonderful yellow ochre wash that glows even on cloudy days. The cityscape enjoys a different kind of wash from the heavy downpours that focus their force on this month when farmers frantically try to gather in the harvest before it is flattened. According to the edge-to-edge television bulletins (as with the earthquakes, the Japanese are experts at monitoring disasters and milking them for every fluid ounce of entertainment), it was due to arrive in Fukushima prefecture at 3 p.m. on the 17th September, and sure enough, the typhoon struck, punctual as the *shinkansen*, on the dot of the hour. The penultimate hairpin bend on our sole approach road completely collapsed in a landslide and our normal sensation of isolation became an actuality. Between the bursts of rain, the skies are less dramatic, though, and September's complex cloud formations have mostly been benign, spectacularly pink in the setting sun.

An alternative mud-compacted track, where the hairpin once

'from lime green to a wonderful yellow ochre wash that glows even on cloudy days'

'spectacularly pink in the setting sun'

was, now serves as our escape route to civilization, and I shall be able to make my third visit to New Zealand as scheduled, returning this time with the Principal of the Institute as my guest here for a week.

Coinciding with the visit of my VIP guest from New Zealand was an invitation for me to attend an *onsen* party at a *ryokan* (inn) some three hours' drive west of here. When I explained the situation the invitation was immediately extended to him and we gleefully set off to share this perfectly timed opportunity for him to sample the 'real Japan'. It turned out to be a bit of an ordeal to be truthful. Clad in dresses and confronted with unspeakable food and the ever-present *karaoke* machine, we coped bravely, he better than I. The best part, for me, was meeting 'Miss Asahi Beer' (ex 'Miss Peachy Fukushima') and my guest made a great hit with her mother! I also met Noriko, the proprietor's daughter, for the first time . . .

11th October 1995

Out driving through the zig-zag mountain passes, now edged with red-and-white poles preparatory to winter, there is the feeling of being on a slalom course long before the arrival of snow. Before the month is out, an almost equally bright red will identify the maples in the surrounding woodland where badly parked cars at the roadside betray the fact that the local scavengers are out in their numbers, raiding nature's larder for its autumn produce in the form of roots, stalks, berries, fungus and chestnuts.

Once a month I have been visiting a masseur, introduced to me at my request by the lady barber I have befriended in Shimogo. His salon close by is festooned with his diplomas in various forms of alternative medicine and he is constantly trying to persuade me to allow him to demonstrate some of these. Fortunately, a head-shake is universally recognised as a negative (at any rate it is here where I need it most) but he doesn't stop trying every time. After a dip in the hottest *furo* (bath), I dry off and submit to his pummelling and finger pressure technique known as '*shiatsu*'.

Peter Westbury

He seems to find a source of merriment in my underwear –

perhaps I should re-phrase that: he finds my underwear a source of merriment for some reason and shows amazement at my western apparel, especially the shirts and cufflinks. He is quite a character with his trim goatee, very internationalistic and is married to a Chinese girl, twice his size, from Shanghai. They are expecting their first baby.

Communication between us is largely achieved by mime but his sessions are very effective and really set me up for an evening back in Shirakawa with the young Filipinas, of whom I have the pick since Jack's engagement to a Japanese girl.

Socks Appeal

Now some explanatory notes on footwear to be incorporated one day into Westbury's 'Alternative Guide' to Japan: Socks Appeal.

1. When entering private homes and certain public buildings like hospitals, clinics and the traditional hotels (civic halls, police stations and 'international' hotels are exceptions) and all national heritage buildings like shrines and temples open to tourists, you are required to remove your outdoor shoes at the interior step of the *genkan* (porch). You have changed space from outside to inside and this division is marked by this small but rigid ritual. It is also marked by the trodden down heels of many shoes as people tend to be in a hurry when they leave.

2. If you want to impress your host, it is regarded as a touch of politeness to pause in the hallway and place your shoes ready in the direction of your departure for when you leave. House slippers for guests will have been placed on the step. In the case of public buildings they are arrayed in pigeon-holes in which, the slippers being removed, you may place your shoes.

3. None of the slippers that are provided cater for the western foot whose length is, in most cases, several sizes larger than they are accustomed to in Japan. This does not get you out of complying with tradition even if it means padding around the dusty corridors of a shrine or temple in your socks or stockinged feet.

4. There is a further change of space when you visit the rest room and you will find a change of slippers, usually brightly coloured to distinguish them from others, outside the entrance. Do try not to risk your host's displeasure by forgetting to change back into the regular slippers, as this would be regarded as bringing something unclean into a clean zone.

5. All this changing of footwear may seem tedious and irritating (which it is, especially when you are in a hurry), but the Japanese place great emphasis on these divisions between spaces and adhere religiously to these practices, even when alone. Without knowing he was being watched, I once saw a man emerge from his house, lace up his shoes, remember something he'd forgotten and, rather than step on the interior floor wearing his outdoor shoes, crawl back indoors on his hands and knees with his feet held high off the ground, retrieve the item and then crawl out again. (You or I would have tip-toed in.)

6. Brides teeter on high-wedge sandals assisted by an attendant on each arm. Apprentice *geisha* (known as *maiko*) have to learn to wear high clogs, a custom dating from the period when the apprentices were children and wore tall shoes to add to their height and in which they had to learn to walk gracefully. Modern day fashion-conscious girls echo the past with their precarious platform shoes but don't seem so dedicated to getting the deportment right. They walk so ludicrously badly, they are a spectacle for the wrong reason.

7. The backless *geta* (sandal-clog) is like a wooden flip-flop incorporating two parallel bars on the underside that, again, increase the wearer's height. Ladies, already restricted in movement by their *kimonos*, hobble along wearing these, their white socks strangely divided by the single thong no doubt adding to their discomfort.

Geta

8. Scaffolders and roofing contractors wear shoes called '*jikatabi*', a sort of cross between an ankle-boot and a gaiter with a cloven bit between the large toe and the rest. These are worn with ballooned-out jodhpurs which you'd think they'd find restricting, hazardous even, but which most probably contain voluminous pouches full of cigarettes.

9. Unless you are a masochist, shop for all your own footwear needs before coming to Japan or back home while on a visit.

Jikatabi

10. Remember to allow for the fact that snow rots leather and your shoes will need replacement. Repair is *not* the answer. The ancient craft of shoe-mending can be tracked down in the backstreets but they are roads of old cobblers.

Westbury Meets East

24th November 1995

Early November sees autumn peaking but it only seems to be a matter of days before overnight frosts and high winds strip the trees of their glory. At lower altitudes, cosmos grows at the side of the country roads where irises and chrysanthemums had grown in earlier seasons. The Japanese symbol of autumn, it costs a fortune to buy in Tokyo. Here in Fukushima and Tochigi prefectures one may see whole fields of cosmos growing wild, pink and red and white. This is the same species that was featured at the Chelsea Flower Show a few years ago in dark chocolate colour and perfume!

Late November has seen the first of the snow and the weather has turned crisp, that British adjective implying downright cold. But it is a dry cold and sunny days are not precluded.

In the town gardens, at lower altitudes, the persimmon ripen on the now almost leafless trees and the spectrum of colour is vibrant on the still present chrysanthemums, from yellow, mustard and orange through to burgundy. Suddenly it seems, *susuki* is growing everywhere, its tall white fronds disturbed by the breeze and catching the sunlight, as spectacular, when backlit, as a firework display. But then, that's what fronds are for.

Back in the summer, Peepee, the appropriately named but misguidedly purchased St Bernard dog, was added as window-dressing to our already over-stocked menagerie consisting of Hamanaka *san*'s two mongrels, his cock, two hens and a

Cosmos in Flower – symbol of Autumn.

caged fox. With no trainer to show the poor animal where to
lift his leg, it is now too late; Bridewell Heath has the run of
him, rather. Although still a puppy, he is now huge and to
everybody's surprise has an uncharacteristic aversion to snow.
I am all for claiming a refund under the Trade Descriptions
Act or, better still, returning him to the shop particularly as
he seems to have taken permanent refuge on my landing where
I have to step over this snoring supine lump of fur to reach
my apartment. At twenty paces, his offensive smell begins to
assail the nostrils and is a grievous deterrent to the already
sparse amount of social traffic on my staircase, presenting a
literally overwhelming obstacle to any romantic opportunities
that might occur. I was pondering a solution, something
humane but final, when this shuffling disaster of a St Bernard
sealed his own fate by biting one of the students. The Japanese
finally saw sense and he has been sent away on a training
course which, however long, will be over too soon.

A few observations on Japanese gastronomy. Actually the title
is badly chosen, rather a contradiction in terms, putting
Japanese food on a bit of a pedestal when all I find I really
want to do with it is put it into a doggy bag. For a dog I don't
particularly like. It is only fair to acknowledge that some foreigners do like the indigenous style of cooking. Raw fish is not
difficult, but raw horse as a delicacy? . . . somehow less acceptable. The Japanese have always been great imitators so it is
possible to find restaurants advertising French, Italian, Indian,
Chinese, Mexican, you-name-it, dishes. When it comes to it,
though, they are not very convincing. Unlike the Japanese imitation leather plastic products that actually smell of leather and
the Hokkaido cheeses that, if stored and treated properly, cheat

'Suddenly it seems,
susuki is growing
everywhere'

Westbury Meets East

the taste buds into believing they are Camembert, these culinary copies are not for those who can make comparisons with the real thing. Another over-riding problem here is that, after some time in Japan, almost everything starts tasting of fish — even the chocolate biscuits and the ice cream!

A warning about electricity. The *shinkansen* apart, everything here is slow. To prove that light travels *slower* than sound, turn on a Japanese light switch and you'll note a definite time delay between the click of the switch and the illumination of the lamp. It might, of course, have something to do with the slower electricity in Japan: 110 instead of the UK's 240. Power madness!

I should perhaps explain my failure to send birthday cards. It may be that I have been looking in the wrong places (this has been known) but I have not seen a birthday card shop since my arrival in Shirakawa, though they do sell cards for special occasions. Jack bought such a one for his son's birthday. (Well it's only once a year. Sorry, Jack.) He judged the pretty pink and blue rather cissy so he chose the smart silver and black,

'Sherlock Holmes Mystery'

only to have it explained to him later that this was a funeral card. He sent it anyway... but to his ex-mother-in-law.

2nd December 1995

Winter has not reduced the avalanche of students nor the advanced booking of guests for the BH Christmas package which will be very much the mixture as before with the addition of a 'Sherlock Holmes Mystery' weekend. Half a dozen of the Kiwi staff have gamely auditioned to play the various parts involved, the only speaking role, if you can call it such, being that of the victim, a maid, who is required to emit a piercing scream. I shall be Watson (well, it *is* my bowler) and Jack has been type-cast as the villain.

Only in Japan?

I AM INGENUOUSLY ABANDONING the chronicle of events to insert here a collection of odds and ends that I've labelled 'Only in Japan?'. Some I find surprising, some are plain daft (annoyingly so); others are brilliant. All are actual and contribute towards making this the fascinating culture that it is.

1. The wonderful sound of a 100-piece orchestra of schoolchildren playing like professionals on the concourse of Ueno's JR station, musicians and commuters alike enjoying the fabulous acoustics of the vast railway booking hall.

2. The *mamenoki* (beanpole) in stainless steel, erected in public places as a conspicuous meeting-place.

3. The attendants at a filling-station on Route 4, between Shirakawa and Kuroiso, burning rubbish, *next to* the refuelling pumps on the forecourt.

4. The Japanese-run Italian franchise restaurant where they serve the red wine chilled.

5. No tipping!

6. Driving the hour it takes to the nearest place you know you can buy marmalade, only to find a notice in the window saying this is the one day this month chosen to close the shop for cleaning.

7. The countdown display at temporary traffic-lights indicating to halted drivers how many more seconds they will have to wait.

8. The electrically heated loo-seat (very, very comfortable and somehow most encouraging – a great invention).

9. Open-plan banks! No bullet-proof grilles; in fact, no grilles at all.

10. The cinema finally located (not an easy task in a provincial town: no 'Gaumont' no 'Empire' blazoned across the

Peter Westbury

entrance), you check the times of showing; decide there's time for a quick *okonomiyaki* – only to find on returning that the foyer's packed with school-children. It's a 'Special Offer' day and the tickets are sold out.

11. Proposed revisions, just announced by the Education Ministry, to the guidelines on sex instruction in Japan's schools, the first up-date in 12 years, taking into account the *enjo kosai*, or dates between male adults and female junior or senior high school students, in which the girls receive lipstick money in exchange for sex, a practice which has been rife for years.

12. The *Tamagotchi*: the biggest craze currently in Japan, with over 4 million sold, they are plastic eggs which hatch into electronic chicks. (They have now arrived in the UK and are marketed as 'Virtual Pets'.) They require almost constant attention for, if irregularly 'cared' for... they die! They are 'adopted' by children (whose study suffers), housewives (whose home life suffers) and, would you believe, businessmen (whose office routine suffers). There is even a spin-off enterprise providing crèche facilities so that the chicks have surrogate care during office hours!

13. The so-called Love Hotels, where customers are not necessarily unmarried couples in search of sex. Married couples, living under the same roof as their parents as well as their children in cramped accommodation with paper-thin walls, need to find privacy for love-making, too.

    These short-stay hotels provide the answer although the curious thing is that, while claiming to be discreet, the Love Hotels are easily identifiable by their garish signs and over-the-top facades which make them look like anything from cartoon castles to space-ships.

14. The low crime rate – the *sarin* gas affair shamed the nation.

15. Medical insurance claims where the charge by doctors to sign the claim form to recover 3,000 *yen* is 3,500 *yen*.

16. The '*sokaiya*', which translates as 'one who gains his livelihood from assemblies', sounding harmless enough but which really means 'someone who is paid by companies to buy the silence of potential trouble-makers

at AGMs, etc.'. Currently, four executives of the country's second largest bank, the Daiichi Kangyo Bank, are allegedly involved.

17. In a country that takes an almost tragic view of 'loss of face', the strange phenomenon of competitors in a TV programme willing to expose themselves to the slapstick ridicule of hurling themselves at a paper wall marked 'X' or 'O', depending on whether they choose 'True' or 'False' as their answer to the question posed, to find that, should they prove to be incorrect, they are covered in flour.

18. The '*madogiwa zoku*', literally 'the ones who sit next to the window'. All the major Japanese companies have them: the incompetents! They remain on the payroll because no-one gets sacked in Japan owing to the impor-tance of not losing face. And they're not going to resign, are they? So they are given harmless things to do (like guiding visitors round the premises). Sometimes they are shunted off to different departments – we've had more than our share of Company misfits shipped up to BH from Tokyo. The only area in which they can be relied upon to be punctual is the canteen.

4th January 1996

It has been a point of principle with me at Christmas time to make the effort to decorate my flat even though almost the only folk to see inside it is the team of cleaning-ladies on their weekly blitz. I have also managed to obtain the necessary ingredients for my traditional Christmas 'Sharpener', a combi-nation of Stone's Ginger Wine, Dark Rum and Ginger Ale. Very warming and on offer to any callers. The Japanese make more of what they call '*Shogatsu*' (first week of January) than they do of Christmas.

For them, life is punctuated with annual beginnings and ends and the arrival of the New Year is still celebrated in the traditional way when Japanese city-dwellers return to their ancestral villages to reunite with their families, visit the local shrine or temple and pray for successful crops and good fortune. Elaborate door decorations (like corn dollies) made from rice stalks and string are placed in the entrances to homes. Visiting is not restricted to the houses of families. Company superiors are called upon, too, and anyone else to

Peter Westbury

whom you have become indebted over the past year. The practice of sending *nengajo* (New Year's cards) has grown in significance so that receiving large numbers is regarded as an indication of high social status. My own season's greeting cards covered most of my desk and I was required to remove them before the next visit by the President in case they exceeded his.

The total absence of guests on the evening of Christmas Day meant that it was possible to throw a Staff Party. It also meant that Ben and I worked like fury while the staff, now numbering 51, took it easy. I even peeled a mountain of potatoes; my last bulk batch had been when I was doing my National Service. Jack was off-site, meeting the new mother-in-law-to-be, having announced his engagement officially on Christmas Eve. His first fiancée is not yet aware of this, her flat still serving as a useful base in Tokyo. After dinner, Mikada *san* insisted on a showing of *The Remains of the Day*, a long and rather tedious film, the story set in a stately home against a background of political unrest in the run-up to the Second World War. There is, however, an impeccable portrayal of the butler by Anthony Hopkins and a memorable sequence where Peter Vaughn, the actor playing the part of his father, is serving at table, a dew-drop at the end of his nose and everyone else in suspense. Superb acting, no dialogue and I wonder how many takes to get it right.

The 'Sherlock Holmes' weekend proved most successful, period bobbies' helmets and jackets appearing as if by magic, on loan from the Japanese 'Sherlock Holmes Society' of all things. We even mustered a deerstalker. The Mystery game culminated in the smashing of the heads of snowmen, a parody of 'The Case of the Six Napoleons'. Fifteen snowmen were needed, so to motivate the staff we set a competition complete with prizes. The description 'snowpersons' was agreed after some haggling but for a long time nothing seemed to happen. There was no shortage of snow but we had not bargained for the arctic temperatures and the Kiwis' vulnerability to the cold. I built four of them myself, including a giant bust of a character that might have been a cross between Malcolm Muggeridge and Somerset Maugham after Graham Sutherland. Ben and Amanda produced two. The rest were cobbled together at the eleventh hour by the Japanese staff with the aid of mechanical diggers. No prizes were presented.

We are all wondering what 1996 will bring; how long will our

Westbury Meets East

jobs last? . . . how long can the place remain open without making a profit? When we raise these questions we are told we don't need to know. We are in the dark regarding an awful lot and one can see the frustration and stress beginning to tell on one's colleagues. I have made a New Year's resolution to start smoking . . . but I don't seem to have the will-power! I also resolved to try passive drinking . . . but I don't think I'm going to be able to keep it up!

I was sitting in Inawashiro's 'Papa Francesco' *ristorante*, a Milanese franchise, recovering from a hair-raising drive through a blizzard on icy roads and munching a Pizza Margarita, when a stranger introduced himself. He had recognized me, he said, from the New Year's Eve nationwide television broadcast which he had enjoyed very much. (Made me glad I wasn't picking my nose). That sort of experience, plus the stack of 'fan-mail' throughout the season, brings it home to me what a unique kind of job I have. If only the Japanese would learn from their mistakes but they seem to enjoy the familiarity of tripping over the same things all the time.

15th February 1996

There have been times during this winter in the mountains of Fukushima, when I have found myself thinking that I could not face another. If anything, it has seemed harsher this time, the roads more hazardous, a real test of your sense of humour. Another heavy dump is whiting out the landscape at this minute. I must try to take a short holiday soon.

I have been on three very contrasting local journeys in recent weeks. The New Zealand staff have been holding up pretty well in the circumstances, homesickness triggered off from time to time by news of the summer temperatures at home if not by pressure from the boy- or girl-friend left behind. One girl has been complaining of migraine symptoms; there is also a complicated domestic situation back in New Zealand and she has been to me a few times for advice. I'm not at all sure that being the father of three children and two step-children qualifies me any better for the job but I frequently find myself needed '*in*

Peter Westbury

loco parentis' as far as the younger staff are concerned. I suppose I should regard this as a compliment though I had hoped the worries of parenthood were behind me. I have to admit that I had started to suspect that the migraine girl's persistent headaches and increasingly frequent counselling sessions ought to be put down to attention-seeking ploys.

At one o'clock one morning in January, my bedside telephone rang. It was Masumi who shares quarters with the Kiwis. 'Jill is in terrible pain; I think she must go to hospital.' So along treacherous roads and on what must have been the coldest night of the year, the three of us set out, Masumi having volunteered to translate. I really motored down that hill, the girls with their eyes tight shut. It might have been mid-day instead of the middle of the night on Route 4, the trucks hurtling along in close-packed convoys, their drivers making no concession to the icy conditions.

The medical team was awaiting our arrival as pre-arranged. Jill was clearly frightened and would not let go of my hand, insisting that I went with her for the thorough examination that followed. I saw more of Jill in that anxious hour than I have ever seen of my own daughters – if attention was what she was seeking, there was no way to avoid giving it. I paid for that unkind thought one hundred fold when the specialist announced the decision to place her on their brain-scanner and I found myself pacing up and down, the worried 'parent', for the next two hours!

The good news is that she was given an all-clear; the bad news, extricated with help from Masumi under careful questioning from the medics, was that the silly girl admitted she had been topping up the prescribed medication for her migraines with additional pills she had brought with her from New

'Illegally pitched dome-shaped tents' on Lake Hibara

Zealand. Anyway, after being kept under observation for a further 24 hours, she returned to BH and was soon back on duty. It will be interesting to see if she ever refers to it again. Kids!

The second outing took place at the beginning of February when I set off for what turned out to be the most expensive haircut of my young life. (Since I started lying about my age, I do actually feel younger – I recommend it.) I had been unable to reach my regular hairdresser because of the impossible conditions on the lake-side route to Shimogo. As a consequence I took pot luck with one of the barbers in Shirakawa, taking the opportunity to do some shopping afterwards. By the time I faced home, the road was completely obliterated by a blizzard and I had absolutely no choice but to book myself into an hotel in the town. I drove back next morning after the snow-ploughs had been out. I paid Y2,800 for the haircut; Y9,864 for the room with breakfast inc. tax. Total? About £78.00!! Beats Jermyn Street.

I took off in the *Pajero* last Sunday with Penny, one of the teachers, for company. We had prepared a picnic so that we were self-sufficient and drove north to Lake Hibara, which takes its name from the drowned village now at its bottom. At this time of year, the frozen lakes are sprinkled with brightly-coloured illegally-pitched dome-shaped tents. Anglers, wearing equally brightly-coloured boiler suits, often matching their tents, drill holes through the ice with enormous hand-held augurs in order to fish. It was an extraordinary sight on this beautiful sunny day, the tents achieving an amazing luminosity against the snowy backdrop. Nobody seems to worry about the illegality of the sport, probably just a device to absolve the local authority from any liability in the event of an accident. We then took a diversion from the main road

```
[The English have difficulty pronouncing Chateau d'Oex:
                Hooroex! hooroex!
                For Chateau d'Oex
                Where all moexke hoex
                While they're awoex.

                What do thoex soex?
                Crime doesn't poex? -
                At Chateau d'Oex
                Whoex hoex! whoex hoex!

                Yes, stroexght or goex
                Or old and groex
                The mice all ploex
                So, have a nice d'Oex!
Even the local Swiss have given in and call it Chateau Day!]
```

Peter Westbury

through exciting snow-laden single-track lanes very reminiscent of the conditions and the terrain in Switzerland almost exactly two years ago when hot-air ballooning with friends at Chateau d'Oex.

Penny's OK, the same age as my eldest and very 'jolly hockey-sticks'. I couldn't believe it when she lent me a Joyce Grenfell recording!

The student groups are harder work now – they have less language ability than previously experienced. I've increased the amount of mime in my Table Manners lessons and omitted the technical vocabulary like 'knife', 'fork' and 'spoon'! No, not seriously. It has been proposed that I extend my March itinerary to include other New Zealand cities in order to research recruitment opportunities there. By concentrating exclusively on Auckland, we have rather drawn attention to ourselves, it being too much of a coincidence for the Japanese officials to swallow when visa applications are filled in by 15 students from the same college taking the same flight.

22nd February 1966

Snowball fights with the students have become part of the routine. Tobogganing, too, has been very popular. Unfortunately, Amanda's video camera did not record the unrepeatable sequence when, near the bottom of the makeshift 'Cresta Run' behind Drake House, the sledge carrying a student and myself hit a bump, my bowler hat left my head, and as we slid to a stop, landed on hers!

But how about this for a crazy sport: orienteering in the snow?! Think about it – all those footprints giving the game away! Penny and I did a trial run with devious plans of walking backwards to confuse those following. We only succeeded in falling botty-cheek deep in drifts and into concealed ditches filled with the white stuff. We were drenched.

Some of the, dare-I-say-it, outsized New Zealand staff have arrived here short of certain items of uniform. It has fallen to me, therefore, to escort them to local outfitters in order to make up complete sets of skirts and trousers.

Talk about the blind leading the dumb. This simple act of shopping was hindered not so much by the language problem

Westbury Meets East

– elaborate charades are a substitute whenever vocabulary fails – but by the system. For example, go back on Tuesday to buy the goods you priced on Monday and they explain that Monday was a special promotion day, pointing at the notice in *kanji*! The outing to buy skirts was, predictably I suppose, the most fun; I didn't know where to look, trying in vain to find middle distance. With all the taking off and putting on, stepping behind screens and observing the shoe etiquette, the girls became giggly and impatient and modesty soon took second priority. I think we may have scandalized the store assistants.

In response to my periodic nagging, fire brigade officers from their base in Yumoto, about 35 minutes away, finally paid us a visit this week to instruct us in how to handle the fire appliances. The pantomime was rather embarrassing, more attention being paid to the business of saluting and presentation than to that of dealing with the flames which, thank goodness, were only simulated. They also demonstrated First Aid procedures. The recommended practices in Japan do not entirely coincide with thinking in NZ or the UK and, regrettably, the officers were not afforded the unquestioning respect to which they are obviously accustomed. However, the exercise did expose the general lack of know-how in this area and our Education Department has agreed to prepare an in-house manual as a consequence.

It also became apparent that we could not rely on the local fire-fighting force to be of any use to us in an emergency. The mainly wooden buildings would have been consumed by fire and the blaze died down by the time they'd have reached us. The officers drove away looking very preoccupied. But at long

Interfering with Shakespeare.

Year Two: July 1995 to June 1996

last there is to be a clamp-down on smoking in the student dormitories.

This week has also seen me in Miyagi prefecture. A Tohoku University professor had invited me up to Sendai. This is the same gentleman who wrote, adapted and directed the production of *Romeo and Juliet* staged here last August. Goaded, no doubt, by other modern interpretations such as *West Side Story*, he had been inspired to substitute Sendai-*shi* for Verona, where street brawls between rival gangs were enacted in the Tohoku *ben* (local dialect). I also remember a very dishy Japanese Juliet in a T-shirt, all the actors being from his Shakespeare Society at the university. The project had been a great success and he now wanted to discuss a version of 'The Dream' with this summer in mind. It is proving difficult to find a mutually acceptable date so with my tongue in my cheek I proposed pushing forward the timing to, say, December, changing the play to *The Winter's Tale* and capitalizing on the immortal stage direction: 'Exit, pursued by a bear.'! Audition details could be posted in the woods.

The well-intentioned offer to show me round the university buildings proved to be unfortunate. The appointed guide, a '*madogiwa zoku*' if ever there was (though I can think of better examples on the staff at BH), was most awfully boring. But I was later treated to a Japanese meal in a top-rated Sendai restaurant where we were joined by the professor's senior colleague who, incidentally, seemed to own half the city's buildings that we passed. From the moment we were introduced he didn't stop beaming, full of *bonhomie*, until it finally dawned on me that he was absolutely paralytic. Prior to the dinner, I decided that for me, too, an anaesthetized state would help me cope best, matching his consumption of *sake* and countless dry sherries and I don't actually recall that the meal was all that bad.

Next day I did have the real pleasure of being driven a little further up the coast to Matsushima and its '1,000 islands', said to be in the top three on the tourists' list together with Mount Fuji and Kyoto. I'm ticking them off slowly.

This year has seen a distinct improvement in my social life and on the 28th of February I am off to Guam to take some overdue leave. The two are not unconnected.

Westbury Meets East

Destination Guam

28th February 1996

I'M FINALLY EN ROUTE for Narita airport to fly to Guam, a US possession in the tropical Pacific, one of the Micronesian islands, located at the edge of the Mariana trench. My early morning departure was hindered by a fresh dump of snow overnight combined with high winds.

Jack had volunteered to drive me to the station and he and I actually had to shovel our way through what has become the notorious Golf Club bend where drifting frequently occurs. Because the Japanese cannot measure the cost of inconvenience every time this happens, they are not prepared to invest in the snow shields erected in such places, but 'one day' they intend to plant a row of trees to grow into a screen. Meanwhile, from mid-November to early April all our vehicles carry shovels. I am now heading for a gentler climate with more even-tempered winds. Travelling once more through the built-up areas of this alien land, I reflect, not on how ugly it all is but how consistently ugly. Most of the towns and cities resemble an unorganized mass of flat-roofed airport buildings of the fifties, rather like the view of Slough from the M4 but with quadruple the helping of masts and scanners and cables and concrete posts. With no pretensions to loveliness, why should there be expectations and it is a measure of my resignation that instead of looking out of the train window, I find I have had my nose in a book. Until, that is, a pretty lissom girl sits next to me, distractingly perfumed. Who needs scenery?

Boarding Continental Micronesia's flight number CO964, I couldn't help thinking that *In*continental would be far more appropriate, judging from the smell from the loos even before take-off. The inflight movie was a Pink Panther cartoon! Life in the fast lane this was not proving to be...

Mischievously romantic guide-book writers taking literary

Peter Westbury

Poolside in the hotel gardens, a cleverly lanscaped network of lagoons and cascades linked by swimmable channels.

licence describe the island of Guam as a 'footprint in the sea'. My own description would be more like a salmon in mid-wriggle but, if we stay with the Robinson Crusoe cliché, I have no real quarrel – Man Friday was certainly abundantly evident among the Chamorro males. The population is a rich blend of Mayo-Polynesian descendants and invaders from Asia, Europe and the Americas. They seem well-outnumbered by the Japanese and Korean tourists who pour in by the plane-load to enjoy the wonderful climate. Day and night, the view out over the Pacific from this honeymoon suite at the Hyatt Regency is just beautiful.

With some experience of honeymoon suites, it is ironic that this, the best for design I've encountered so far, finds me in my current unmarried state, but the booking had been made through a third party with instructions to go for the luxurious. I wish I could have afforded it years ago but then I never dreamed I would be holidaying on a Pacific island, ever!

29th February 1996

This calendar oddity, the focus for predatory females every four years, was spent lazily poolside in the hotel gardens, cleverly landscaped to part-conceal with exotic foliage a network of lagoons and cascades linked by swimmable channels. Exhausted from reading and being served drinks and barbecued food with hardly the need to move, I rallied to dip my body in the Pacific, forgetting how sticky ocean-bathing is. My reading rate slowed at one point when some really very attractive sun-worshippers entered the scene, chose their spot, peeled off and preened themselves, oiled their bodies and finally settled to some serious tanning. Their womenfolk, also gorgeous, followed suit thirty minutes later! I think a Japanese skin is what I'd like to order for my next life.

St David's Day and a Jungle Hike

Chamorro guide:	Hi, Mr Peter, I'm Aldon.
Me:	Hello.
Aldon:	You English?
Me:	Yes, as a matter of fact.

Peter Westbury

Aldon: Well 'ceptin' you, we got all Japanese on
           board today, so we're goin' to give it them in
           English! (His little joke.)

(Statistic: 90% of visitors to Guam are from Japan.)

So, driven by Buddy, we collected other paid-up jungle hikers
calling at what seemed like every hotel on Guam and Aldon
gave us the *spiel* but, of course, in Japanese, believing I understood. There were two 'honeymoon' couples, a family of four
and eleven nineteen-year old girls. No complaints from my
direction. The bus bumped along pot-holed roads taking us

Westbury Meets East

inland to a point where we transferred to 4WD vehicles for the stretch that would take us off the map.

At the lunch time picnic spot, the Chamorro boys and I swam under a curtain waterfall while the girls pretended not to notice.

A Japanese army sergeant became a local legend when, during the Second World War he took refuge in these mountains during the American liberation, hiding himself in a cave. Not realizing that hostilities were at an end, he remained there for many years thereby providing the guides with some much-needed colour with which to regale tourists. Apparently he's still alive today, now in his eighties, making occasional return visits when he is treated like a hero. We all sat huddled in this poky cave which we'd reached by threading ourselves through a tricky narrow tunnel, vertical in places, not for the claustrophobic. Aldon explained how the sergeant had kept himself alive with berries and water from a nearby spring, sleeping on a short uneven slab of rock, not exactly the living conditions anyone would choose but, fairly bearable in the light from our portable lanterns. Then we were instructed to turn off the lamps. There was not a chink of light and it all went very quiet. It was one of those moments of truth and after an eternity lasting about half a minute, I spoke the one word that everybody was thinking; '*Shinjiraranai*' (unbelievable). We crawled out a lot faster than we had crawled in.

The sudden rainfall is as unpredictable here as the power cuts. Neither is featured in Guam's holiday literature, which in any case, is not 100% accurate in what it says. If I'd taken any notice of their advice to leave formal wear at home, gate-crashing the US Navy band's Farewell Gala Concert, a glamorous occasion attended by the island's big-wigs in full evening dress, would have been out of the question. It was a great evening, the military orchestra looking (in Aldo Ray's words) like so many glasses of milk!

2nd March 1996

I had never parasailed or jetskied before and reckoned it was time. It is always the logistics of new experiences that interest me almost more than the activities themselves. Suspended in a harness ('Don't buckle that too tight man, you'll squeeze your nuts!'), I was surprised at how quickly and simply the parasail release mechanism operated. Eric and Earl dunked me in the bay a few times, washing off the protective sun-block so that my legs lobstered a little. Well, a lot actually. I'm writing this at a beach table outside the jetski 'base', a kind of Third World corrugated-iron roofed shanty with a fresh water trickle for a shower. Someone has brought out a feast of hamburgers and french fries and, another first, I've just sampled root beer, a carbonated soft drink reminiscent of a TCP gargle. I wondered whether this flavour was intentional or whether it had just been stored badly. The can was labelled 'Old-fashioned MUG'... I thought, 'Yes.' The jetskies are wide-bottomed for rookies like me. After a few circuits, keeping obediently within the buoy-demarcated shark-free zone, I must say it palled a bit and I've classified it for the future as more of a spectator sport, especially since the arrival of four extremely dishy young Japanese goddesses, wearing the skimpiest of bathing suits, to take instruction just over there at the water's edge. Not a wide bottom amongst them. It's all enough to make a happy man very old. Actually, as an aside, I do seem to be coping better with this age thing, lately. I'm down to 53 now; next birthday I plan to be 52.

3rd March 1996

The final day was spent seeking shade in the lush gardens of the hotel. In the evening, at a spectacular Las Vegas-style stage show at 'The Sandcastle' nightspot, an amazing illusionist, performing with doves, tiger cubs and, in his finale, an adult Bengal tiger, was wonderfully supported by a cast of singers, dancers and show-girls all in the best possible taste, extravagantly costumed and professionally presented.

Westbury Meets East

4th March 1996

A very early start was required for the return flight to the real artificial world awaiting me back at Bridewell Heath. The snow had not left the mountains of Fukushima-*ken* and it was soon back to the old winter routine and out with the shovel.

9th March 1996

Attempting to keep an appointment with the masseur, I was halted by an 8-car pile-up only seconds ahead of me. The temperature had dropped so dramatically from above zero to minus nine degrees that the drivers had been unprepared for the suddenly treacherous surface. Reversing gingerly and turning back was a better option. I dined out alone at 'La Marée de Misaki', in Shirakawa. I eat there whenever possible; the chef, Itoh *san*, produces some splendid dishes. Although the menu is in *kanji*, I have learned the magic phrase – '*omakase shimasu*' (I leave the choice to you) – and he has to serve something special!

I completed my day off by visiting a new Filipina bar in Kuroiso where I fell in and out of love with a girl who looked, in turn, like Brooke Shields, Dorothy Lamour and Marty Feldman as the evening wore on and the alcohol wore off. I returned safely along deserted roads in the early hours in time to start another day in the life of a butler.

11th March 1996: to New Zealand

In the past I had always been in a panic at Ueno, switching railway networks in a headlong dash to reach Narita on time. This morning, knowing there would be time to spare and carrying a *bento* (pre-packed lunch) in my shoulder bag, it was my plan to investigate the district which I knew included a park. It was a beautiful spring day as I emerged from the concourse, having invested a large sum of money in a storage locker for my big bag. There was blossom on the trees and peonies in full bloom in the shrubberies in contrast to the bleak winter landscape back on the mountain. Unfortunately, though, contained within the park's perimeter, apart from the impressive Toshugu shrine and *pagoda*, I discovered a zoo, a maintenance depot, several refuse dumps and Tokyo's equivalent of Cardboard City with its makeshift blue polypropylene

Peter Westbury

tarpaulin bivouacs. The combined smell totally ruined my appetite and the tramps and the loonies benefited from my discarded picnic. At noon, a thousand amplified gongs disturbed the peace and hundreds of pigeons and I decided in unison to make a move, they to another part of Tokyo to scavenge lunch at a more tranquil venue, and I to continue my journey to New Zealand, first stop Wellington, to meet the people who have it in their power, if they are so disposed, to assist me with future recruiting. Before I could leave the park bench, a Shinto priestess approached and murmured a quiet prayer over me: I didn't protest – I need all the help I can get.

My disappointing lunch time detour in Ueno Park has left me with three hours to kill before check-in at Narita. I've yet to find an airport designed for lesser mortals like me to wait in comfort. It's too early for them to accept my heavy bag at the counter, so rather than lug it around I've found a position next to a window. My view is very restricted, though, and all I can see of the actual aircraft is their giant tail-wings moving sedately beyond the hangars like enormous artificial sharks' fins in slow motion. My brain is dulled by a cacophony of incomprehensible Japanese voices. I've lost concentration on my book and the English newspaper is only full of the London bombings and the Wales' divorce terms – tragedies both.

Westbury Meets East

Research Down Under

13th March 1996: Wellington

I HAVE SOON LAID TO REST all the pre-conceived notions that had been fed to me labelling this city as the epitome of England or Scotland in the fifties. They are in the nineties here and make no mistake. They have the technology, as they say; it's simply that they don't shout about it, taking a very relaxed attitude about most things. They do possess a passion for equality and for rugby and all that they both entail; and this passion they wear on their sleeve. But it is more likely to be a denim sleeve than that of a three-piece pinstripe. The politicians and bureaucrats that I came to meet could not be described as behind-the-times. They effortlessly matched the 'all-talk-and-no-action' qualities of their contemporaries worldwide. As a consequence, my meetings with high-powered sounding officials (in Education and Tourism) and with Pacific basin do-gooders (like Asia 2000) were ill-fated, in spite of their pious brochures. They were all of them quite without teeth and had no money to spend; only being good at political capital. So after two very frustrating days of presenting my case to a series of polite listeners who might have been exemplary graduates of the Japanese Nod-But-Do-Nothing School for Decision- Makers, I was no further forward. Seeking to ease by making respectable the visa application process, I had approached these people to discuss a number of possibilities: the inauguration of degree courses in Tourism to incorporate a 6-month work experience module at Bridewell Heath; student exchanges with our Tokyo University or Language Institute; and sponsorship within the framework of the NZ Hospitality industry to give trainees exposure to the expectations of Japanese tourists from first-hand experience in Japan. My axe got nowhere near the grindstone.

This evening, I felt I deserved some light relief. Usually arriving in most places 'too late' for the funfair or 'too early' for the carnival, I was amazed to find that I'd landed in Wellington *while* it was holding its Festival of Art & Music. I booked into a con-

Peter Westbury

cert by 'Le Quatuor', a brilliantly inspired and zany string quartet of musical clowns who included Vivaldi and The Stones, Bach and The Beatles, reggae and recitative, opera and flamenco, Maori war dance and classical ballet, cossack and slapstick, country and western in their 90-minute non-stop repertoire plus half-an-hour of encores. Catch them somewhere if you can. I walked afterwards to a waterfront venue called 'The Boatshed' to listen to some jazz that proved unremarkable. What was memorable, though, was the Maori barman. Tall even for a man, riveting as a woman, he was statuesque, his bosoms too firm and perfectly proportioned to be other than false, but good value from the management's point of view as he doubled as barmaid and bouncer.

14th March 1996

More abortive meetings this morning but I took some time on this sunny afternoon to investigate this city further and made an unexpected discovery while walking in the Botanical Gardens. By way of contrast to the rather ragged rose-beds, which included a variety unknown to me – Sam McReady's 'Sexy Rexy' – there was an example of a Japanese watergarden, in the off-centre of which an eternal flame flickered in a stone lantern 'donated to the people of New Zealand by the Abbot of the Toshogu shrine in Ueno Park, Tokyo'. What a coincidence! (You're making it up. No I'm not.)

I joined a so-called 'Heritage Tour' conducted by a Kiwi who was either a vicar/part-time bus driver or a bus driver/part-time vicar – he didn't seem too sure himself. One way or the other, we had the angels on our side as he swung us around the steep and winding roads of Wellington as if trying to compensate with physical excitement for what must rate as among the most boring places of interest in the world.

Tolerated, it would seem, right in the city's centre, shoulder-to-shoulder with staid civic buildings, are the euphemistically named 'bath-houses', their lurid graphics and signage in European and Asian languages leaving none of their questionable delights to the imagination of a clearly cosmopolitan clientele. Or anyone!

15th March 1996

'Good morning, Ladies and Gentlemen and welcome aboard

Air New Zealand flight number 417 from Wellington to Dunedin. This is Captain Drew Anderson speaking to you from the flight deck and we have some rather squally weather conditions for you today for take-off and the prospect of not much better on arrival at Dunedin.

'This means we may encounter some bumps as we climb through the cloud layer to ten and a half thousand metres and descend through the front that's sitting over Christchurch. One other thing – the runway here at Wellington is being re-surfaced. This is done by fusing sections of tarmac together. The work is half-completed. It's been my experience that, with the sort of load we're carrying today, we're likely to feel some jarring as we roll over the step in the runway approximately halfway down.'

Even without these additional hazards, Wellington rates as one of the world's trickiest airstrips with the sea at both ends and along part of one side. The hills on which the city is built also make the approach blind and visual confirmation of the accuracy of the navigational aids must come as a great relief to many first officers (not to mention the passengers) as the tarmac comes at last into view. There has not been enough room to build the customary air traffic control tower next to the airstrip so it is some distance away; its address is actually a street with a street number like your house or mine. Anyway the man was right to warn us, the take-off was uncomfortable, but hilariously so – like riding on square wheels. At least we could see where we were going, unlike the arrival at Dunedin where the instrument-landing through low cloud was less amusing.

My hosts met me at the airport and we motored for three hours, taking the right turn out of Milton, now the southern-most point I've reached on this planet, to Queenstown where we booked into a small hotel, our base for a weekend's hiking and rock-climbing. I felt that I should bungy-jump, too, but the moment soon passed.

16th March 1996

The mountain range known as 'The Remarkables' had a dusting of snow this morning and looked, well, remarkable. The cable-car gave us a cheating start on our climb to Ben Lomond but we only reached as far as the saddle for the summit was in low cloud. Queenstown is a great centre for outdoor activists without being too bluff and hearty; you get the impression that

Peter Westbury

The 'Remarkables' and Queenstown.

the polite extrovert would be most welcome and there were many examples of these from Scandinavia, Russia, Scotland and Japan. They will be put to the test tomorrow: St Patrick's Day! One can eat out well and inexpensively in Queenstown and the whole weekend was a wonderful unwind in the middle of my recruiting researches.

18th March 1996

I enjoyed very constructive meetings today with two Heads of Department at Otago Polytechnic in Dunedin. The Head of Tourism lives with her husband in an amazing mansion built for one of the founder families of the Cadbury business. We are going to develop a course in Hospitality and Restaurant Studies to include work experience at Bridewell Heath. I met an enthusiastic response from the students, which augurs well for my return here in September.

Dunedin is the smallest of the four cities to which I have now paid short visits and seems also the least worldly. Out on the peninsula one can visit the only mainland breeding colony of the albatross and a sanctuary for yellow-eyed penguins, seals and cormorants on which you can snoop from a hide. If, on the other hand, you wanted to hide from a snoop, then you wouldn't choose Dunedin at all because it does give the impression that it is small enough for everyone to know everybody's business and a stranger sticks out a mile. The Octagon in the city's centre is a useful focal point and from which most places of interest may be reached on foot, though it's unlikely anyone would want to slog it up Baldwin Street which is noted in the Guinness Book of Records as among the steepest streets in the world (1 in 2.86). A rugby ground, one repertory theatre (if not, two), a prestigious art gallery of glorious design that lures top-circuit worldwide travelling exhibitions... I bet I could even find a *karaoke* bar if I tried hard enough. But, best of all, Dunedin has Belpepper's Blues, a curiously named eating-house carved out of an old railway station waiting room, that has a magical menu worth planning your whole itinerary around.

19th March 1996

Peter Westbury

I flew up to **Christchurch** where one is more aware of contrasts. Architecturally interesting in the centre around

Cathedral Square, the flat roads then grid outwards, initially lined with shops and offices and hotels and restaurants but soon edged with a succession of light industrial warehouses providing space for body shops and body shops, two kinds, the mechanics and panel-beaters of the former sharing communal doorways with the strippers and hookers of the latter, jowl by cheek.

But there are also riverside walks and recreation parks, where I noticed one rapt lady tactually communing with nature as she progressed slowly along an avenue of trees, embracing each as she went. A commercial hot-air balloon pilot is currently in trouble here over a forced descent into the sea recently when some Japanese honeymooners came to grief. But on a more cheerful note there are thriving art galleries and theatres in this cultural oasis of western entertainment and I was lucky to be able to catch up with the musical *Chess* which I had missed when it was showing in London.

20th March 1996

I received a most encouraging response to my internally advertised presentations at two Colleges of Further Education here and succeeded in finding, after a day of interviews, six suitable candidates for positions starting mid-May. On the journey by taxi from the Polytechnic to the hotel this evening, as we travelled past those warehouses and the plethora of massage parlours that it was impossible to ignore, the driver gave a running commentary, extolling the attractions of Christchurch's ladies of the night. 'Mind you . . .', he paused, 'I have to admit that some of them are real dogs!' I have stayed in.

21st & 22nd March 1996

My visits to **Auckland** are now following a familiar routine thanks to the kind hospitality extended to me by the Head of the Department of Hotel & Restaurant Studies (in spite of the demands made on him by every Tim, Nick and Barry connected with the 'new building' project which has been his 'baby' from start to the hoped-for finish in July), but mostly to the invaluable practical help of his secretary who now stage-manages each visit for me. With a little playtime choreographed into the programme this time, I've been able to explore a little

Westbury Meets East

more of this 'City of Sails', to give it its proper epithet. Auckland, larger and busier than Wellington, has a self-importance, seeming to take itself rather seriously and often mistaken, not surprisingly by virtue of its size, population and appearance for the very capital. The imposing canyons of Queen Street and Albert Street, the choice of several Five-star hotels, the tower blocks housing major international companies, the prominent university buildings, the theatres, the concert hall and the waterfront all contribute to the sureness that this is where it's at. I met up again with Suzy to whom I'd been introduced in the Aotea foyer last September. We took in a violin concerto this time and the minute it was over, dashed across to the Town Hall where I'd managed to pick up two cancelled tickets for a gig by Whitney Houston's auntie: Dionne Warwick! The following evening saw us at an hilarious production of *The Mikado*, a hugely ironic coincidence, given that I'd be back in the Land of Koko and Nanki Poo in a matter of hours, where the comedy still unfolds.

20th April 1996

Fish-shaped windsocks.

In contrast to the breathtakingly crisp whiteness of the forestry near the mountain top (yes, it snowed again last night), I travelled this morning across the drizzle dulled plains of Tochigi-*ken* where the landscape visible from the train window is now dominated by newly irrigated paddy fields. Soon the countryside will resemble so many grass-edged mirrors reflecting the sky. Festooned colourfully once more in the farmhouse gardens are rows of giant gaudy fish-shaped windsocks strung between poles to commemorate the approaching Boys' Day Festival on the 5th May. When the wind drops they resemble outsize novelty condoms hanging limply out to dry.

I'm taking a week off, one of three owed to me before the end of June though I've no hope of squeezing in the other two. I was tempted to travel Japan a little but confess that my continued lack of confidence with the language plus the certainty that my money will go further abroad have pointed me in the direction of the airport to see what is on offer . . .

The Philippines One

21st April 1996

HAVE YOU EVER FLOWN PIA? With the slightly terrorist undertones implicit in its name, small wonder that
the plane filled up with sinister-looking moustached
Asians with tea-cloths for headgear – and that was just the
women. There was also an above average number of
babes-in-arms and masses of cardboard boxes tied up with
string, just a few of my least favourite things. All it needed
was Ketelby's 'In a Persian Market' to come over the intercom
to complete the scenario. Terribly bazaar. The aircraft was
routed in hops via Bangkok to Karachi. I was to alight at the
first stop – Manila – not without some apprehension, as all
news coverage from that particular capital seems always to be
publicising the city's dangers.

The truth is that a random selection of headlines taken from
the *Philippine Star* (e. g.: 'Fifty Kidnaps New Record for January
to April'; 'Doctors sued for Negligence'; 'Customs Officials on
Graft Rap'; 'British Tourist Murdered'; and 'Muslim Extremist
Groups Clash with Government Troops'), could easily be
representative of newspaper reports just about anywhere in the
world today. Apart from an electrical storm during which the
in-flight movie projector got shaken to bits, the leg from Narita
to the Philippines passed without incident. My room at the
Bayview Park Hotel gave neither a view of the bay nor of the
park. But I am jumping ahead.
Last night was actually spent in a Filipino home! Sitting next
to me during the flight had been Ludy who was appalled that

Manila.

I had not booked hotel accommodation and managed to transfer her nervousness to me. The upshot was that I found myself accepting her invitation to her home in Parañaque. Married to a Japanese after only one month's acquaintance, it transpired (later) that she returns monthly to Manila to act as match-maker to Filipinas seeking Japanese husbands. She'd have offered me a longer stay *and* fixed me up with her sister, no doubt, but luck was on my side as she was going to be busy using her house to set up her latest party-plan marriage introduction service for a client expected the next day. I was introduced to the said sister, a bit on the chubby side for my taste, plus cousin upon nubile cousin – no men in evidence. They were very, very kind to me. We enjoyed a very family-style supper (and breakfasted together this morning) with me adopting the role of stand-in *tatay* (daddy) to this household of pretty young ladies in their teens and twenties: Mar-lyn, Mariza, Liza, Donette, Jhun, Annalisa and Maylynne. They sang for me, as they shared their food, with happy faces and natural laughter, characteristics I had enjoyed while in the company of their fellow-countrywomen in Japan and partly what brought me here. What they also have in common is an eye to the main chance of a romantic way out of their poverty... The night was uncomfortably sticky and noisy, the loud hum from the aircon exceeded from time to time by the cats' fracas in the yard as they defended their territory. These alternated with sounds from a phantom insect, outside but immediately under the window, playing castanets. I must have dozed off eventually, only to be woken by a cock crowing and for a moment I believed I was back in Japan listening to Hamanaka *san*'s menagerie stirring below my balcony at The Residence.

When it was time to leave they all said they wanted to marry me but I told them I was too young. Then, I reassured them: '*Napaka ganda mo.*' (Tagalog for: 'You're so beautiful'). They looked at each other very strangely and I hoped I'd not made a gaffe but it turned out that the Filipina in Japan from whom

Rizal Park and the waterfront.

I'd learned the phrase had come from this very Manila suburb and, to their amazement, I had reproduced their local accent! Vicente the driver arrived and together with Ludy and her sister we set off for Roxas Boulevard along which most of the hotels are strung. They helped me find a bank and this place, the Bayview Park Hotel, where I'm very comfortable although from the inside of the hotel I might just as well be in central London. From the window, though, I can just make out the figure of a man sprawled on a truckle bed on top of a corrugated iron roof, shaded from the sun by clothes hanging from washing-lines none of which you are likely to see in Park Lane. The best part of being in the hotel is the plumbing; in this humidity, frequent showering is essential. Last night and this morning, the bathroom arrangements had been very primitive, water being gravity fed from a tank in the yard and, judging from the slow trickle from the shower rose, supplies were low. It is a mystery how eight girls sharing such facilities manage to look so tasty. December, by the way, is the coldest month and it never goes below 25 degrees Celsius.

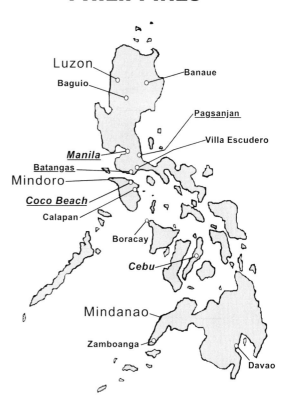

Sketch map of the Philippines.

22nd April 1996

After patiently sitting in a travel agent's office for what seemed like most of the day making plans for the rest of my stay, I ventured into the hostile streets. Each bank I passed had two or three uniformed security men with machine-guns covering the entrance. I put off the idea of a raid. The heat was on in more ways than one and after only half-an-hour out in the sticky mid-afternoon I retreated to the hotel's air-conditioning, having only investigated Rizal Park and the waterfront. As I stepped over or round bedraggled tramps and pedlars, I decided this was not a district to venture through after dark.

Westbury Meets East

I was right not to have worn the YSL shirt with the tailored slacks. In denims and a tee-shirt I felt over-dressed.

A few facts about this country whose 7,107 islands are collectively known as The Philippines: only about 500 of them are more than one kilometre long and only around 2,500 of them have a name. With a population of 67 million and rising, the economy is said to be improving and it probably is, though the 70% who are officially classified as being in the poverty trap doubtless have their own opinion and Manila's dusty and smelly streets, strewn with detritus both inanimate and human, bear witness to the on-going struggle for survival. With the newspapers shouting of continued crime, violence and corruption, it was no surprise to read today's headline announcing that another police colonel-in-chief has been sacked for diverting some 5.7 million *pesos* into his own Swiss bank account, an impressive figure whatever the value of the currency!

Of the last three Presidents, they say Marcos was bad, Aquino was worse, Fidel V Ramos much better. There is an apocryphal story concerning the Marcos family going on holiday. The President, his wife Imelda (she of the hundreds of pairs of shoes), the two daughters and young son are on board their private jet together with a trunk-load of money. High above Manila, Imèe, the elder daughter asks: '*Tatay*, if we threw this money out of the aircraft and down to the people of Manila, would it make them happy?' 'No', said her father, 'it would not.' Then her sister, Irene, asks the same question and receives the same reply. Finally, the young son, 'Bongbong' (nickname of Ferdinand Jr), asks: '*Tatay*, would it *really* not make the people happy if we threw down all this money to the streets of Manila?!' 'No, my son, it would not. But now, were you to choose to throw your mother out of the aircraft . . . *that* would make the people happy!' Coryn Aquino really didn't handle the presidency too well; after a short while, the people who'd elected her reckoned she wasn't up to it. But she'll be at least half-remembered because when she came to power, she re-named the International Airport the Ninoy Aquino Airport after her assassinated husband and half that name is, of course, hers.

Peter Westbury

23rd April 1996

President Ramos' grey Mercedes (licence plate No 111) made a spectacular swerve right in front of our bus at the Makati turn and accelerated slap into the thick traffic congestion that choked Roxas Boulevard for as far as you could see in spite of or perhaps because of the efforts of the motor-cycle traffic cops.

Though he has been the most popular among recent presidents, he is still vulnerable to physical attack and so the man we saw in the back was more than likely a decoy. We, that is to say two Korean ladies, a couple from Hong Kong and myself, were heading out towards Tagaytay to see the world's smallest volcano known to be active. Taal volcano is situated in the middle of a lake forming a very picturesque outlook for the wealthy occupants of Forbes Park, the Beverley Hills of the Philippines and where the presidential private estate is located. En route we passed along the western edge of Lake Lugano, Asia's largest lake. At 90,000 hectares, they say you could put Singapore into it twice, though they don't suggest how or even why you should want to try!

The bouncing creaking bus took us to Las Pinas where the parish church of St Joseph boasts the only bamboo pipe organ in the world, so we obediently shuffled inside and up to the loft, duly admired the amazing construction, listened to a brief recital and shuffled out again clutching a free postcard which I later mailed to Carlo Curley (the world-famous organist whose name you may remember from the Bridewell Heath opening gala concert).

We stopped twice more on this tour, firstly for the others to purchase

Bamboo Pipe Organ.

Roadside fruit stall.

diesel-exhaust coated mangos, bananas, pineapples and coco-nuts from roadside stalls; and secondly, for a visit to a Jeepney factory, to my mind the highlight of the day. Jeepneys are part of the Filipino way of life. They are stretched jeeps, anything up to twenty feet long and powered by reconditioned Izuku or Mitsubishi engines shipped over from Japan for the purpose. (The Japanese have a similar trade with Australia; in the case of New Zealand they ship out the whole second-hand car.) The bodywork is made of uncoated galvanized iron, some panels being shiny. The curved sections such as the wheel arches, the bonnet and the roof are hand-beaten into shape using wooden mallets and crude earthen moulds fashioned out of the factory floor. After assembly, the personalized decoration of the bodywork can colossally affect the final price, up to $US 12,000 being paid for the most elaborate. By far the majority are used as taxis. To distinguish ownership, each driver chooses an identity proclaimed on a signboard above the windscreen and painted in very bold Edwardian pub-mirror advertising style lettering. Thus you may see Lord Jesus Christ coming towards you, or St Augustine, or Mother of Perpetual Help. Another I noticed: simply – Kenneth. Once licensed you're in business at one-and-a-half *pesos* for the first 3 kilometres and half-a-*peso* for each kilometre thereafter. Passengers signal the driver to stop pretty well anywhere at the roadside; they then board and later leave the vehicle through the central rear doorway with the help of handrails. If you prefer comfort then you pay to travel by air-conditioned coach or modern taxi.

Peter Westbury

24th April 1996

If you drive south for two hours out of Manila through the heavily polluted air which, even at daybreak, seems redolent with cooking and diesel fumes far worse than in Tokyo, you will reach Batangas city and port, where a series of primitive ferryboats take it in turns to brave the sea. Prior to embarkation (a rather grand word for a simple process), small boys show off by repeatedly diving from the outriggers. Taking the ferry on a bearing of 180 degrees, you finish up on Coco Beach on the island of Mindoro. As you approach the shore, with the flames and smoke from the oil refineries fading from sight in the rear distance, the lop-sided bosoms that form the silhouette of Mount Halcon slowly reveal themselves through the haze. We shipped a lot of water on this morning's crossing but life-jackets are reassuringly included in the fare; they are clearly expected to be needed. The vessel itself, with a crew of four, fourteen passengers and sundry Coco Beach staff and families on board, served also as cargo carrier, so the deck was shared with a miscellany of essentials from spare parts to food supplies to mail and newspapers. This deck had no sides, just parallel seating facing inwards, covered bow to stern by a ridged canopy, the whole constructed in the main of bamboo and clear plastic sheeting. At the Coco Beach landing-stage, we all stepped onto a floating platform, which was then manually hauled to the temporary-looking jetty. There are no sides to any of this – I imagine they lose a lot of luggage when there's a swell. The narrow strip of beach gives on to a village complex of thatched bamboo buildings set in 10 hectares of very lush hillside, the dream of a Danish-Italian whose architects

'Small boys show off…'

Above: Shoreline seen from Batangas Jetty.

Below: 'At the Coco Beach landing-stage.'

obeyed his instructions to blend with nature: there is no concrete in sight.

My guest suite turned out to be half a bungalow on stilts; the other half was occupied by my 'service family', Leno and his wife Evelyn, whose duties will include fixing the mosquito net and silencing the gecko 'talking too loud' at night-time. Lying in my balcony hammock some 20 minutes after arriv-

ing, I found myself thinking, 'I've gate-crashed Paradise. It only needs a butterfly...', when a large yellow butterfly fluttered into view. I dozed. When I awoke, I thought I should go and see what Paradise had to offer the undeserving intruder but my smugness was short-lived. Each of the delights that had sounded so inviting in the brochure, like the revolving lookout restaurant with the mad chef or the boat trips to Sabang or

'My guest suite...'

Puerto Galera, were either unstaffed or under repair. It seems that Paradise is closed on Wednesdays. So, instead, I booked a *shiatsu* massage for 6.30 p.m., poured a 'sharpener' and steeled myself for a dinner of Filipino dishes followed by an early night as the boat back to Luzon sails at 7 a.m. and I must be on it, Ruby, the travel agent, having fixed me up with a change of hotel and a blind date next evening. As it happens, I shared the supper table with some dishy Scandinavian scuba diving fanatics and what with one thing and another it must have got very late. I remember a backgammon board being produced at some stage but the next thing I knew I was groping through the mosquito net to kill the alarm clock. That was surreal: waking up naked inside a muslin tent into which I had no recollection of having crawled.

25th April 1996

Back in Metro Manila, I booked into the Pavilion Hotel, a barn of a place but conveniently placed, took lunch and a late *siesta* by the rooftop pool and then freshened up to meet Noddi, Ruby's friend back from America. ('Big Ears' appeared later in the shape of Wolfgang, Ruby's German friend exiled in Gran Canaria, a shifty Shylock look-alike if ever there was and a two-timer to boot. How do the girls fall for them? . . . and Ruby Santana is a looker.) In the end the four of us finished up at 'Josephine's', a traditional Filipino restaurant and cabaret spot where a wedding party was in full swing. There appeared to be no objection to strangers joining in as long as we reciprocated by going along with the practice of pinning money on to the bride and groom.

The meal was excellent and the cabaret, too, up to the point where it seemed expected for me to participate in one of the dance routines, a complicated and potentially ankle-cracking ensemble involving bamboo poles and called the '*Tinikling*'. I did succumb to persuasion, but in return for their diligence in helping me master the tricky timing, I insisted on teaching them the famous Westbury knee-pass as performed in the best *karaoke* bars the length and breadth of Shirakawa. You'll be glad you weren't there.

The 'Tinikling.'

26th April 1996

The lady between my legs moaned out loud and grabbed my thighs to steady herself as we rolled, taking in water over the sides of the shallow dug-out propelled by the two swarthy boatmen. The driver had collected us at 8 a.m. for the journey to Pagsanjan Falls where, we were assured by the brochure, we would enjoy 'a thrilling boat-ride through rapids in canoes handled by expert oarsmen'. Well, it was exciting but Noddi was a moaner and complained at the cost of everything (not that she was paying), the silly 'baka' – or should that be 'kalabaw'? (There are two varieties of domestic cow-like animals in the Philippines.) Anyway, the cab-driver and I had a good

This page, previous page bottom and following page: The Journey to Pagsanjan Falls.

Westbury Meets East

laugh over it later and he will be a useful contact for next time. Because I will be back – with a companion of my own.

✽ ✽ ✽

27th April 1996

Ludy, the match-maker, was taking the same return flight today. The Japanese suitor had selected his Filipina bride and paid his deposit. And then cancelled! Cold feet are cold feet in any climate.

'Silly *kalabaw?*'

Westbury Meets East

Radar Trap

9th May 1996

THIS EVENING, while hastening to the dry-cleaners, the solution to the shirt-ironing problem, I was caught, very politely, in a **Radar trap** for the first time anywhere. I was, it is true, spectacularly exceeding the very unrealistic speed limit but whereas previous arrests following chases by patrol cars had only resulted in cautions, this time it seems I am the victim of technology, the hard evidence of a radar print-out being embarrassingly incontrovertible, leaving no room for either doubt or clemency and the unfortunate policeman cannot just file it – he is compelled to follow strict procedures. As I did not have my driving licence with me at the time, itself an offence, I have to present it and myself *ashita* (tomorrow) at the local *keisatsusho* (Police station) to discover the outcome. The police officer's name sounded like 'Magnakata' but it was actually closer to 1915 than 1215. He said he looked forward to seeing me next day at 4 p.m. and was so excited at his catch that he almost forgot to produce his little kit for finger-printing my left fore-finger across the corner of the evidence peeled and stuck to the charge-sheet. We bowed farewell to each other several times and I repeated '*ashita la vista*' over and over but he didn't seem to get it. I arrived at the dry-cleaners to find them shut.

10th May 1996

It suited me better to go in the morning. The *keisatsusho* was swarming with offenders producing licences and paying fines. Over-dressed and over-accessorized in my butler's daytime uniform of three-piece morning suit, bowler, gloves and watch-chain, I approached the counter, swinging my umbrella. Where there had been, perhaps, half a dozen receptionists, suddenly there was no-one! Eventually, an unsuspecting lady clerk, emerging on

Peter Westbury

some other business could not fail to make eye contact and so there began the usual game of charades, aided and abetted by laborious use of the pocket dictionary. Peace talks with the North American Indians might have been like this. Soon we had gained an audience but not much in the way of progress. The wisdom and know-how of a senior officer was clearly required and Chief Inspector i/c Traffic, Araeke *san*, who had been cowering over in the corner of the open-plan office, braved the arena, only to escort me immediately to a separate interview room where we could be more private and where his loss of face at not being able to speak English would not be apparent to his subordinates. He picked up the telephone and sent for assistance. Assistant Detective Inspector Endo *san* from Crime Division appeared in the doorway and immediately recognized me! Not, I should point out, from his investigations of local villains but from seeing me on local Fukushima TV. This had a profound effect on his colleague who had been sitting silently deliberating on how I was to be punished. (They carry firearms, these people.) There was an embarrassing pause. I asked Endo *san* whether we had a problem. He said 'Yes, but not a big problem'. Minutes passed while the Chief Inspector stared at his notes. I could hardly plead 'Not Guilty' against the succinct evidence of the radar machine so I reiterated that I really was most sorry. I hoped my dignified grovelling would reduce the amount of the fine, which threatened to be substantial as, according to the tally sheet in the open folder, my name was among the previous day's top performers.

Another pause. Finally it was decided: whereas my guilt was not in question, in view of the fact that I was such a highly respected person and ever-so-famous, there must have been some administrative error – in which case they would let me go! Isn't that terrible?! Enough to make the absent Magnakata go and commit *jisatsu*. The last word on this episode is that I feel sure I will be seeing more of Detective Inspector Endo. 'If ever you are in any trouble here is my private telephone number'. That means a *karaoke* night, at the very least; which will cost me more than double the fine!

11th and 12th May 1996

This second 'Ambassador's Cup' Golf Trophy weekend involved the first visit to Bridewell Heath by Her Majesty's newly-appointed representative whom it was a real privilege to welcome.

Westbury Meets East

When it comes to the *post mortem*, I'm totally convinced that it will be confirmed that the florist mixed up her orders and we received the displays prepared for the grand opening of a *pachinko* parlour (pinball casino), such were the arrangements of gaudy clashing blooms. By contrast, the Refectory stage where all the prizes had been spread, was a dowdy mess and my guess is that it would have been outright winner if entered in the Faringdon High Street worst-dressed shop window display competition – a distraction for victims of traffic jams in that town before the one-way system. But these areas were not our responsibility. We just kept smiling and pouring the drinks and nobody commented on these obvious cost-cutting moves by the powers in the background. We worked like fury and at the finish it was voted our most successful event yet. But a pity about those finishing touches.

On the Sunday we served 167 golfers a five-course lunch in one hour and 20 minutes *concurrently* with the speeches and prize-giving, giving a wider significance to the word 'handicap'.

That same morning I had the fun of driving the *Cima*, its pennants flying, Union flag on the starboard wing, the Meatball on the port, down to the dry-cleaners in Shirakawa and parked right outside. True I had first dropped off the

Rehearsing for the Ambassador's Cup event.

Ambassador's wife at the station, on her way to an overlapping engagement, but it was a joy to see the faces of the shop assistants when they realized the limousine was for my shirts.

Name-dropping is no crime – I've always believed it requires a great deal of skill. That the Ambassador's wife possesses such skill in abundance was apparent during our descent from the mountain when it was 'Lady Thatcher this' and 'The Princess of Wales that'. She was very amusing company and I tried to reciprocate with the tale of my recent skirmish with the local traffic police. She then rather unexpectedly passed on a motoring tip to confound speed cameras: you simply wrap cling-film over your licence plates! She also revealed herself to be a keen race-goer and will be presenting the Epsom Cup at Tokyo's racetrack next month. She seems to handle a large share of the Ambassador's duties herself and I have the impression that the dear man has little say in the matter of who does what. She creams off what appeals to her and leaves him with the rest: 'Behind every great man there's an exhausted woman', she quotes from a conversation with Princess Diana.

Virginia Bottomley and Michael Roberts are on the list of imminent eminent guests. I, too, have been invited to tea . . . 'if we're in'!

A postscript: His Excellency seemed to recognize me on his arrival . . . and I him. That's because I designed some fitted bedroom furniture for his house in Church Crookham about four and a half years ago. Neither of us let on.

14th May 1996. Chiba

At 5 a.m., having shaved, and showered, I gave my *bodigardo* a shake. He took some time to revive and the thought did cross my mind as to how effective might he have been in an emergency after last night's bender.

He then drove the requisitioned BH bus the short distance to the airport for me to meet and collect the fresh arrivals from New Zealand, replacements for those of the staff leaving later this week. We have this routine well worked out. Okawa *san* and I leave Bridewell Heath in the afternoon, joining the expressway by the Shirakawa access and remaining on motorway roads for nearly four hours all the way to Chiba where we install ourselves in the University guest rooms, handy for the airport and the early morning collection. We're an odd couple by any criteria, the one a Black Belt 7th Dan (ex *Yakuza*) and the other an English butler, nothing in common save the need to eat, drink and sleep. I call him my bodyguard but he's actually on loan from the President. I seem to take more care of *him* that he of *me*. We take it in turns to choose somewhere to eat.

This time he selected a Japanese restaurant and I groaned inwardly, though it might just have been my stomach protesting in anticipation. (To be fair, we have explored most of the neighbourhood over a period of time and the choice boils down to Japanese, pseudo-Italian or McDonald's. Once, we set off to sample the cocktail bars, in the Five-star hotels that serve the Exhibition Hall district, and it was only next day that we realized that we hadn't actually had anything to eat at all; in some way preferable.) Okawa *san* ordered from the menu written almost entirely in *kanji*, the odd (distinctly odd) English word appearing here and there. Miniature dishes appeared containing unidentifiable but inevitably fishy things described as 'titibits'. A giant mug of beer assisted their disappearance. 'Yakitori' was next – or should that be 'Yukkitori'? Actually, not so bad: strips of chicken skin served with spring onions and topped with whole boiled potatoes that you prise apart and into biteable sizes with *hashi* (chopsticks) using a reverse tweezer action. Then we were each brought a bottle of warm *sake* (rice wine) to help the side-dish of cooked-in-their-pods green vegetables, a sort of cross between mange-touts and peas, which you release with your thumb straight into your mouth. Next came tofu, swordfish and sausage floating in gravy. Not sauce. Gravy. Appetizing stuff. We could have had some 'finally ground' chicken (poor bird) and indeed may well have done, more did follow, but my memory lets me down at this stage. I'm not sure what we find to talk about each time; it's as difficult for him as it is for me. I always seem to come back to asking the names of his children; he must think me very forgetful. He's only got one! A son – or is it a daughter?

I do recall purchasing a bottle of whisky and some crisps at Okawa *san's* suggestion from a convenience store on the way back to his *tatami* room. But do please note that it was *I* who shook *him* awake this morning. These bodyguards!

25th May 1996

Peter Westbury

Looking through some press cuttings today, I came across the *Telegraph*'s obituary of Princess Chichibu, widow of the brother of the late Emperor Hirohito. I was reminded of the visit to

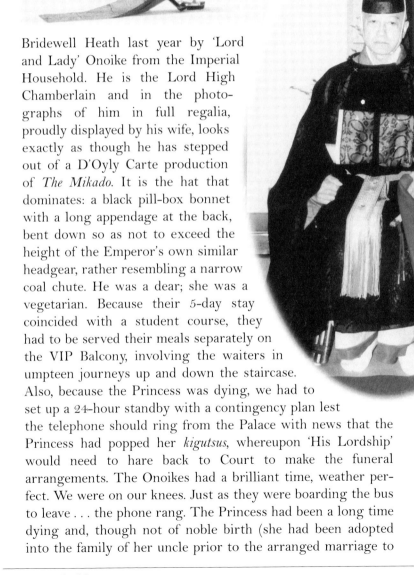

Bridewell Heath last year by 'Lord
and Lady' Onoike from the Imperial
Household. He is the Lord High
Chamberlain and in the photographs of him in full regalia,
proudly displayed by his wife, looks
exactly as though he has stepped
out of a D'Oyly Carte production
of *The Mikado*. It is the hat that
dominates: a black pill-box bonnet
with a long appendage at the back,
bent down so as not to exceed the
height of the Emperor's own similar
headgear, rather resembling a narrow
coal chute. He was a dear; she was a
vegetarian. Because their 5-day stay
coincided with a student course, they
had to be served their meals separately on
the VIP Balcony, involving the waiters in
umpteen journeys up and down the staircase.
Also, because the Princess was dying, we had to
set up a 24-hour standby with a contingency plan lest
the telephone should ring from the Palace with news that the
Princess had popped her *kigutsus*, whereupon 'His Lordship'
would need to hare back to Court to make the funeral
arrangements. The Onoikes had a brilliant time, weather perfect. We were on our knees. Just as they were boarding the bus
to leave . . . the phone rang. The Princess had been a long time
dying and, though not of noble birth (she had been adopted
into the family of her uncle prior to the arranged marriage to

Westbury Meets East

the Emperor's brother), had nevertheless had the grace to hang on long enough not to spoil the courtiers' holiday.

Peter Westbury

A Night in Shining Kaneyama

26th May 1996

I HAVE JUST SPENT the longest night of my life. I cannot have disgraced myself too much last September when I first visited the Ebisuya *Ryokan* at Kaneyama *Onsen* because I found myself once more on the guest list for an evening party at this tiny resort inn which translates as the 'Money Mountain Hot Spring Tavern', situated in the far west-ern reaches of Fukushima-*ken*. Jack joined me this time as we drove through gorges and passes and the unspoiled villages of the valleys beyond Tajima. After the routine with the shoes, we were shown to the *tatami* room. *Tatami* means a night on a *futon*. A *futon* is a thin mattress spread flat on the floor. A *futon* on the floor is not going to guarantee you a good night's sleep and if you are not going to get a good night's sleep then there is a strong case for partying through. The other guests were waiting for us downstairs so we quickly changed into our *yukata*, a wrap-around unisex dress designed for shorter folk than us, and descended to the party room. Disadvantaged by a garment that forces you to display a lot of leg and,

A Night in Kaneyama

occasionally, knicker as you sit cross-legged at the low tables, the ordeal by mouth followed, by which I mean auricular as well as prandial. The speeches! Jack and I were separated. 'Divided we fall', I thought. I had been persuaded to sit at what might be called the high table, had it not been so low, next to the evening's chairman, a man called Yama-guchi ('Mountain fashion store?') who was a bit of a pain in the *oshiri*. Having arrived late, instead of occupying the vacant flat cushion, he inserted himself between me and the other two top table guests, with whom I had been communicating in French and conversation completely petered out. That everyone is expected to get up and say a few words, I knew from the previous visit, but I didn't expect to be first. Standing self-consciously in this dress (a lovely blue), I launched into my prepared speech, regretting that I'd allowed my glass to be topped up so often. '*Watashi wa mata kokoni koreta kotowo totemo ureshiku omoyimasu*'. I hope you're impressed. Polite in the extreme, this roughly translates as 'I most unreservedly assure you that I am highly delighted to have been invited here again'. Roughly. I would challenge anyone to memorize and repeat that, syllable for syllable, after a half of bitter never mind three bottles of Sapporo beer and half a pint of *sake*!! Unfortunately, all they'd wanted from me was my name and occupation!

Having survived that embarrassment and endured incomprehensible speeches from everybody else (Jack was pretty unintelligible, too, by this time),

Kaneyama *ryokan* situation

a tray was placed before me with a selection of the most beautifully presented, unmanageable and indigestible-looking 'titibits' about which the Japanese enthused, watching my every mouthful.

It was the complete kit: whole desiccated fish (you start by biting off the head; then you crunch it up); *miso* soup with mostly unidentifiable delicacies submerged in it (I was grateful to probe something that turned out to be half a potato), cold green bean-stalks, steamed cress (why do they bother?), bamboo, raw quail's egg, shredded carrot (the least unpalatable, I majored on this), tofu topped with wood-shavings? . . . etc . . . etc.

After the traditional *banzai* (three cheers to signal the end of the feasting!), at which no-one shouted louder than I, the inevitable *karaoke* session was announced and we all adjourned to the bar. A more relaxed atmosphere soon prevailed, courtesy of a trillion whisky *mizu*, the Japanese drunkard's staple tipple – whisky and water. The above average vocal talent was purely imaginary, but the womenfolk were definitely transformed from gold-toothed simians to sylph-like maidens that you wanted to rush off and marry. The performers included the lady proprietor, her son Yuruzo, his sister Noriko and her friend Kumi, a comely wench with a gifted voice and a mischievous sense of humour. She and I gave a rendering of Sade's 'Smooth Operator' that you would hardly recognize. Actually,

A more relaxed atmosphere.

it received a tumultuous reception and I record this in my customary unbiased fashion. I recall a reciprocal massage and palm-reading at some stage. It was Noriko, however, who held my gaze (should that be 'glaze'?) and seemed more than a little interested. Her brother had the most amazing *alto castrato* voice which gave a wariness if not a *frisson* to the communal bathing in the hot pool under the stars at 4 a.m. He was a really nice chap, perhaps only giving me the once over on behalf of his sister. But doing that he certainly was.

During some weak moment earlier (there were several), I must have thought it a good idea to agree to an early morning fishing session. It was my first experience of fishing and will most certainly be my last. 6 a.m. saw me at the river's edge but Yamaguchi *san* was ahead of me. With his down-turned mouth he strongly resembled what he was trying to catch. So far he'd had no luck and his humour was not improved when, within 35 seconds of casting and with purely accidental skill (if it can be called that), I had landed what proved later to be the largest of the small catch.

(There is no evidence of this fluke. The snapshot was 37th on a 36-exposure film – the 'one that got away'.) Yamaguchi *san* disappeared off and I soon tired of the so-called sport. Needing to depart early, I had been confident that we would manage to avoid the Japanese breakfast but on returning to the hotel I was dismayed to be served all the tummy-turners they could possibly assemble on one large tray. The least offensive of these was a sort of rice porridge flavoured with something that might have been a kind of pease-pudding bean-curd paste with a spinach flavour, coarse in texture, unsoothing to the stomach, totally evil in colour and quite incompatible with the early hour of the day and the mostly liquid consumption of the previous night. I longed for some coffee. I hallucinated eggs, bacon, toast, butter and marmalade.

We paid our bills, retrieved our shoes neatly awaiting us in the *genkan* and were waved off by the staff. Feeling decidedly delicate after just two hours' sleep and minimum solid sustenance, Jack and I arrived back at the Manor House and walked straight into a health check! 'Everything normal!' said the nurse disappointedly. Oh well, there's life in the old dog yet.

2nd June 1996

Peter Westbury

Almost exactly one year ago I was preparing to travel to Gifu

City. The journey by rail was fairly daunting as it would involve three changes each way and the itinerary, which had been faxed to me by my hosts along with the train tickets, seemed rather tight given the timing of the connections. Anyway, they reassured me that the platforms were not very far apart and I set off, bowler-hatted, morning-suited and really excited to be seeing something of another part of Japan at last. Part of the excitement was the chance of seeing Mount Fuji, a 'must' for foreign visitors, on the middle section of the journey. I made the transfer in Tokyo well enough, although the platform number on the faxed schedule had been incorrect, settled in my reserved seat and kept my eyes peeled for the famous mountain. The *shinkansen* absolutely flew westwards along the southern coastal region before looping upwards to Gifu-*ken*. The tea plantations resembled giant green caterpillars following the curved terrace contours to form a vast distorted maze. But – no Mount Fuji. I began to think I'd taken the wrong train but I learned later that for a large part of the year it is only visible one day in ten because of the haze. Never mind, perhaps I'll catch it on the return journey. After changing at Nagoya, I was met by car at Gifu

Hotel Nagaragawa, a riverside watering-place.

To the tailors of Gifu City

station and chauffeured to the Hotel Nagaragawa, a riverside watering-place.

It was something of a pleasant surprise, as well as a morale booster at the time, to have had my speech to the International Guild of Tailors so well received. Fifty minutes on the Lifestyle of the British Gentleman (with hats) followed by question-time. I have just come across the day's programme buried in a desk drawer and had it translated. Coming last on the day-long agenda after such heavy-weight topics as 'A Study of the Economic History of Gifu and its Future Direction', it is perfectly clear in retrospect that my speech was welcomed purely for its light relief. The word they used in the Japanese title was *kodawari*; the nearest my translator can get to its meaning is 'The British gentlemen's personal code of behaviour and his natural flair for knowing what is right'. A bit toffee-nosed and tending to beg the question, this title went rather deeper than my material. What they got was: 'The British Gentleman, his background, his up-bringing, his education, his clubs, his attire and his Lifestyle'. What *I* got, in addition to the incredible and truly unexpected fee (£370.00) plus my travel and hotel expenses, was a wonderful western style dinner (at which I was obliged to make another impromptu speech) and the unforgettable experience of watching *ukai* (cormorant fishing). I can do no better than quote from the explanatory notes so thoughtfully prepared for me by Ms Yoneda, my charming interpreter: 'Cormorant-fishing is a traditional method of catching fish using trained birds and the practice is thought to have

'Cormorant fishing.'

started in the 7th Century. The season lasts from the 11th May to the end of October. The fishing is done in the evening as small wooden boats drift downstream, each boat carrying a blazing torch in an iron basket suspended off the bow to lure the fish. The boats are usually manned by two fishermen and two boatmen. The master fisherman skilfully manipulates as many as a dozen cormorants, around the neck of each of which there is a ring on a rope about ten feet long. When one of the birds comes up to the surface with a fish (which it cannot swallow because of the ring), the fisherman pulls in the rope and makes it disgorge its catch.'

While the tailors threaded their way to the bar after dinner, I descended by elevator to the *onsen*, making the acquaintance of a charming Japanese lady on my way but she was off to her next appointment. Unfortunately the two ladies in the picture were nowhere to be seen. I found them in the hotel brochure! In fact I enjoyed a good old splash and a soak entirely on my

Nowhere to be seen.

Westbury Meets East

The hotel *onsen*

own before donning my *yukata* and retiring for the night. On reaching my room, I found Yoneda *san* waiting to see if she could be of any further use. You have to hand it to them – they are so thoughtful.

Next morning, one of my breakfast companions told a Chinese laughing-story of the photographer who was describing the technical difference between two snapshots, one of a girl dressed in 'pantaroons', the other in a mini-skirt. It was clear, he explained, that the girl in the mini-skirt was over-exposed. Encouraged by my polite laughter, he told the story again – four times, his own mirth increasing with each repetition. You have to laugh! They are as bad as we English. They do like a joke they know.

The culinary tables were turned at breakfast. I have described the traditional Japanese breakfast menu already – sheer purgatory. Attention focused on the *gaijin*, everyone waiting politely for me to begin, anxious to witness my enjoyment. I'm afraid I felt unequal to the challenge and I'm sure that I disappointed them.

And so it was time to say farewell to Gifu, known in Japan as 'The City of Apparel'. The tailor who doubled as my taxi-driver whisked me back to the station. 'How's business?' I enquired, half expecting to receive the stock London Rag Trade reply: 'Don't ask!'. Instead, the Gifu equivalent: 'You cannot fight the gods!'. Already.

On the first leg of my return journey, I got the direction right but boarded a slow train instead of a fast one, which made a nonsense of the remaining connections. But I'd had a great adventure and although Mount Fuji remained coy... I really couldn't carp.

Peter Westbury

On the Trot

3rd June 1996

CONTRACTS EXPIRE at the end of the month and nothing has been said about renewals as yet. If they do want me to stay I shall have to send home for further supplies of Imodium. There is a Japanese equivalent, should you ever need to know. It is called 'Trot' – perhaps the reverse of what one might expect, thinking about it. Maybe the chemist mis-interpreted my mime?

Booms from the Japanese Army's firing range just a kilometre or three away, combined with penetrating metallic percussion from Hamanaka *san*'s workshop only a few feet below my balcony window, put paid to any hopes of catching up on my sleep following yesterday's very late night. So I put on a tape that included Holst's 'Planets' and the Anvil Chorus and gave them some competition while catching up with some domestic chores. I encountered the Army on the move later in the day, a fragmented convoy weaving its way through Shirakawa look-ing completely lost. This reminded me of the only other time I have stumbled upon the soldiers, which was while driving in the mountains last winter with Ben and Amanda. We had tried to find a short cut but soon realized the track was taking us above the snow line. Suddenly, we had penetrated the defences of a trainee platoon on manoeuvres! They seemed very star-tled by the appearance of these intruders, *gaijin* to boot. It's not as though we were well camouflaged, BH vehicles being a pretty green rather than macho. Anyway, we brazened it out and asked for directions. They asked to see our map! (Perhaps they are simply not standard issue in the Japanese Army?) Having established that the way ahead was un-negotiable, Ben swung the estate wagon round and straight into a ditch. This seemed to make the militia feel less bad about their lapse in security as it was now we who appeared foolish. They laughed

Westbury Meets East

a lot and made no move to help but by slapping the car into reverse gear and bouncing on the bumper we were soon sliding back whence we had come.

Referring back to the events of yesterday evening from which it has taken me most of today to recover, I had been invited with three other members of the permanent staff (*how* permanent?!) to a reception and buffet party organized by local businesses to wish good luck to the Japanese 'Porsche' motor-racing team entered for the 24-hour Le Mans later this month. Mr Suzuki, the driver, was the centre of attention, less because of his success in the French heats back in April, of which there was film footage, but more due to his very pretty escort, a dolly bird with so little on that the padding stood out a mile. ('This little dolly, made in Japan . . . almost every night.' – line from *Fiorello*, a sixties musical.) Her main role in public was to hold a large 'elf DIESEL' umbrella over his head during his interminable speech. Long before the end, her arms gave out. *While* he was actually speaking, I was asked to reply with a few words on behalf of the sponsors! They request these favours absolutely at whim as if it is the most natural thing to be asked to address a banqueting hall of at least 280 people (I say 'at least' because that was the number on my draw ticket with which I later won a tee-shirt) with next to no notice. Of course, it is impossible to refuse so you accept with aplomb while panicking inside. Izumi *chan* ('*chan*' is a more intimate title than '*san*' and is an endearment frequently used in an office environment or among friends), the pretty clerk in Accounts with whom Chef has been, er, with, was one of our group and agreed to interpret my improvised little speech a sentence at a time provided I promised no 'difficult' words. We borrowed the umbrella from Miss United Padded Cups and bounded on to the stage, each with a radio mike. Up with the umbrella, pantomime of 'Funny, no rain!' and suddenly we were a 'turn', as Felix Bowness would have described us. Finally, having proposed the toast to the driver and his team ('*Gambatte kudasai. Okiotsukete. Kanpai!*') and turning now to the main audience, I borrowed a quip from an old school chum, circa 1954, 'Do remember: if you're drinking and driving, first make sure you have a car!' They loved it.

In the draw, Izumi and I both won a commemorative tee-shirt (I've mentioned that twice now; I'm so unused to winning anything) and everybody received a calendar. I had

Peter Westbury

mine autographed by Suzuki *san* and his pit-stop popsy as we left.

It was my night really. Later, in a newly-opened *karaoke* bar to which our hosts insisted on introducing us, I was greeted by the owner as if we were old friends, having been in the place only a few evenings previously!

I sang a duet in Japanese, well to be truthful just the chorus, with a lady of a certain age whom I'd never met before and, together (*horresco referens*), we rated top score of the evening – 93 on the 'clapometer'!

Much later, absolutely starving and alone, I was at last able to order a club sandwich at an all-night road-house. I had not trusted the food on the buffet table, my stomach demonstratively protesting at all the iffy food sent its way recently. And I very much regret to report that my romantic involvement with the other half of the triumphant duet had been curtailed at a critical moment when I had the first suspicion that the 'Trot' capsule I had downed before setting out might indeed be a Japanese laxative after all!

Westbury Meets East

Road-testing the Tudor 2+1

5th June 1996

ANOTHER LARK! Tonight I'm road-testing this bed for Hitachinomiya-*denka*, His Imperial Highness the Prince Hitachi, the Emperor's brother and fourth in line to the throne of Japan. He will be coming to stay next week so I am trying out the King's Bedchamber in the Manor House for him to use. The imposing bed is a copy of a Tudor tester-bed. It has a carved canopy with cornice and frieze and two elaborate columns for footposts, the lower parts in square section and the upper turned and featuring distinctive cup-and-cover mouldings. The head panel incorporates the Bridewell Heath coat-of-arms in exquisite marquetry. This hardly used model (the 'Tudor 2 + 1' shall we call it?) comes in wine upholstery with oak trim. Vroom, vroom! You can probably appre-

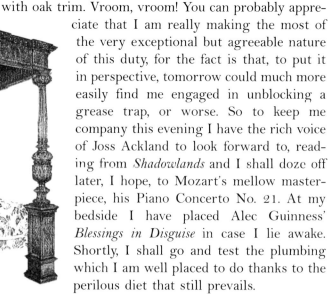

ciate that I am really making the most of the very exceptional but agreeable nature of this duty, for the fact is that, to put it in perspective, tomorrow could much more easily find me engaged in unblocking a grease trap, or worse. So to keep me company this evening I have the rich voice of Joss Ackland to look forward to, reading from *Shadowlands* and I shall doze off later, I hope, to Mozart's mellow masterpiece, his Piano Concerto No. 21. At my bedside I have placed Alec Guinness' *Blessings in Disguise* in case I lie awake. Shortly, I shall go and test the plumbing which I am well placed to do thanks to the perilous diet that still prevails.

The bathroom is Victorian in style as is the whole vast bedroom and sitting-room. It is all rather like a grander and later

Peter Westbury

version of a Regency suite at the Royal Crescent Hotel, Bath, though a bit more on the masculine side. Around the T-shaped room runs an ivory frieze of dainty unicorns, contrasting with the heavy furniture which includes a wonderful pair of lioness chairs and some Roman stools upholstered in red and gold. Two fat-bellied bombé chests flank the impressive mantelpiece above which 'The Monarch of the Glen' stares out. Chased gold-collared Bohemian water-glasses surround a crystal decanter on a silver tray so I'll have something suitable in which to serve myself juice in the morning. A framed facsimile of the Magna Carta hangs in one recess; and 'Touch', a reduced size copy of one of the 'Five Senses and Old Age' series of tapestries that hang in the Cluny Museum in Paris, graces another.

3 a.m. – the night has revealed deficiencies in suspension, ventilation and cornering. I am hot and uncomfortable. The mattress has a pattern of ridges and will need a cover. The journey to the bathroom was hazardous in the dark and I stubbed my small toe on a giant footstool that I had forgotten was at the end of the bed. The French fittings were confusing: it was a long time before I realized that the hand basin tap marked '*Chaud*' had been connected to the cold supply so it was never going to run hot.

Time off during rehearsals for the Emperor's brother's visit.

The tap marked '*Froid*', it follows, had been erroneously connected to the hot supply – what you might call a Froidian slip! The free standing bath on its ball and claw feet and complex shower attachment was great fun but the mixer tap had a mind of its own and, without a screen, the water went everywhere.

I have an exhaustive list of faults that will need ironing out before the 14th if this room is going to be made fit for a prince. I shall call a meeting when the office opens. In the meantime I shall go home and get some sleep!

❀ ❀ ❀

2 a.m. and still sorting out the table plans.

Peter Westbury

7th June 1996

I'm not sure that it's a time for rejoicing, exactly, the frustrations of working here are, if anything, on the increase and the staff diet is certainly still far from the *cordon bleu* cuisine that tempted us here, but it was revealed today that, if we wish, our contracts are to be extended. All salaries have been frozen, however, so we will, in effect, be accepting a reduction in income because the *yen* has slipped from its high perch on the exchange rate charts and most of us have financial commitments outside Japan. But there are other aspects than money to consider and I have started to discover a life here outside Bridewell Heath . . .

14th June 1996

I welcomed Prince Hitachi on the steps of the Manor House this afternoon and he returned my greeting in English in a high-pitched electronic voice and shook my hand. He looks out through his enormous *megane* (spectacles), blinking so frequently that one understands why photographs invariably show him with his eyes shut. A cross between a scrubbed-up version of our staff kitchen chef and Mr Magoo, he shuffled his way meekly round this facility like an automaton, accepting the interminable ordeal by Mikada *san* guide-speak with great grace – or should that be resignation? He must have known what to expect; they had been together at University and in touch since, many times. His nickname, '*Uchujin*' (man from outer space), together with his voice and manner combined to give the impression of a charming, well-dressed, spaced-out robot. He was no trouble at all and most appreciative of every attention. His college contemporaries, both male and female, proved to be a motley crew, life having been kinder to some than to others. Their parents had been of a hierarchy that had made history and headlines in World War II as admirals, ambassadors, generals, etc. They sat down to a splendid dinner, a replica of an historic menu of 1906 when, according to Mikada *san*, something or other important had been celebrated.

They knew how to relax and enjoy themselves and I was kept busy after dinner steadily pouring whisky *mizu* in the King's Suite where they all sat around reminiscing until quite late . . .

The check-list, following my personal 'road-testing' of The Bed, had included the need for a mattress cover. One had originally been recommended by Ben and Amanda who had tried out the half-tester in the Queen's Room when it was first thought that the Prince would be accompanied by the Princess. Of course nothing had been done and when I pressed the matter my request was greeted with feigned surprise and eventually the admission that they had great difficulty in grasping what a mattress cover was. A pad, perhaps, a fitted sheet? Ah! A mattress *cover*! It would have to be ordered from Tokyo –

Westbury Meets East

such things were not available locally. On the morning the Prince was due, a parcel arrived. After all the careful description and translation, we received, yes, an incontinence sheet. Did my Japanese colleagues perhaps know something about His Imperial Highness that I did not?! On the grounds that he would be more likely to be kept awake by the crackly sheet than by the ridges of the mattress pattern, I made the decision to leave it off.

... Having tidied the room after the drinks reunion and established that a 6.20 a.m. wake-up call was wanted, I wished His Highness 'Good-night' and withdrew, leaving him in the charge of his guard and chamberlain, your friends and mine, Messrs Suzuki and Kobayashi, the broker's men. Pantomime similes do leap to mind quite frequently at BH. Pantomimes and circuses – Westbury: ringmaster and shoveller.

I knocked punctually on the door of the King's Suite the following morning, entered, drew back the curtains and served morning tea. The prince was already up, shaved and dressed, but the bath was bone dry. I would not normally be so indiscreet as to mention this fact but I was asked later by his erstwhile class-mates whether there was any evidence that he had taken a bath. They explained that, as a student, he was renowned for his aversion to bathing and they were curious to know whether his habits had changed. They had even been to check the bathroom themselves. But my theory is that the bath was dry because he had found it more comfortable to sleep there than in the bed!

Peter Westbury

This Onsen *Thing*

18th June 1996

ACK TO THIS *onsen* thing, I am at the Ebisuya *Ryokan*, once again, in Kaneyama. Since I was last here (26th May), the party room has been partitioned up into sections and I am now sitting on a *zabuton* (very flat cushion) on the floor in front of a traditional Japanese dinner, all by myself! It was Noriko *chan's* idea to invite me here again. I didn't really know what to expect – hardly a candlelit table for two – but I didn't think I'd be on my own. The room is perfectly empty, save the low table in the exact centre. There are no plant pots or anything else in which to secrete the ornate but unappetizing food, most of which consists of rather indigestible stalks. The customary very dead baked fish, the roe spilling out of one of them like ants' eggs as I split it open, sit next to the uncooked variety. I'm not sure which is worse. Anyway, hopes of a romantic evening are dissolving fast and not for any alcoholic reasons. We have exchanged *omeyagi* (gifts) in the time-honoured way. There is nothing spontaneous about this process; the gift

industry represents a major slice of the Japanese economy. Similarly, there is the obligatory custom of presenting your *meishi* (business card) to all and sundry, thus keeping busy the paper factories and the print-shops. My presents to Noriko were all consumable and I'm beginning to wish I'd hung on to them. The prospect of a midnight feast of chocolate truffles and sparkling champagne would have kept my spirits up. If only there was some *bread*!

I had arrived at the agreed time of 3 p.m. and been shown to my room. The idea, ostensibly, is for Noriko to teach me some Japanese in return for me giving her lessons in English. The

Westbury Meets East

first topic should have warned me that romantic interlude this was not to be: with the help of four large wallets of photographs, she proceeded to describe the details of her father's funeral. (In a mental flashback to my youth, I remembered the postscript in a letter from Rosario, a sweetheart in Barcelona – 'P.S. Carmen wish me send you her remains.')

Prior to this dinner, I have had time to dip my lone self in the *onsen*, have a relaxing *hirune* (forty winks) followed by a pre-prandial 'sharpener' that I smuggled in, just a small one, you understand.

With a little unexpected time to myself, I have the opportunity to explain this *onsen* phenomenon in more detail. The *o-furo* (communal bath) is filled with water from natural hot springs higher up the mountain through bamboo pipes. The *onsen* is for both cleaning and relaxing BUT both functions are quite separate in the Japanese rule-book and you must ON NO ACCOUNT take soap or allow suds into the shared bath water. So you squat on a low wooden stool at one of a row of low shower taps and, having filled a scoop from the tub, you soap yourself all over and then rinse well, rubbing yourself down with the *te-nugui*. This is a token strip of towel about 12 inches (30cms.) wide and 30 inches (75cms.) long, just the size not to make it once round your nether regions but nevertheless supplied to conceal your nakedness initially and with which to dry yourself later, wringing it out several times as it becomes sodden. The surprise is that the sodden thing actually does work and fails only in the modesty stakes. The *yukata* (cotton gown – mine was 'big size' this time, with a snuff-coloured hexagon motif on a cream background; brown does nothing for me) should be wrapped left side over right before securing with the *obi* (sash), a word not unheard of in English crossword puzzles. Not believing it to be particularly important, I am sure I have sometimes mistakenly wrapped right over left.

Peter Westbury

I have recently learned that this is how corpses are dressed ready for cremation. The *yukata* may then be worn for dining or lounging about, even out of doors but mind who you smile at. I would have preferred the blue but apparently, at Ebisuya *Ryokan*, at any rate, the blue is colour-code for *se no hikui* (short-house). Japanese bath-house fantasies as featured in Bond movies have as yet to manifest themselves in my experience but hope springs eternal and every now and then I tempt fate by giving it a sporting chance.

Still no sign of Noriko; I'm glad I slipped my notepad into my document-case. Thinking this evening would follow the pattern of the two previous visits, I had prepared some key phrases for the usual impromptu speech: 'wonderful ambience', 'kind family', 'unique experience' – you can imagine the sort of thing, nothing about the food – but there's not another soul in evidence. I've had a little walk around to bring circulation back to my buttocks and I've experimented with different sitting positions when, every so often, my back gives out. But there seems nothing for it but to contemplate the four identical opaque paper panelled walls. However hard I concentrate, I cannot remember by which one I entered as the doors, which slide, are homogeneous with the walls. Unless someone comes soon, they'll find me in hysterics . . . . (Denoting the passage of time – leaving me to chat among myself.)

It was explained to me recently that a relationship with a Japanese really amounts to a prolonged greeting, a continuous process in which the *gaijin* is asked many questions of an increasingly personal nature. I can hardly wait. Actually an Englishman I met who has lived here for 20 years told me that he gave up learning the language for conversational purposes because all that the Japanese ever showed interest in was his age and the size of his feet. I actually take some comfort from this, knowing that women are strange creatures. My first wife married me for my wrists; the second for my buttocks. I feel things may be moving in the right direction.

Noriko has just put her head round one of the walls (it was *that* one) to recommend that I take some rest (!) before we go together later tonight to a traditional public *onsen* under the stars . . .

And so it came to pass that, after selflessly forcing myself to

Westbury Meets East

stay awake until the other guests finely (i.e. in a fine state, not like the 'finally' chopped chicken from Chiba!) went drunk to bed at 2 a.m. Noriko and I slipped out quietly, holding hands in the dark (and the rain) to find our way to the historic public baths, which turned out to be nothing more than a stone shed with a concrete lined pool about 10 feet long by 5 feet wide and 2 feet deep. One 'end' was for the gentlemen, the other for the ladies. Mould lent character to the walls.

As there were just the two of us, Noriko modestly waited outside while I immersed myself. I had to go through with it; it was, after all, the highlight of my stay. Ten minutes from having left the hotel we were back in the warmth of the foyer wishing each other *'iiyume o'* (sweet dreams), a chaste as well as chastening experience!

The 'distinguished *Noh* actor' who had introduced himself grandly during the obligatory *karaoke* session I was trapped in while waiting for them all to go to bed, turned up at breakfast in work overalls and went off with his hungover mates to lay cables or something. Noriko and I spent most of the day parked in the rain, happily enough exchanging *non sequiturs* from language primers, the personal questions delving no deeper than discreet enquiries concerning the whereabouts of the pen of my aunt or a transparently spurious interest in how my postilion had come to be struck by lightning. She is really very sweet. But then so are the others, in Tokyo, Omiya, Kuroiso and Aizu Wakamatsu . .

22nd June 1996

Since my visit to the Philippines, my stock has really soared in the local Filipina clubs where I've been place-name dropping shamelessly. I have also benefited by a relaxation in their rules regarding off-duty dating and I've spent some memorable afternoons harmlessly playing sugar-daddy to a few girls at a time in restaurants, shopping malls or funfair parks. As their work visas limit them to a six month stay, I have seen quite a few pretty faces come and go, some of them skipping off to the

Peter Westbury

big cities, others back to their homes with the hope of returning again to Japan. It is impossible not to have favourites and
I've been seeing more of some than others. I've also been visiting one club more frequently, where the girls and the cabaret
(and the prices) are streets above the rest. It was an obvious
choice of venue for my birthday outing and I decided, in order
to satisfy his curiosity as all he'd received from me in response
to his enquires as to my social life was an inane grin, to invite
Jack along. He was in a rut, let's face it, with his fiancée's
mother wholly hostile to her daughter's alliance with a *gaijin*
and he was getting nowhere. I thought it was time to intro-
duce him to Faye.

We had a great foursome: Faye, Jack, Choco and I. Choco is
an outrageous flirt with a scorpion tattooed on her left breast.
I like her a lot. She is the only Filipina I've met who did not
have a hard luck story to tell of sick parents or needy brothers and sisters. She raises one eye-brow and her dazzling smile
is slowly transformed into the sexiest of grins, the unspoken
questions entirely in her eyes. So I was rather pre-occupied
with Choco and consequently failed to notice how well Jack
and Faye were getting along. It wasn't until we were driving
home much later that he told me this was the girl he intended
to marry!

Diary:
Year Three
July 1996 to June 1997

Mistakes and Identities

1st July 1996

F OR THE PAST TWO YEARS I've been living in Japan
(largely on Imodium and rice) and it may be the moment
to reflect on the little I've learned. I was rushed out here
at very short notice without the time to acquaint myself with
the contents of those guide-books that tell you all about what
to expect. This was a mistake. What I have learned, I have
learned from painful first-hand experience.

I knew that the Japanese were entrenched in a much-
publicized 'different' culture, that they live to work rather than
work to live. That they would be efficient and well-organized,
I felt confident. The short notice should have been a clue. It
is one of their characteristics to act at very short notice, usually when time is running out and forces a decision. Their sense
of anticipation is nil. The outsider is advised (should that be
warned?) – I am quoting from a guide-book I picked up last
week – that the Japanese are 'strongly into the group thing'.
In theory this is so that responsibilities are shared; in practice
this has given rise to a procedure in which they really excel:
decision-postponement-making by committee. They sit in
meetings saying not very much, frequently pausing for
thought, nodding to signify only that they hear what is being
said and not that they agree or plan to do anything about it,
sometimes nodding because they are, in fact, asleep, and then
convene to await the deliberation of the President or Chairman
or the Director- General so that it all boils down to a decision
by one man anyway, though not before many more interven-
ing meetings. This is why business, that could be concluded in
five minutes, takes five months and leads to exasperation for
the non-appreciative outsider. Everything is at a glacial speed
or slower. This slow process is as much ingrained in them as
quick action is ingrained in me. It came as a surprise when I
learned that there is no future tense in the Japanese language
but it does explain a lot. Planning ahead, as a concept, is at a

Westbury Meets East

serious disadvantage without the word-tools to go with it. This has helped me to understand the situation though not to accept it. After all, having a past tense has not made them any better at hindsight! They still make the same old mistakes.

The impossibility of predicting the future provides them with the logic for leaving everything until the last minute. Every *gaijin* I meet confirms this from his own experience. I can hardly believe that I have signed on for another year but there is always the feeling that things may change and that 'Future Tense' will be a thing of the past.

2nd July 1996

I've been shopping for some bits and pieces to accessorize the *apato* since I'm to be staying on for another year.

[Actually, they've accepted my proposal to extend the notice required by both parties to two months, a more realistic length of time for them to find a replacement should I resign and for me to find alternative employment should they terminate or not wish to extend my contract].

So now, hanging on my walls, I have an original semi-abstract still-life in oils by Hideo Ikeda (a 61 year old artist who studied in Europe and whose one-man exhibitions received some acclaim), two prints (one by Gustav Klimt and the other by Bernard Cathelin), a water colour of Temple Island, Henley on Thames and a *noren* (door curtain), depicting a warrior, given to me by Noriko *chan* to guard my bedroom but which is traditionally hung to show you're open for business.

6th July 1996

Considering the number of sunrises I've witnessed since coming to work in the 'Land of the Rising Sun', it is a wonder that the significance of the national epithet has only just dawned on me! It was an early start again today and now, after a hearty breakfast of sultanas and compressed fish-flavoured cardboard in a Tokyo business hotel, I am back on the train heading for home. I came up yesterday on a PR exercise to meet representatives from Diners Club and a finishing school. Last night's company-funded stop-over gave me the chance to meet up again with two delightful new young friends, Satoko

Peter Westbury

and Mieko. (We last met back in February when they came to BH for the ski–ing. I drove them to the ski-field in a blizzard. It became even more of an adventure when the car started to die due to freezing diesel.) Our rendezvous was the foyer of the Westin Hotel at Yebisu Garden Place, which is only a short walk to the *trattoria* they had thoughtfully chosen for our supper together. Our difference in ages? – *mondai arimasen* (no problem). We laugh a lot. I feel thirty years younger. I help them with their language practice and they help me keep my ego in check. Everybody benefits. I increase my stock of two-word sentences, which we devised to conceal my total ineptitude at mastering the Japanese verb structure and the girls seem to enjoy their involvement in the conspiracy, accepting it for the face-saving memory trick of a slow learner. One of them left early for a date; the other was happy to stay chatting until the small hours, not having to work today.

But I must be back at the village following a rare tip-off from the Tokyo office to say that the President would be down for his birthday some time this weekend.

7th July 1996

Today was the President's birthday and he arrived sartorially immaculate, as ever. Having had a birthday recently myself, I was well-rehearsed to greet him with; '*Tanjobi omedeto gozaimasu!*' (Birthday congratulations.) He beamed. Mind you he had something to beam about with four young escorts in tow, imported from the Ginza for the weekend. We had one of those evenings in the Refectory when everything went really swimmingly. The butler spilt a glass of dessert wine down himself but, that apart, it all went like a dream.

Later, in the Snooker Room we entertained members of the Churchill *Kai*, a very distinguished group of elderly amateur painters. I had been in conversation with an incredibly jolly guest who told me she had been one of only two lady Public Prosecutors out of a total of 18 in Japan and another very expensively dressed lady who was an opera singer, when the latter's husband, a retired senior banker, joined us. He declared that I would be most welcome to make love to his wife, once, provided that he could bring his sketch pad. He specializes in nudes. I expect he could have showed me a wrinkle or two.

Westbury Meets East

The ex-Public Prosecutor intervened, thereby saving embarrassment on all sides.

No sooner had the eminent senior citizens withdrawn to the pub, than the President's group arrived by way of dazzling contrast. Jack and I had another of those 'pinch-me- is-this-really-happening' sensations as we heard the special request for us to teach these four sophisticated, slender, long-legged, well-heeled and provocatively dressed tarts the basics of snooker! We behaved, of course, impeccably... But then the President *was* watching and, to paraphrase my friend Beth's classic remark, 'Whose birthday was it, anyway?!' The grins on our faces took several days to fade.

9th July 1996

I have made it a policy to bring my own slippers with me when attending hospital. The short plastic jobs stacked in *genkan* pigeon-holes make a *gaijin* feel even more of a freak. Today I hoped to have avoided the usual long wait by asking Izumi *chan* to telephone ahead and make me an appointment but the place is on overload and I'm obviously still way down the list, if one exists. In this waiting area, on the backless bench next to me, is a deaf chappie they've been shouting at but most of the time the atmosphere has been convivial with jolly reunions and much cackling from sociable old ladies among the regular patients. I have just spotted my usual nurse – I call her *Tenshi san* (Miss Angel), I don't know her real name and she does not seem to mind a little flirting. There is suddenly an overwhelming smell of drains but I seem to be the only one to notice; maybe their sense of smell is on a par with their eyesight.

Anyway, in case you didn't like to ask, I've been coming here because of a skin allergy so I'm hardly top priority. I think I must have been affected by something in the water causing irritation and peeling around my face. With my son's wedding celebration approaching I thought I should obtain some treatment in case I'm taken for a leper at the feast. On that first visit I was waiting for three hours. Eventually, the *kangofu* (nurse) beckoned me in to an extremely untidy room lined with framed photos of rashes taken from many angles and of every body part and orifice. Stripped to the buff (I'm only here for

Peter Westbury

my face!), I become an object of curiosity to three pairs of eyes. The *isha* (quack) riffles unhurriedly through Obunsha's senior Medical Dictionary (Illustrated) umpteen times, then tries in vain to match me to a photograph (*any* photograph!) from case-books consulted at random from stacks spread higgledy-piggledy all over the desk and floor. Periodically he gives me a prod. It's trial and error, clearly, just a stab in the dark (or should that be a dab in the stark?). So far, my *mondai* (problem) has remained unidentified for which, in some measure, I'm grateful as these illustrations are on full view to me and any one of them would really test the squeamishness of fellow-guests at a wedding breakfast. The prescriptions seem so far to have been in the nature of an experiment. They have been many, varied and costly, part of the experiment being to test my bank balance.

Each lengthy consultation has been divided pretty evenly between page-turning, mis-diagnosis, communication difficulties and much giggling. At one point I was asked whether I wore make-up. Well, I suppose I could have been an actor. (But I never had the Latin!)

This time I have come away with 21 tiny tablets, costing just £44.00, about one quarter of the average price of a few hours in one of the alternative 'stress clinics' known in these parts as Filipina bars!

17th July 1996

Venezia, a delightful 19-year old Franco-Polish fashion model came into my life for a few magical afternoons this week when we posed together and generally acted up for the camera-team, here to shoot a Burberry commercial. It remains to be seen if I and/or my bowler hat (which looked very fetching on *her*) will be featured in the catalogue. 'Venezia' is the professional name of Anna-Venezia Karowska. Come what may, I have some wonderful snapshots for the scrap-book as reminders of the incredible rapport we shared for a few hours that put me on a high for days; plus the standing invitation to the family-owned *hotel-particulier* in the Rue de Grenelle when I'm next in Paris. We shall cook for each other – we've already agreed on the dinner menu. It is almost in my mouth . . .

Burberry shoot, Venezia
wearing MY bowler hat.

Seedy CD ROM

19th July 1996

THE VILLAGE OF BRIDEWELL HEATH is a gift for Japanese film-makers who can take advantage of an authentic-looking British location to form the backdrop for fashion-shoots, product launches, full-length features or whatever. Rarely does a week go by without an invasion by teams of cameramen, lighting technicians, wardrobe assistants and models who proceed to festoon their equipment, their cables, their gear and themselves about the furniture, the stair-case, the cloisters and the gardens. I am often too busy to do much more than greet them, make sure they have access to where they want to film, pacify the staff whose routine will be disrupted and finally wave the group off when they leave.

One group, with the grand title of 'Japan Corporation' but actually standing out as being even more casual in appearance than the average (which is to say, downright scruffy), arrived last March to make 'a film about a school'. Something else that distinguished them from other film-makers was the fact that they had in tow a bunch of extremely mature, not so say nubile, models that they were going to have to do more than shake a stick at to transform into teenage schoolgirls. The producers had obviously gone part of the way to lending credibility of their own to the fictional setting of 'St. Elmo's' (why the patron saint of fire, I do not know; perhaps they thought they were hot stuff): the unit had brought with them customized school uniforms complete with blazer badges and plaid skirts. The Director outlined his schedule giving the gist of the story and we left them to it.

I have failed to mention that some time before Christmas I had been moved from my minuscule cubby-hole of an office within the general Ops. Room to the luxurious expanse of the President's Room. To put the right perspective on this, it had been a matter of expedience, not magnanimity. More space was needed in the Ops. Room; the President is an infrequent visitor

Westbury Meets East

now; move the butler out of one and into the other. Better still, leave the door open and he's on show to passing guests even when he's at his desk. But I don't want to appear ungracious; I cannot imagine I will ever occupy a more opulent office. In pseudo-Victorian style, the furniture is all reproduction but of superb quality. The mahogany playing-field size partnership desk topped with panels of tooled leather is supposed to be a copy of one in the Trump mansion. The Regency settee immaculately upholstered in figured satin, the Pembroke side-tables decorated in exquisite marquetry, the semi-circular chiffonier, the display cabinet housing the priceless collection of Etruscan pottery, the lamps, the paintings, the clocks, the leather armchairs . . . all add up to surroundings designed to impress the visitor, if not to intimidate, very much in keeping with the Shogun tradition.

I realized the suitability, from the point of view of the story-line, of using my office, normally a private room and regarded as off-limits to film-crews, as the Headmaster's Study and offered it as an idea to the 'St. Elmo's' director for consideration. He not surprisingly jumped at the chance and that is how I came to be involved in what, it only slowly dawned on me in my *naiveté*, was very likely the making of a soft porn movie or what, I gather, is known in the modern idiom as a seedy CD Rom. I suppose I should have twigged when they asked me to take off all my clothes! JOKE *ONLY*!

CD-ROM
for Macintosh

[Actually, these days they can use all sorts of amazing computer wizardry to remove your clothes, facial hair, anything! . . . they need neither an airbrush nor your co-operation.]

What they in fact did was to ask me to play the part of the Headmaster and to give the girls a ticking off, though to this day I still have no notion as to the nature of their misdemeanours. So, of course, 'in good faith', as the allegedly guilty usually plead, I simply entered into the spirit of the thing. It was only next day when some of the Japanese staff were becoming curious as to what was going on that I thought it best, in all seriousness, to cover myself by writing a memo to Mikada *san* expressing my disbelief that our Company would hire out Bridewell Heath as a location for any purpose that might damage its reputation.

A copy of what we take to be the final marketed version of this CD Rom marked 'Complimentary', arrived yesterday. Those who played the game last night – it's a sort of quiz – assured me today that it is all incredibly boring, all the girls remain fully clothed and the very worst thing about it is the character of the Headmaster who is described on the sleeve as 'seedy'! Hardly 'complimentary'!!

Fireworks at the Massage Parlour

25th July 1996.

LITTLE HOSHI *san*, the masseur, invited me over to his parlour last night. The village of Shimogo was holding its annual *hanabi matsuri* (fireworks festival) and I would be meeting the village elders as well as his friends and neighbours at a very traditional party. He was anxious that I should not have to drive back late so insisted on providing me with accommodation. Naturally I was touched and honoured.

If the fireworks display was simply the bait – fine by me. If actually seeing the fireworks had been important to me then I was going to be in for a disappointment. That they did really happen, I know, because I could hear random explosions so they weren't some Zen concept of non-fireworks – all in the mind. I can think of plenty of cases, too, where you're much better off *not* seeing what you're hearing; it's just that a firework display is not one of them. Not to sound piqued, I trust, but you do not quite get to appreciate fully either the colour or the spectacle from the sound alone. The whizz-bangs did have a stronger element of surprise, it is true, unheralded by any light-travels-faster-than-sound pyrotechnic warnings. As a consequence of this, though, a number of drinks were spilled, regarded each time as either disastrous or amusing depending on how far down the alcoholic road the victim had progressed.

Each guest had arrived with a liquid contribution varying from the harmful to the lethal. It was obvious that the lines of supply had not been co-ordinated as there were no two bottles, cans, jars or receptacles the same. It was also easy to estimate that quantity was going to be a problem. The measure of success of a Japanese party is the time it takes for the needle of the social barometer to swing all the way from 'Dry'

Peter Westbury

(sober) through 'Change' (getting silly) to 'Saturated' (dead drunk) at which point everyone has fallen asleep. Even taking into account the small amount required by most Japanese to reach this euphoric state, there was, frankly, not an awful lot to pour and it looked as though it was going to take an alarmingly long time for everybody to fall asleep at this party. During the getting silly stage, in the early part of which each guest had taken his turn to be photographed wearing my straw boater, an impromptu dance took place. An elderly gentleman with a serious shortage of teeth, Hoshi *san's* father, I think, whom I'd assumed to have an arthritic hip (he'd used his arms to propel himself around the floor on his backside when I'd met him before), suddenly sustained a miracle cure. Someone had persuaded him to perform the *dojyo sukui* which I cannot translate, only describe. He leapt up and left the room carrying some improvised accessories. A chant started up, led by the local mayor, who had arrived in his pyjamas, in anticipation, I assume of early oblivion. Soon everyone was clapping and stamping to the rhythm: dum-dum DUM, dum-dum DUM. Then the little old one-time cripple re-emerged through the split in the *noren*, to gracefully re-enact for us in nimble dance steps the traditional story of the fisherman dragging the muddy river bed to catch eels in his basket.

Over his head he wore a drape, partly secured by his spectacles and leaving his face exposed. Up each nostril and in front of his lower gums he had pushed the opposite ends of shortened *hashi* (chopsticks). His face had not exactly been his fortune to start with; he now looked repulsive, but intentionally so. His dear little wizened wife followed him cackling with glee, her eyes sparkling, her gold fillings catching the candles' light. They completed two circuits of the floor, sharing these moments of glory and finally making their exit to prolonged applause. Party-piece over, the limp was re-instated.

Emergency supplies of alcohol arrived, drinking resumed and gradually, true to form, unconsciousness

Westbury Meets East

prevailed all around me and I found I had nobody left to talk to. I was cross with myself for not having the foresight to check where I was meant to crash out for the night, but supposed it didn't really very much matter.

6th August 1996

Narita to Changi. '*Na miss kita, mabote*, Meriam' (Meriam, I miss you very much). Meriam is 22 years old, half-Spanish, half Indian and has recently replaced Choco in my affections. She shares my bed from time to time whenever our schedules allow which is to say not as frequently as we'd both prefer. Her arrival at the *apato* very late last night to wish me a safe trip before my early departure this morning took me nicely by surprise. But pretty comatose as a result, I was at some risk on my three-part journey to Narita by *shinkansen*, metro and *Keisei* line, drifting into sleep several times but managing to awake at the crucial times to change trains. Strap-hanging on the Tokyo metro, I thought I was hallucinating when I saw my own face staring back at me from a poster and then remembered that some of us had posed for a Japan Rail advertising campaign promoting Bridewell Heath. I never had such an experience on the London Underground!

It is now about midday and it feels as though I'm 'arm-chair-motoring' high in the sky, sitting *upstairs* in this Singapore Airlines Boeing 747–500 Megatop. Gus said his course was an introduction to another world – how the rich live – though I did believe at the time that he meant someone else would be paying. I'm flying indirectly to the UK, stealing a stopover in Singapore for a few days' relaxation before continuing home to meet up with the family and friends for my son's wedding.

I'm travelling 'Raffles' class which basically means you have two of the prettiest flight attendants to make you feel like a king from the moment they hang up your jacket to the serving of champagne on request throughout the trip. The arms of the chairs are housings for gadgets of amazing complexity: folding video screens and audio equipment providing eclectic in-flight distractions from Edina and Patsy to Richard Gere, from full length features to Nintendo games. 'We offer you 300 hours of entertainment and only a 13 hour flight. Sorry.' – runs the apologetically boastful advertisement. Not having slept a wink last night, I'm not wide awake enough to master the

Peter Westbury

accessing instructions for this great variety of choice and the headphones are stuck on Japanese pop music which the captain keeps interrupting in hesitant English to broadcast warnings of turbulence that he will be taking measures to minimize by flying increasingly higher. So now I'm relaxing over this luncheon, possibly the best that any sky service has to offer, such is the reputation of this airline. Strange to realize that it is actually an *airline* that has provided the best meal I've had in three days, during which time breakfast, lunch and dinner have either been improvised or skipped altogether due to pressure of work. All the same, I shall be leaving the *soba* (cold green noodles).

Meriam's home is 34,000 feet below at this minute. She comes from the Philippines where she lives with her father, Mariano Ravellarez, a fisherman, and her younger brother Manuel. There is no mother. Her name was chosen by her father from the New Testament and mis-spelled, hence Meriam. Her elder brother's name was also chosen from the Bible. Melchor lives elsewhere with his wife and baby son. I like Meriam very much. She is a bit of an enigma (aren't they all) with her child-like directness combined with her wry, knowing smile. 'Don't go', she said this morning with wide brown eyes and reminding me very much of the singer, Sade, as depicted on the sleeve of her 'Love *deluxe*' album. Meriam has a mole *avec* bristles with which she does tormenting things; just the one... on her chin. Lilian is 26 and Chinese and removes my tray. I doze... when I wake up it is Nashatta who is standing over me. Also 26, she is a stunning Malaysian. We discuss entertainment in Singapore and she thinks I would like 'Studebaker' a night club and disco. She offers to meet and escort me there as she says it is difficult to find. Am I dreaming this?

7th August 1996

A lazy morning was followed by a half-day city tour to get my bearings, taking in 'Little India', the merchants' quarter that is under renovation, a Chinese temple or two, a Hindu shrine with amazing statuary, the Government buildings with the well-known cricket ground and stylish pavilion in front and, of course, the famous 'Raffles Hotel'. A visit inside the Hotel was not included but while the other passengers were being led to the tourists' shop, I used the main entrance to take a look at the Foyer Bar with its 'Writer's Corner' and thence to

Singapore skyline.

the Long Room. I've always maintained that doors are there to be opened which tends to happen as long as you look the part. Which is how I came to be sitting in 'Raffles' and sipping a 'Singapore Sling', the drink for which the place is renowned. And very over-rated, I must say. The drink, that is. The hotel is extraordinary, having been extended under Japanese ownership to approximately five times its original size.

Entering 'Studebaker' that evening with Nashatta on my arm was the ego-trip of a lifetime. If I'd thought her stunning in

Raffles Hotel.

Ornate portal to
Hindu Temple.

Merchant's House,
Little India.

Peter Westbury

uniform, she was nothing less than statuesque out of it. For our date she wore a beautifully cut black trouser suit, under the jacket an olive-bronze shot-silk halter-neck top. The stuff of cat-walks. I'm perfectly sure my attempt to appear blasé fooled no-one. The fact that we left together later was something I might have fantasized over but never have predicted. Nor that we would have continued to enjoy each other's company into the small hours.

8th August 1996

Who could possibly resist a day-trip entitled 'Kukup Tour'? To be fair, nothing actually went wrong. You exit Singapore by bus and enter Malaysia where the border notice reads: 'WELCOME. DEATH FOR DRUG TRAFICKERS (*Sic*). BE FOREWARNED.' You are on the tourists' trail to look at rubber, coffee and cocoa plantations, a pewter factory (where I purchased a letter-opener that created difficulties for me with Heathrow Customs officials on my return journey) and a 'water village' where, to give some local colour it is confided to the traveller that drug trafficking takes place under cover of coastal fishing. I had fancied buying myself a Malacca cane but saw there none.

In the evening, Nashatta and I enjoyed the atmosphere of a stroll together along Boat Quay and a drink in one of the myriad bars. Then for a meal back at the Orchard Park hotel.

Drug-trafficking or local fishing?

9th August 1996

Just time this morning for shopping and a haircut (alas no Korean touches) before continuing my journey to England to catch up with family matters and to steel myself for The Wedding. I have my speech prepared . . .

17th August 1996

Somewhere in the Thames Valley. Considering the potentially explosive mixture of in-laws and out-laws among the guests at this wedding, sufficient to have put my mother off attending, it all went surprisingly well. What would have happened had I disregarded my daughter's plea not to go ahead with my speech, is quite another matter. But I'm coming to that. If I can take credit for nothing else (and I can't because the whole thing was in the capable hands of Derek's mother, her Spanish boyfriend and the bride's parents), I can at least say that, in spite of it being among the funniest pieces I've written, I did succumb to doing the right thing, only leaking the best bits when it was all over. I have had some mileage out of it since, mind, but only among audiences sufficiently far removed or unconnected to take umbrage. Like in Japan!

Both my exes were there and family from all sides. You see it already sounds like a battlefield. 'You'll keep a low profile, dear, won't you', said my mother. 'Yes, Mum, if the trenches are deep enough'. My only offence, on the actual day, I found out much later, was to have worn The Hat – a wonderful parti-coloured extravaganza of an affair, a jester's cap-and-bells, which I wore with white tie and tails. This was my son's wedding; he was going to have no difficulty pointing me out.

The picnic on the hilltop paddock overlooking the river and the horses' apostrophe, the buskers imported from the London tube to provide background music, the hand-picked words for the ceremony in the improvised bower, the participation by actors from the Weekend Murder Mystery Company, the village hall supper and the Dixieland Jazz quartet made an altogether formidable ensemble act lasting from midday to midnight. There were no speeches at all. The early morning flight in a hot-air balloon, my sole contribution to the programme, was called off because my pilot friend had suffered a damaged knee in a recent accident.

Peter Westbury

And so, with all identities bar one buried in anonymity and the joyous unmarred occasion now safely locked in the past, here is the dis-allowed speech from the Father of the Groom: 'Bride & Groom, Distinguished Guests, Ladies & Gentlemen, I think I can honestly say that I've enjoyed this Wedding Day more than any of my own. You don't relax a lot at your own Reception because there's all the worry about your speech. This time it's everyone else who has my speech to worry about. This very special occasion has afforded me the wonderful opportunity of meeting up with my own family once more, as well as with the in-laws and the out-laws and it has been splendid seeing everybody hitting it off together, instead of just hitting, er, together. I'm very fond of saying that blood is thicker than water; it's also true to say it has a lower boiling point. But when it comes to "The Family", I am a great softy and this very date is a most nostalgic one for me as it is the anniversary of one of my own weddings. You could say it is my second wedding anniversary! [No-one, not even my second wife, had realized the significance of the date!] Yes, twenty-two years ago today I married the lady who was to become Derek's, er, step-mother and I'm pleased to say that she is with us now: that's her in the jacket with the giant poppies. I'd recognize her anywhere. "What was your name again?" We were never in agreement over the date on our mislaid marriage certificate so each year we used to celebrate (if that's the right word) on different dates depending on who got in first. Then there'd be all the customary recriminations – "you forgot again!" – "But it's not until tomorrow!" – that sort of thing. We're much better friends now, separated by divorce and half the planet.

'Actually both my exes are here. I understand my first wife is going out with a man called Jesus. I knew I'd be a difficult act to follow. If he's here perhaps he could do something about the wine.

'As for me – I'm now approaching my third divorce, though I've not actually met the lady yet.

'Today's bride and groom have certainly planned an unconventional kind of a day. In the absence of a passing Druid, my ex-brother-in-law, Uncle Trevor, pronounced a few words. He didn't have to understand what they meant – just pronoun' 'em (as Spike Milligan once said).

Westbury Meets East

'I ought to say a word or two about the happy couple but

I'm still trying to remember her name . . . That's it: Butch! No, that's what my mother calls her. Just a minute . . . I had a letter from her not all that long ago . . . yes! Bernie. "Welcome to the family, Bernie".

'Now I've never met the "other side" before today and I've no doubt they're wondering what their daughter, er Bernie, has taken on. But before you start feeling sorry for them, we've no idea what *our* boy has taken on either! We *may* be middle-class inebriates but how do we know they're not chartered accountants or *bank managers*?!

'Have you ever thought how strange it is what attracts one person to another? My first wife married me for my wrists, my second wife for my buttocks. Hardly surprising when the second marriage lasted twice as long as the first. Once proclaimed the best in the county, they are by no means my worst feature today, though I'm beginning to think I should have them pleated. Now I promise not to go on boring you to tears – I know what it's like to have an audience audibly doze off in front of me. In Japan I deliver what has been voted the single most boring lecture in the whole teaching curriculum and, I may tell you, against some pretty fierce competition.

'Thank you for listening, those of you who are left. I hope I've not offended or embarrassed more than I usually do.

'I sincerely add my hopes to everyone else's for the future and the continued happiness of Derek and er, Thingy'.

26th August 1996

Heathrow to Changi to Narita – back to school! In London it's 2.45 p.m. but here at 37,000 feet, courtesy of Singapore Airlines it is still lunchtime. We are a little north of Budapest (where as a matter of coincidence but no real consequence I have recently placed an order for a consignment of Tokay 'pudding' wine – 4 *puttonyos*) but will swing south-east before the Carpathians to fly over Belgrade and on to Turkey, pointing for Singapore and the eventual transit stop before the home run to Japan.

Tania and Car-Lynne, two willowy-waisted charmers, have just served pre-prandial drinks, which have gone a long way to blunting the effects of the airport goodbyes at which I'm not very skilled. Charlie Parker has also helped to blur the edges with some very mellow jazz and after lunch I shall drift into a siesta, flanked by the two delightful Hong Kong Chinese

Peter Westbury

girls with whom I've been chatting.

Or, instead of concocting this agreeable fiction, I could have shared with you the reality of swollen legs and stiff body, constantly squawking infants, the frequent metallic click of the loo door right next to me and the sudden explosive roar of the suction flush mechanism.

Travel broadens one, it is claimed; sometimes it just flattens.

15th September 1996

Auckland. Another suitcase, another town but strange to think that this time the town is almost the furthest away it is possible to be on this planet from the people and places I was visiting for last month's wedding. Perhaps stranger still is the happy

Take-off.

Westbury Meets East

And landing.

coincidence that my son Derek and his bride, whatsername, had also made it to Christchurch by the time I arrived there last week, but then some folk will go to enormous lengths just to pin me down to my promise of a hot-air balloon ride! We did fly together, a very sedate affair but with a very unusual flight path. It reminded me of the occasion in Tuscany when Roberto had agreed to take an 80-year old wheel-chair bound lady for a birthday flight in his Raven. Her house stood in a large garden and conditions were right to use it as the launch-site. With some difficulty, the lady was lifted, wheelchair and all, into the basket where she could barely see over the edge. The whole shebang took off and Roberto followed his usual pattern of gaining altitude to show his passengers the weird shadows cast by the *crete* in the early morning light and then descending to explore the erratic currents of the ground winds caressing the contours of the dry valleys. After about an hour of this, Roberto was on the lookout for a likely landing-spot and to the amazement of everyone – the co-pilot, the companion and the retrieve crew, but not the little old lady – he placed the basket back again with great aplomb in the *Signora's* own garden. Of course, the skill of the pilot played a huge part but the chances of that situation happening are extremely rare; the octogenarian, however, simply assumed that it was all part of the normal service!

Our flight in Christchurch also doubled back on itself to the park from which we'd ascended but as we had only been airborne for 30 minutes or so, the pilot flew us on further towards the city and then back to make a meticulous landing in the university car park, taking advantage of the empty spaces at that hour. Two days later, after months of waiting for the case to be heard, it was announced in the local newspaper that the

Peter Westbury

verdict had gone against our pilot who, last year, had been forced to ditch in the sea following a sudden deterioration in the weather causing a fatality, and in addition to paying a steep fine he was suspended from flying for 6 months. One error of judgement is all it takes; a rather sobering footnote to our little adventure.

The recruiting presentation and interviewing went well and I also had time to research uniform suppliers, make the acquaintance of Emiko, a Japanese holiday-maker staying at the Millennium, find 'Il Felice', a recommended Italian *ristorante* and see Shaw's *Caesar & Cleopatra*.

In Dunedin, I revisited the wonderful Belpepper's Blues in addition to interviewing 18 candidates for positions at BH.

Now I am at the Centra on Albert Street, Auckland, having had to decamp from my usual base at the Park Hyatt to make way for an invasion by Japanese businessmen; they are everywhere. Then I will have to move yet again, the third time in five days in the same city, to the Sheraton. I mustn't become too blasé at the chance of sampling all these Five-star hotels at the Company's expense. My luck seems to be holding out this far and it is great to be back in New Zealand mixing pleasure with business.

Suzy is out of town this weekend so I went alone last night to the ballet – *Coppelia*. The ticket office managed to sell my ticket twice and rather than make a fuss I accepted the only alternative, mountaineering to the back of the gods where I had enormous trouble hearing the words! I mentioned this in the first interval to the lady sitting next to me and she thought I was serious. For sheer whimsy the story is unrivalled but hearing the familiar music and seeing the beautifully costumed and choreographed stage presentation was a great treat, starved as I am of such delights back in Japan.

From this level 26 mini-suite at the Centra I have an incredible view beyond the roof of the new Sky City Casino to the Westhaven Marina where the boats bob at their moorings at the southern end of the 'Nippon Clip-on' road-bridge. A crane cradle containing two workmen has just dropped, spider-like on its fine cable-strand, from a platform near the top of the slender concrete column that is the Sky Tower, still under construction. Nearing completion, it will give the Southern

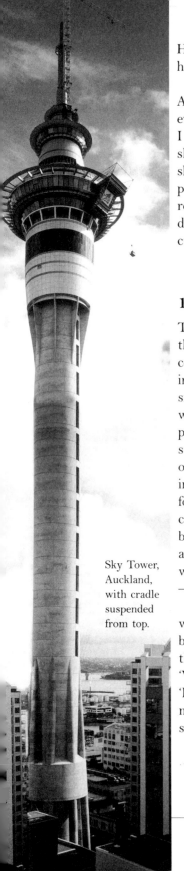

Sky Tower,
Auckland,
with cradle
suspended
from top.

Hemisphere one of its most impressive landmarks and house the inevitable *cliché* – a revolving restaurant.

This is one of the rare days when the sun has shone on Auckland. It is a matter of record that it has rained here everyday for the past twenty-nine. The room has darkened, I notice, causing me to look up and out but it is only the shadow of the Sky Tower that has moved. The shiny ASB skyscraper opposite frames the left-hand edge of the panorama and I have just realized that I can wave to my reflection in the polished one-way glass of one of its windows set on the angle. I shall remember to draw my curtains later.

17th September 1996.

To 'Sails', the Auckland Yacht Club restaurant, as guest of the Institute of Technology, my host on a high following completion of the new headquarters. But are new buildings ever complete? We compared horror stories of snag-lists and delays, taking some solace in the fact that we were both of us similarly involved with the almost daily parry and thrust of dealing with wriggling architects and stalling contractors, he seeming to have no real advantage over me by being able to communicate with them directly in their native language. He was on his usual excellent form, always the amusing companion. He came up with a collection of politically incorrect throwaway lines like 'the bar with the Scottish "Happy Hour" – 5.30 p.m. until 6'; and an unrepeatable story about a Pakistani demolition worker with two bottoms; both his employers were Irish – you may be able to work it out from that.

Finally: a builders' merchant was puzzled when, every weekend, a customer would call and pay for 120 bricks to be delivered to his apartment address. Three months of this and the merchant's curiosity got the better of him. 'What are you building, mate?' 'A barbecue', was the reply. 'But you live in an apartment block!' 'Sure do – and what's more I'm on the 14th floor but another seven months should do it.'

6th October 1996

Tochigi *ken*. I am parked in a field on the bend of a rock-strewn river that is flowing quite fast after the recent rains. Above the rush of the water, Mariko Takahashi is singing from the tape-deck entirely for my benefit, the words of her ballads unbelievably moving considering I can understand none of them. I picnicked at this spot exactly a week ago, on the way to visiting the roller-coasters at Nasu with Misty and Melody from The Kirara Club. This time it is the meeting place for a late lunch date with Meriam, one of the delightful redeeming features of living in this Asian society. But as I'm running a tad early, there's a little time to reflect on the past week.

The die is cast for the next batch of Kiwis and Ben and I have been working flat out preparing individual 7-page letters of invitation for faxing to the incoming group chosen to start in mid-November. Ben and I have adopted a 'believe it when you see them' attitude, the Company still running a big risk with the Immigration authorities.

The butler trying to pull a few strings.

To give a personal welcome to Keiko, a recent newcomer to the staff who has been brought in to take over the role of Purchasing Officer from a young man who plays Beatles music and sleeps a lot and has been promoted to the Sales Department, I took her to my favourite local restaurant for some *unagi* (eel) which Itoh *san* grills to perfection. Keiko's command of English (unlike Meriam's 'pidgin') is excellent and she has the face and figure of a classical ballerina, exquisitely petite, but an architect boyfriend in Tokyo.

It was a very agreeable rendezvous, nonetheless and I am sure there will be others. It was quite early when we wished each other goodnight (she lives in Shirakawa with her parents) so I

popped into the Kirara to see the girls. Since Jack's most recent engagement, to the Filipina, Faye, he and I no longer hunt in pairs as he is nervous that she may learn of his fickleness, whether real or concocted out of jealousy, on the regional club grapevine, where they've not much else to do than gossip. Meanwhile, my Tagalog is improving and I'm picking up a lot of information for my next trip to the Philippines. I've been rather neglecting my Japanese lessons and thought it time to take Noriko for another drive in the country. So we shared a pleasant enough day on the western edge of Fukushima-*ken* south of Aizu, taking in an art gallery, a craft museum and a fairy centre, all too *kawaii* (cute) for me by far. We shared a mystic moment at a shrine where we held hands and made a wish but there's something missing. She is really very sweet and clearly warmly disposed but, the same age as my son, I have the strong suspicion that she sees me as a substitute for her late father! Does that mean that Meriam sees me as a surrogate *grand*father?!

Peter Westbury

A Visit to the Dentist

8th October 1996

A VISIT TO THE *Haisha* (Dentist). It seems such a short while ago that I chose this title from a list of options for my English Language 'O' level examination essay! Today, 40 years on, give or take a decade, I found myself in Mr Takamoto's open-plan surgery in Shirakawa, reclining in one of four adjustable chairs and facing up to Japanese-style conveyor-belt dental treatment. The patient does not have to move chairs, neither do the chairs themselves move. It is the mechanics who are mobile, working by rote in teams to apply their particular specialized skill at the required time. The thought did occur to me that Mr Takamoto might be cashing in on some exploitative apprentice scheme because the helpers did seem extraordinarily young and there were no less than eight of them.

The first one I met had the most difficult task, coping with my *totemo kagirareta* (very limited) ability to communicate but after much blinking and blanking I was duly processed and then introduced to the elderly head man who examined my notes and declared 'Hmm – same age.' Lying in my teeth (how appropriate), I responded with: 'Well YOU are wearing well, at least!' at which he beamed, but there the compliment stuck. I made a mental note not to come back if I had the choice.

For the real tasks I was in the hands of three very young female assistants who, masked and gloved against contamination, were rendered android in appearance, the whole scenario beginning to resemble a robotic assembly line. But my imagination allowed me to fantasize, picturing them as extremely beautiful behind the surgical disguise and I lay back, Z-shaped, to take their assault like a man. One handled the drilling and scraping, another prepared the mould, the third whispered softly in my ear the equivalent of 'Please rinse'. We established that my health insurance policy does not cover dental work but I won't know until I return on Friday just how huge the final

Westbury Meets East

invoice will be or whether, for immediate cash settlement, they will be lenient.

Having reclaimed my shoes in the porch (the slippers provided were the daintiest yet, smaller, even, than those supplied in hospitals), I emerged into the rain, my bill so far for what, after all, still remains a gap, a mere Y3,980, which is £22.00 at today's exchange rate. 18 months ago this would have been £35.00 which has really brought it home to me how much my salary has been eroded in UK terms with most of my personal outgoings requiring settlement in sterling.

11th October 1996

I am absurdly early for my dental appointment. 'On time is late' was a doctrine hammered into us at school by the deputy headmaster, a little Napoleon of a man. The result, in my case, has been to make me almost manically hot on punctuality, costing me months of my life wasted waiting for others. Fortunately, I have brought with me something to read; no traditional back numbers of 'Yachting World' or 'Country Life' in *this* waiting room.

As the place begins to fill up with mothers and hordes of small children, 'Peter *san*!' comes the summons over the speaker system and I am soon back, prone, in the factory and covered with a fleecy blanket as if I was one of the tinier patients. A printed cartoon hippo yawns on the blanket, smugly displaying ALL its teeth! The dental nurse abandons me for a while; the conveyor-belt system suffers an hiatus and I fall asleep.

When I wake I find the team grouped around me and though they are masked as before I can tell that they are a different bunch of apprentices to those I met on Tuesday. They take it in turns at practising their respective procedures. Then it dawns on me: of course! . . . dental *practice*!

Assembly completed, there was another Y4,600 (£26.00) to pay, to which I should add the £30.00 I handed the dentist in England who bodged the filling which led to the problem. But now, feeling a little like a 007 adversary with my new highly-polished metal bridgework in place, I am, thanks to all concerned, part English and part Japanese imitation!

Peter Westbury

4th November 1996

This autumn has seen few distractions from the routine into which the village has settled. Even the soprano concert two weeks ago has become something of a set-piece simply requiring us to follow the pattern of the original, though we were very pleased to welcome a talented and attractive young pianist, Yuki Sunahata, to accompany Ms de Rothschild as replacement for her harpist when he became indisposed. Not only prettier than him, she has a base in Yokohama, considerably nearer than Powys, and I'm invited to visit in a week's time. I'm also intrigued by the recurring visits of Sashiko —— —— who singled me out to take her on a sight-seeing drive through the forest to see the leaf-change and on to Tonohetsuri, a gorge with an old arched suspension bridge that swayed and undulated erratically, throwing her off-balance and providing convincing justification for clutching my arm for support. From there I drove to Ouchijuku, a village of thatched houses said to be of the Edo period but denounced by Kiko —— —— (another regular visitor, a paediatrician, who has rather latched on to me) as a fake. Sashiko is a most distinguished looking lady of aristocratic bearing, in her early 40s, I would guess, though at times she looks barely in her 20s. She alternates flirtatiousness with shyness in a most tantalizing way. It would be very agreeable to meet her again in the right circumstances . . .

There has been a palpable increase in the repeat bookings of a number of what I will call 'enthusiastic' lady guests to Bridewell Heath who each lay claim to individual attention from the moment they arrive. Frankly, there is danger in numbers and I have grown more and more aware of the physical difficulties of keeping them all satisfied and apart. While in the majority of cases it is all very flattering and innocuous, with others pursuit seems more persistent and the suddenly plentiful perks of my resumed single status could be seriously under threat.

The strict two-metre distance rule laid down in The Butler's Official Guide-book (Section III; Guests. Para (ix) – female advances, polite avoidance of) is of no help when it is my clear duty to 'please all of the people all of the time'! I am a martyr to the cause.

Westbury Meets East

A martyr to the cause.

14th November 1996

The gay Filipino co-manager of the Kuroiso club had kindly invited Jack and me to his birthday lunch-party in the staff quarters above the premises. Jack had Faye's approval as she, of course, would be there and I was persuaded to escape from the village for what would be three hours at the most over an unbusy lunch-time period. The girls – Dali, Benni, Kati, Meriam, Nella, Mari and Faye – all looked so unsophisticated in the daylight and sharing the meal had a real family feel to it, reminding me of supper with the sisters and cousins in Parañaque. We rather lost track of the time and, haring back along the notorious Route 4, we had the bad luck to hit heavy traffic. While extricating the *Pajero* from a traffic jam with the idea of trying to find an alternative way, I managed to reverse into an invisible little defenceless low-slung Eunus as it was just tucking itself in round the back of me in a similar manoeuvre. No damage to the *Pajero* but the caved-in door of the sports car looked very expensive. My pride was dented, too; the first prang I've had in Japan and it isn't even winter properly; only the second knock in 38 years of driving. Well, they do say there's no such thing as a free lunch!

2nd to 5th December 1996

New Caledonia, Coral Sea. To reach the mis-named 'Ile des Pins' (discoverer Captain Cook was, it is popularly claimed by the locals, looking at the wrong species of tree when he christened the island – not the only mistake he ever made), you take a 25-minute flight by Latair 48 from Noumea's Magenta airstrip on the main island of Nouvelle Calédonie, this French possession in the South Pacific. It is a most beautiful place, you could say idyllic scenically though the architecture doesn't amount to a great deal – not so much as a shutter to provide a bit of character.

The climate is about perfect except for during depressions which occur during December through to February (the 'cheap' season) when wind and rain lash the islands and outdoor activities have to be put on hold. Scheduled flights arrive daily at the main airport of Tontouta from Paris via Tokyo.

My colleagues who were booked in here last week were unable to participate in the water sports and had a thoroughly miserable time. Each of the officers on the staff at BH has been

Westbury Meets East

packaged off to this resort on the President's orders to see what there is to learn in 3 nights and 4 days from the phenomenon known world-wide as Le Club Med! Fortunately for the discerning or, if that sounds too toffee-nosed, those for whom follow-my-leader morning-to-night organized group activities are anathema, there is, right next door, another phenomenon, known world-wide as 'Le Meridien' as well as other inviting low-key natural playgrounds to which one may escape.

Which is how, on my last full day, with the wind blowing in what is left of my hair, I came to be bouncing or, rather, jarring along at speed (I was sat above a rear wheel arch) in an open-windowed 20-passenger bus with nine Japanese couples on their honeymoon, all of us fleeing from the holiday-camp atmosphere. The nineteenth passenger, Miyuki (also Japanese), a petite and pretty 34-year old *divorcée* (as it transpired) and I made up the full complement, each in the party presumably drawn by the list of attractions on offer at this Pine Island: rain forest caves, clear pools, fine powder sand bays, turquoise sea-lakes and a lobster lunch at Kuto beach. As the only two 'singles' on board, there was an inevitability about Miyuki and me pairing off and before the day's excursion was over we had made plans to have dinner together. We made two stops for snorkelling, the first involving wading across a tidal estuary to reach a wonderful beach. The second was on an isthmus, the ocean on one side, a secluded lagoon on the other. Not unromantic for a first meeting . . .

Chatting over dinner, Miyuki explained that she had thought about visiting Guam but chose to come to New Caledonia to avoid tripping over hordes of her tourist compatriots! I found this place more lush than Guam and also more *civilisé* which is rather to be expected from the French European influence. As to ownership, the visitor is left in no doubt about that, owing to the presence of the *gendarmeries* and *bidets* and the smell of the Gauloises or perhaps that should read the other way round.

I had to fly back to work the following day but we exchanged telephone numbers late that night with the thought going through my mind that I should invite her to Fukushima to stay for the Year End Party at Bridewell Heath.

I had overflown these islands in September 1994 on my way back from my first recruiting trip to New Zealand and I remember thinking how inviting they looked. I never dreamed my job would bring me here nor that I would be charmed by a diminutive Japanese girl with an elfin smile who appeared completely out of the blue.

Peter Westbury

8th December 1996

No snow yet, mercifully, but our winter accessory, Pepe the St Bernard has arrived back after completing his training course. I wouldn't say there has been any noticeable improvement in his personal hygiene but he has obviously been trained to bark and growl at strangers. This would not be of any consequence but for the fact that he still persists in sleeping on my landing and Meriam's attempts at arriving discreetly are quite futile as she tries to step over this horrendous howling hearth rug at two o'clock in the morning. I might just as well borrow the megaphone from the office and make the announcement.

But it's Pepe's breath that's the shocker. You don't have to be all that close for it to knock you over. I'm seriously thinking of having a metal disc struck to replace the 'Bridewell Heath' one on the chain round his neck: 'Hidewell Breath'. Actually I can think of at least three of the Japanese staff to whom this could equally apply – perhaps I'll have a few made. Perhaps Pepe could carry Listerine in the brandy flask!

19th December 1996

The dreaded 'White Christmas' at Bridewell Heath has been advertised and promoted but where is the snow? Unlike the two previous Yuletides on this mountain top, it looks like being a snowless occasion. In spite of the decorations, which have been up since the beginning of the month, I have failed to kindle in myself the spirit of Christmas.

I thought I might benefit from playing some musical favourites from the past this evening but halfway through the Humphrey Lyttelton Story that I have on tape, the tears were suddenly streaming down my face, not at all the desired effect! Well, I suppose it's simply that time of year when even the most cynical of us is vulnerable to nostalgia.

Tomorrow I shall collect Cenita and Maria-Helena, two Filipinas I've befriended down in Shirakawa and show them over the Manor House and round the village. They are far from home, too, at this tricky time of the year. Next week, I'm thinking of donning the recently acquired 'Santa' outfit and surprising them in the club late on Christmas night. I've been practising '*Maligayang Pasko!*' (Tagalog for 'Merry Christmas') and '*Feliz Navidad!*' (the same in Mexican). I copied them off the poster outside Fr Martinez' church.

Westbury Meets East

20th December 1996

Amazing! We woke up to a white world this morning – just in time! The first of our 'White Christmas' weekend package guests arrive tomorrow: typical bloody Japanese last-minute timing!

By the afternoon, several inches covered the village of Bridewell Heath and it did look magical. Never having seen snow before, my two young Filipina guests were entranced. After the tour I found them some hats and coats and a friendly snowball fight ensued before I drove them back down the hill. This evening, a few of us got together and sang a few carols. I think it's going to be alright.

21st/22nd December 1996

With her parents this weekend came a lovely young lady with a mischievous smile called Harumi. She first caught my eye during my social dancing lesson and I labelled her *sukoshi o-tenba* (a bit of a tomboy). But for the evening's dinner-dance – shot of her parents. she was transformed into a princess and won the prize for the

best-dressed guest, which I had to present (very tacky, I know, a Japanese innovation). She also won the hearts of a few of my Kiwi staff. There cannot be many butlers whose arduous duty it is to dance with the guests – all terribly unconventional – but then the whole job here is far from your average textbook butlering.

While dancing together and out of earshot of her parents, she asked me to stay in touch and to meet her in Ueno next month if I can, to be at her coming-out party with her friends. She will be 20. My experience shows that a *gaijin* has only to be his naturally courteous, complimentary and amusing self to be attractive in the eyes of Japanese ladies. Japanese men are rarely any of these things and certainly not all three; they do not treat their women-folk like ladies in the western sense. It is also my good fortune that age and looks do not appear to be a factor, but then I can count the number of handsome Japanese men I've met on the finger of one finger.

Two's Company...

28th/29th/30th and 31st December 1996

THIS 'Year End' has been made both memorable and ageing by the game of cat and mouse triggered off by the potentially detrimental concurrent visits to Bridewell Heath by two of my lady-friends: Atsuko ———, the doctor from Utsonomiya and Miyuki *chan*, she of the elfin smile. To claim that I handled the situation with dexterity would be to ignore the part played by luck but then I do believe you largely make your own luck and I certainly owe no thanks to the Japanese staff handling the guest reservations and who thought it all an enormous joke. Atsuko has been closing in for some time, the gifts increasing in value to the point of embarrassment; for Christmas it had been a splendid antique *haori* (a traditional Japanese silk jacket). Miyuki, no longer an unknown quantity and infinitely more fanciable, if truth be told, had accepted my invitation to come and stay for the New Year's Eve festivities which had been scheduled for the 28th and 29th to line up with the weekend. The next thing I heard was that Atsuko had booked herself in for the same nights. I then persuaded Miyuki that we'd have more chance of spend-ing some time together if she could stay over for the staff party on the 31st as we had only a few other guest bookings for that night and it promised to be fun. No problem. She agreed straightaway. *Sugoi* (Great!). I next checked on their accom-modation. They had both been booked into the same guest-house so I had that changed – Miyuki into 'Drake' and Atsuko into 'Nelson'. I still had the two overlapping days to cope with when I would have to weave and duck and dive or cut myself in two for part of the time.

The first evening saw all three of us in the Snooker Room and at the same time. I played it straight down the middle, explaining separately to each that while on duty it was my obligation to do my best to ensure the satisfaction of all guests and that I hoped she would be understanding. Atsuko made

Peter Westbury

the first move by feigning tiredness and insisting that she would expect me as a gentleman to escort her to her suite to make sure she did not come to grief on the treacherously icy paths. Put like that, I graciously concurred, taking her arm as we edged our way down steps and slopes. She clung on tight declaring that, if we were going to slip then we would slip together, except she naughtily modified the vowel sound in the middle of the verb to make it sound like 'sleep'! Well – my name's Simpson not Samson, I thought, and Miyuki's still up in the Snooker Room waiting for me to go back. So very firmly, I bade Atsuko goodnight in her doorway and, to put her off the scent, headed on towards The Residence and my *apato*. Whereupon, to my dismay, she started following me, soon catching up and linking arms.

For once, I was overjoyed to hear Pepe's unwelcoming growl and Atsuko finally acknowledged defeat. We said goodnight for the second time and after allowing several minutes to elapse I returned to the Snooker Room to provide Miyuki with a gentlemanly escort to 'Drake' . . .

Fortunately, the ladies were involved in separate classes on their second day and I was actually free to be hospitable to some of the other guests. I couldn't believe my eyes, though, when I entered the Refectory in the evening to find Miyuki and Atsuko *sharing the same table*. Some well-intentioned cretin had noticed they were the only two ladies dining alone and suggested that they might like to sit together. I kept getting this burning sensation in my ears.

For the second evening running my duty took me to the Snooker Room. This time, Atsuko was clearly prepared to sit it out until I left. I was genuinely very tired and decided by 10.30 that I'd had enough. Simultaneously, Atsuko collected her coat and followed me into the snow, grabbing me tight. 'If I fall over, will you slip with me?' We reached her porch and I explained I needed to get home for a good night's rest. She looked at me disbelievingly but seemed to accept the situation and I finally made it to the apartment.

I had already let Miyuki know not to expect me back. At 11.15 p.m. the telephone rang! It was Atsuko! She had persuaded some moron in the office to let her have the number of my private extension and was checking up on me! Thank goodness I was there. Meriam laughed her head off.

Next morning it was time for Atsuko and almost every other

Westbury Meets East

guest to depart by BH transport supplemented by specially chartered coaches. I went out to say my goodbyes in the usual way and found Atsuko in the BH bus craning her neck, looking around in vain, expecting to see Miyuki somewhere on board. Cornered, I admitted 'No, she's not leaving quite yet'. I stepped back into the snow, the automatic door closed with a sound like a sigh of relief (or that might have been me) and the bus started off for the station.

As a precautionary measure, I had arranged with the reservations staff, in the event of their being asked, to advise Atsuko that the place was fully booked for the nights of the 30th and 31st.

Unfortunately, this had not been conveyed to the bus driver who insisted Atsuko would have no difficulty in extending her stay if she wanted, in fact she could use his mobile phone to do so. The reservations clerk tapped on my door nervously to break the news that the plan had mis-fired. I was unbelievably calm. Numb would be a better word. I prepared myself to welcome the dear doctor back when the bus returned.

Fate, however, was to lend a hand. When Atsuko checked with her hospital, it was confirmed that she had been rostered on duty for the next two days, in accordance with what she had originally agreed. She would have to spend New Year's Eve on the wards!

Which is how, after all, the Butler of Bridewell Heath came to spend a few very relaxed hours with the elfin-girl from nowhere, sharing the dawn of 1997.

3rd January 1997

The things we do for England. In the course of this winter's in-house entertainment, I impersonated a number of very different roles.

Firstly, the season's programme required me time without number to be padded up and coaxed into the 'Santa' costume, to play an OTT nauseatingly winsome Father Christmas, mostly for the benefit of visiting parents with children in tow as well as for the amusement of the Tokyo staff who came up for the annual party. It's hardly the sort of thing you can add to your c.v. even if I was confident I had fooled any of the young guests (which I'm pretty sure I hadn't). It did remind me of the Selfridge's Father Christmas faced with a know-all kid who, when asked if he believed in Santa Claus, said 'Nah!

Peter Westbury

It's the same as the Devil – it's yer Dad!' I suppose it wasn't too much of an ordeal posing with ladies of various ages sitting on my red-flannelled knee but, of all the accumulated photographic evidence of this caper, it is the scandalous poses with Cenita & Co., the leggy lovelies of Shirakawa, that are the most killing. The beard does little to conceal my blushes.

By contrast, my second disguise was very sober. For this year's mystery drama I had been promoted to Sherlock Holmes, only because I now possess a tweed jacket since shopping in London in the summer. They still refuse to spend any money on period costumes so once again all the kit was borrowed or improvised. There was more of a plot this time and more acting required of the amateur thespians, if lying still in a pool of tomato ketchup can be labelled acting. As 'The Butler' I was on the list of suspects. My re-emergence later, doubling as 'Sherlock' was about as convincing as my Father Christmas had been and immediately eliminated the viability of the butler

Christmas Eve – downtown Shirakawa.

Westbury Meets East

Santa and the stocking-fillers

having 'dunnit'. All it did was to emphasize the fact that we are still extremely short-staffed. Jack, as the villain yet again, received some extremely rough handling at the moment of his arrest by two of his waiters dressed as policemen who dealt him some very life-like blows as they took the opportunity to put the boot in for some or other unfair treatment they felt he had meted out recently. This went on for rather longer than rehearsed once Jack realized what was happening and retaliated with equally realistic vigour. What with bloodied noses and all, they quite stole the show.

At Hogmanay, for the address to the haggis, I brought out my 'wedding hat' – the jester's cap-and-bells. Now you don't get *any* of this at Club Med! Maplin's? Possibly.

9th January 1997

For some time now I've been shaving my shoulders regularly. Meriam agrees that it definitely makes me look younger.

We have to face up to the fact that her visa runs out very soon. She has two choices: to return to her family in Luzon knowing that she is unlikely to be able to return to Japan; or to 'go missing' to Tokyo. She is looking to me for a solution but I don't have one. I, too, am a stranger in these parts. I shall miss those long stray black hairs in my shower.

18th January 1997

Yokohama. Like most experiences, it's who you share them with that makes all the difference. That and the weather. It was a glorious day when I set out to meet Miyuki. I had heard a lot of travellers write off Yokohama as a nothing sort of place but I can only believe that that was perhaps before the amazing Minato Mirai urbanization project was in hand adjacent to the harbour district. Either that or they weren't blessed with as informed a guide as Miyuki who really knew her way around. Taking the *Tokyu Toyoko* line from Shibuya, I headed out through Naka-Meguro, the East Croydon of Tokyo and alighted from the train, not at Yokohama station but at the stop beyond, Sakuragicho. We had arranged to meet at the foot of the Landmark Tower. This is an extraordinary edifice and an absolute must.

Peter Westbury

A bit pricey even for a viewing tower, it is nevertheless

compelling. This is Japan's tallest skyscraper (though there are plans to trump this before the Millennium), with 74 storeys, 70 of them above ground level, the exposed height being 296 metres. To reach the 'Sky Garden' observatory you are whisked up to the 69th floor from the 2nd floor lobby in 40 seconds by the fastest elevator in the world, travelling at 750 metres per minute at the optimum point. I had Miyuki and a clear day and from the 'Sky Garden' with a pretty girl and a clear day you feel like a million dollars and can see to kingdom come, picking out the Tokyo Tower, the distinctive outline of the Grand Intercontinental Hotel (supposed to have been inspired by the shape of a billowing spinnaker, though some liken it to a wedge of Edam cheese), the Bay Bridge and Yokohama's wharves and warehouses and stadium, right over to the distant north-west horizon and Mount Fuji itself.

Landmark Tower.

Chinatown beckoned for lunch but instead of jumping on a bus, we took the Sea Bass passenger ferry service from the Conference Centre Pier to the docking quay at Yamashita Park, just a 20-minute ride. The Chinese 'special', a famous crab recipe, was not a success. We made up for this in the evening at the Royal Park Hotel restaurant high up in the Landmark Tower once again, combining our need to eat with the spectacular sight of Tokyo at night.

Most of the afternoon had been spent at the Moto-machi Shopping 'Shrine' where Miyuki paid homage to the great god of Fashion, being particularly devoted to the pursuit of handbags. There were plenty of other attractions had we

Westbury Meets East

wanted; perhaps they can wait for another time.

I reckon that if you only had, say, two nights in Japan based near Tokyo, you could do a lot worse than plan a day-trip to Yokohama Harbour and one to Kamakura. The two are linked by the *Yokosuka* line and Kamakura is, I'm told, awash with shrines and temples, not as hectic as Kyoto and a lot nearer. That's where I'm hoping we'll be going tomorrow.

19th January 1997

We woke up to a change in the weather and after a lazy morning took the train to Shibuya and a showing of *Evita* which premiered here last night.

28th January 1997

Harumi's appearance today seemed to sum up the predicament of the young in present-day Japan as, *kimono*-clad for her coming-out, she teetered restrictedly along the Tokyo pavements in, or rather on, her *geta* (traditional tall wooden sandal-clogs), a fan in one hand and her mobile phone in the other! In return for my present she made a gift to me of an *o mamori* (amulet) that I am to wear to ensure good health and long life.

Her friends were quite zany and we all bundled into a van driven by one of them to go to the Sunshine 60 building at Ikebukuro. This is another viewing tower/office block on the top floor of which Harumi and I posed together for a lightning sketch artist to produce our likenesses. Mine was too flattering but I guess I was the one paying. To amuse her friends, Harumi had brought photos of her second visit to BH last weekend ('. . . and her mother came too!') when the Kiwis took advantage of the publican's absence to throw an impromptu fancy-dress party and we dressed her up, very fetchingly, as Snow White. I went as the Seven Dwarfs, smiling, sneezing, scowling, etc., in rotation. I was on my knees, of course, an almost permanent condition for one reason or another.

Peter Westbury

Left: 'Snow White' with 'Happy'.

Right: 'Snow White' with 'Grumpy'.

4th February 1997

Today, down in Shirakawa, I test-drove a Mitsubishi 'Avalon'. Dead and buried are the walnut fascias of yesteryear: the dashboard was – a hologram!

The Philippines Two

8th February 1997

10 p.m. It is the eve of my departure to The Philippines and although this will be my second trip, I admit to being slightly apprehensive: but, as my Canadian colleague would drawl, 'It's your choice...' – and it is. But one continues to read and to hear of violent and corrupt happenings there. This came close to home last year when a cousin of mine died in Manila under very suspicious circumstances and I have made the decision to trust no-one, not even Cenita, the Filipina with whom I'm travelling and who says she loves me. Misty, her friend here in Shirakawa, told me last week that her own cousin has a 50% chance of survival following an unprovoked attack by a gang near his home in Quezon City. Cenita herself could very easily knife me in my sleep in case my clothes will fit her brothers! I am exaggerating, I hope, but the thing that all *Japayuki* (the word used to describe the *Filippin-jin* who forsake the wonderful climate and their virginity to come and work in the *karaoke* bars) have in common is that they are from needy families, which fact seems to justify their chosen profession. Usually there will be at least one parent absent (dead or missing) and a minimum of eight children over a narrow age span; typically, one child will be an unmarried mother, one will need urgent and expensive hospital treatment and another the fees for further education to improve her chances of employment in a respectable occupation.

They will all live together in 'The Provinces' in one flimsily constructed shack whose roof is unlikely to withstand the next typhoon. The older ones help the incumbent, probably ailing, father or mother to farm the land with inadequate tools, repair the primitive fishing nets or run the flyblown roadside fruit stall. The young ones swim in the insanitary river estuary. It is all heart-breaking stuff if you choose to believe it. But as it is the *Japayuki's* mission, indeed their *raison d'être*, to send as much money home as they possibly can, the same well-

Peter Westbury

practised plaintive litany is recited to the customers and the gullible Japanese men hand over their *yen*, make them pregnant, marry them for a few months and the next sister takes over the role of breadwinner.

So forgive me, Cenita, you lovely child, do not expect me to be taken in by the love charade.

9th February 1997

Narita Airport. Overdressed in anticipation of a flight upgrade (sometimes it works): sunglasses and cream wool scarf by ELLE homme, ill-fitting lightweight cream jacket by obscure Chinese designer destined to remain undiscovered, matching slacks from the menswear floor of Seibu Department Store in Koriyama, brogues by Church Bros, bow tie by Hawes & Curtis, hat by Christy's, watch by Adidas, luggage by Delsey; my usual 'Englishman abroad' profile, in fact, but this time the flight was over-booked and firmly in Economy Class I remained. There is a late change of plan and I will now meet Cenita on the 14th in Davao domestic airport when we will fly on to Cebu.

Finally airborne for the Philippines. My enjoyment of 'Tin Cup', the in-flight movie, was greatly enhanced by changing the headphone channel and smothering the banal dialogue with Hector Berlioz' *Symphonie Fantastique*. Made a mental note to employ this useful technique in future when appropriate. Northwest Airlines ('We fly to more than 300 destinations in the United States and Canada!' – reminded me of the ads my children used to refer to as 'boaster posters'.) dropped me off at Manila where I have a choice of a five-and-a-half hour wait for the next connecting flight to Davao or to find a stop-over hotel. It is 11 p.m. Suddenly I'm very tired and the optional prospect of sliding into a bed for the night is very appealing BUT 'it is the Chinese New Year, sir, and finding you a room will be very difficult!'.

Thus spake Baz Atienza, my taxi-driver, with all the customary doom and gloom more expected from an English plumber defending his estimate. So it was after many telephone calls plus the payment of an extortionate sum for the short drive to 'Traders' on Roxas Boulevard that I finished up in a US $170 a night suite – the 'last' hotel room in Metro Manila, 'sir!'

Chinese Temple

On Samal Island

Durian -
fruit of the gods

Waling-Waling
Orchid

10th February 1997

Manila. I needed the assistance of a travel agent to help me to (a) find an alternative, less costly, hotel for one more night and (b) re-arrange my internal flight plans. So in the late morning I walked to the Bayview Park Hotel where, last April, I had met the very co-operative Ruby Santana. The travel office was under new management, which was how I got to meet Vena instead. Vena, short for 'Ravenna' which for some undivulged reason she hated, wore her teeth parted. By far her best feature was her neat bottom; her strangest, her square toes with pointed painted toe-nails. She juggled with several phones at once and eventually sorted me out. The hall porter was able to provide me with Ruby's new contact number and office address and it was while I was on my way there that I was accosted by Lorenzo. Were I to hold auditions for someone to play the definitive pimp, I could not want for anyone better suited to the role. Short in stature, wide and swarthy, square-faced with a prominent forehead, greased hair and a pencil moustache, he had perfected the art of the fast sidle. In his crumpled over-sized lightweight jacket he shadowed me closely for block after block and I could not shake him off. When I reached Ruby's office she was, unfortunately, off-duty and not due in until tomorrow. When I re-emerged from her building, there, still, was Mister Sleazy. At first he engaged me in conversation with promises of favourable rates from his black-market money-changer cronies. Having established that I didn't need this service he assumed that I was, therefore, loaded and offered me unsubtle invitations to meet girls 'very cheap'. When I showed no interest he immediately up-graded the merchandise; now I was offered introductions to *part-time* hookers who, in the daytime, worked as shop assistants or bank clerks. Credited with such respectability, the girls' status was now better suited to a visiting gentleman 'like yourself'; so now, having felt he had 'dealt with' my objections, he proceeded to commandeer a passing taxi in which he escorted me to an even seedier part of the city. What followed was both embarrassing and somewhat poignant.

Lorenzo gave directions to the driver and we pulled up outside a number of addresses to descend from the cab and duck through back-street slum dwelling doorways to inspect rows of whores, each claimed by the pimp to be a 19-year old virgin 'of good background, very clean'.

He became more and more exasperated as, at stop after stop

Westbury Meets East

I ducked out again to jump back into the waiting taxi, shaking my head. At one stage he even offered me his ex-wife and then remembered she was out of town! I don't know how I was introduced (in Tagalog) in one house, but one mother woke her sleeping 16-year old daughter for me to judge her suitability as a wife. It is really too sad. As my 'personal friend', which he assured me he was, he could not understand my reluctance to allow him to provide me with a companion with whom to travel to 'dangerous Davao' for my own safety's sake and for his peace of mind! Was I not being very unreasonable? The only danger seemed most likely to be that created by the Moral Defender activist groups bent on spoiling his trade! Apparently, they were particularly militant in Mindanao where I was headed and I should, therefore, according to Lorenzo's logic, travel accompanied. As a potential customer I was proving very difficult to please. By wasting his time I hoped he would abandon his efforts and this proved to be the right ploy but I could not help noticing that it was only the pimp who was disappointed each time this old man shook his head and left. Not the girls!

The postscript to this escapade (I escaped and Lorenzo paid) was that I could swear it was one of his 'virgins' that I spotted at the airport next day in the company of probably the grossest man I've ever seen (his posterior overlapped on to three of the orange pressed plastic seats in the waiting area) wheeling a baby in a pushchair. Fast work.

Dinner at the hotel with Vena was distracting enough to make me forget to ask her to explain her aversion to being called 'Ravenna'. She did, however, convincingly demonstrate the desirability of triangular toe-nails. But not during dinner.

11th February 1997

A.M. The traffic is flowing surprisingly well today as I look down on Roxas Boulevard, so-named after the popular President Manuel Roxas and built on land reclaimed from the sea. From nineteen storeys up, still in my 'Trader's Club' suite, I overlook the harbour, the marina, the Imelda Marcos Cultural Centre and the Westin Philippine Plaza (to which I'll return next week); I'd prefer to overlook in a different sense the burned-out theatre complex and an empty concert hall which has never been used owing to a superstition surrounding the number of site-workers who died during its construction. But

Peter Westbury

it's time I checked out and positioned myself at Manila's domestic airport for the Philippines Airlines flight to Davao.

Another first: the airline meal was self-service and on the ground! It came in a miniature re-cycled paper carrier bag and tasted as if it, too, had been re-cycled. 'Carry-on' baggage is one thing – but 'carry-on' flight meals?!... only in the Philippines. The in-flight magazine, '*Mabuhay*' (long life), available from tables in the airport snack bar, was dated December and contained many topical Christmas feature articles. Departure was delayed so I passed the time of day with two fellow-passengers who kindly assured me that both hotels I'd chosen in Davao and Cebu were likely to prove inconvenient, one being uncomfortably close to the runway and the other three hours distant. The nearness of my visit to the celebration of the Chinese New Year (the Year of the Ox) had once again left me little choice.

11th February 1997

P.M. From Manila to Davao it is only an 85-minute hop by an A300 but, add the 90-minute delay (for no obvious or announced reason) and that flight time seems endless, especially as you have already devoured your normally occupationally therapeutic flight meal in the waiting lounge. A welcome distraction comes in the shape of the diminutive Filipina with wondrous legs in the adjacent seat; but that is her man across the aisle.

Baggage claim at Davao is a free-for-all as they don't run to a carousel. It's like Day One among the bargain-hunters in the January sales. The passengers raid the carts as they arrive, two at a time, jeep-hauled from the plane. But it's an unequal struggle and the practised handlers are easily the first to reach the carts, tipping the contents on to the concrete floor. Loss of dignity seems no issue here so I elbow my way in to regain early possession of my suitcase, easy to pick out amongst the proliferation of cardboard boxes and soon I am on my way by air-conditioned bus to the Insular Century Hotel to shed my crumpled clothing for a shower and restoring massage, room service supper and an early night.

Westbury Meets East

Mount Apo. As usual under cloudy conditions.

Peter Westbury

12th February 1997

Davao. Were it not constantly cloud-covered (you never see a better-than-hazy photo of its outline), Mount Apo, at 10,311 feet the tallest mountain in the whole Philippine archipelago, would dominate Davao City which itself claims to be the largest city in the world in terms of land area (244,000 hectares). The city is the capital of Mindanao, the second largest island after Luzon, and has its own dialect, though Tagalog and English are 'understood' if you believe the guide-books. The mountain slopes are forested and you come upon geysers and sulphur pillars, rainwater lakes and rivers with thundering waterfalls and cascades. Giant pitcher plants, orchids, ferns and berry-bearing bushes crowd under moss-covered trees. Davao, so-named by the early inhabitants from their word for fire (*daba-daba*) conjuring images of tribal wars and sacred rituals, has also become famous for the *durian* (fruit of the gods), reputedly an aphrodisiac but with an unfortunately repulsive smell. Anthony Burgess famously described the experience as being 'like eating custard in a public lavatory'. Nonetheless, some London hostesses, anxious to be on to the latest craze in foodstuffs, are willing to pay the importer's price tag of around £17.00 per *durian*, though how they get it home is a bit of a puzzle. I was once asked to vacate a taxi in Montmartre while bearing a particularly ripe St Albray back to the *septième arrondissement*. The *durian* is twenty times worse and I cannot imagine bus conductors or neighbours putting up with the stench. (Later, in Sabah in April, Miyuki insisted on trying *durian*-flavoured ice-cream. She very soon complained of a fever and headache and then remembered that you are not supposed to eat *durian* and drink alcoholic refreshment at the same time. People have died!) I cannot see it catching on unless it is marketed as a cure for sinusitis.

I learned nothing of this from today's City Tour. The know-nothing driver, straight from the jungle, was useless as a guide. He couldn't even give me a population statistic for Davao, simply stating that it was the largest in the Philippines. From the scant information he supplied I could have provided no details of Mount Apo's height above sea-level, just that it is impressive. The three-hour trip took two hours and would have taken even less had he not made a detour into the country to the Crocodile Park where he obviously receives a commission. But, as I had never been to a crocodile park before, I concurred. My first visit to one-such has not filled me with any great yearning for my next.

The approach roads to the city from every direction (we tried several in attempting to avoid the grid-locked traffic) were grimed with dust and diesel fumes and lined with smart sub-divisions alternating with shabby packing-case shanties, the former being bought up by foreign millionaires for renting to the rich, the latter being improvised by the local poor for their own occupation. The highlight of the tour was a stop-off to take a stroll round Victoria Shopping Plaza of which they're obviously very proud, a sort of Butts Centre, Reading but with more security. I was actually quite grateful for the opportunity to find a pharmacy for some Strepsils – I think it's all this dust. The whole journey was made to the sounds from a very bad quality tape, probably pirated, of early Barry Manilow numbers, the driver singing along initially with enthusiasm until he eventually correctly interpreted my prune-faced expression and mercifully put a sock in it. Otherwise the tour took place largely in silence.

Now, at 5 p.m., I'm relaxing by the pool after a swim. Peering over my freshly squeezed mango-juice I have a view of the bay partly screened by palm trees and shrubs. It is very pleasantly warm and I cannot help thinking that I would have been more profitably occupied here all day. I've just watched a man shin

Westbury Meets East

up the nearest palm tree so easily that he might have been walking up an escalator. Now he's at the top and partly obscured by the fronds. What's he up to? From his vest he has magicked a small saw and he appears to be selecting a branch. From this angle it looks very much as though it is the same branch on which he is sitting! Now he's coming back down . . . empty-handed. I've watched him do this twice now; most intriguing, but I'm none the wiser. An ancient freckled pot-bellied American just waddled by. 'Looks like rain', he drawled. Nothing would surprise me.

Tomorrow: the Countryside Tour.

13th February 1997

I have saved up details of the Crocodile Park (such as they were) until now because, of course, surprise, surprise, here we are on the Countryside tour, first stop: the Crocodile Park! It really doesn't amount to very much and the look on my face must have put my guide and driver on the defensive. 'It was only opened in 1994', I was informed.

There is one 18 feet long monster that mostly sleeps but nevertheless, close to, has enough menace to give you the primeval creeps. Other enclosures contain much smaller fry. It's all over in five minutes – hardly worth the detour. Twice!

Léo Petilona, the genial chauffeur and Marévil Salaver, the pretty, skinny, guide who prefers the use of her nick-name, 'Bhing', made excellent companions. Bhing is bright, with a college education behind her and the facts at her fingertips; Léo was entertaining, a story to suit every occasion. When a sudden downpour had us scurrying back to the car, he told his very long tale about a priest in bed with a young couple who had come to him for instruction before marriage. No, they were together in the bed because the couple had missed the last bus; a violent storm had all but drowned the village and the roof of the priest's house leaked everywhere except above his own

double bed. The bride-to-be was apprehensive about sharing such accommodation as she was saving herself for marriage but the priest solved the problem by offering to sleep in the middle between the girl and her future husband thus allaying temptation. As an added precaution the priest recommended that she kept her hand on her ha'penny (her *peso?*). And so it was that the storm grew worse and the thunder and lightning more and more frequent. It is the custom in the Philippines, every time that lightning occurs, for people to make the sign of the Cross. Amen. The priest had a huge grin on his face when he waved them off next day.

Our own storm abated and we headed for Malagos, Calina, to the Philippine Eagle Nature Centre to see '*Pag-asa*' (meaning 'hope'), the rare and endangered bird bred by artificial insemination. (I get so much more of a thrill from seeing the hawks circling free over the trout farms of Shirakawa than from watching this sullen caged creature, so still it might have been stuffed; but I told myself good work of propagation is being done here at the Centre and they need visitors' money to help support the programme.) Bhing and Léo and I got on famously and moved on to the Yuhico Orchid Farm in Greenhills where they grow the exotic *waling-waling*, pride of Davao, discovered by a German scientist on the slopes of Mount Apo. It flowers from April to September so – I missed it! But we had a goodish lunch and headed back to the city so that I could change some money.

I have no doubt that I chose the best hotel in which to stay. Perhaps a more central choice will be the 'Marco Polo' but it won't be completed for another couple of years. The hoardings that advertise current film releases are interesting: they are all hand-painted.

I invited Bhing and Léo to dinner so we had a separate outing in the evening and I met Bhing's mother and younger brothers and sisters (no father) when we called to pick her up. She is so natural, very virginal, just delightful. There's a lucky young man in the background, no doubt, although she made

no objection when I linked arms for our photograph in front of the altar at the Chinese Temple. [On my return to Japan I sent her a set of prints of our day together and received a charming letter back saying I was now her friend and she no longer regarded me as a client]. So that evening, in a well-chosen traditional Filipino restaurant, we had some wonderful *lichon baboyi* (roast pork) and a lot more I couldn't identify. Although the three of us really tucked in, they left with bulging doggy bags; they have many to feed at home. '*Walla pongannuman*' ('You're very welcome'). Unfortunately, their choice of entertainment afterwards, deferring, perhaps, to the fact that I was from Japan, was to take me to a *karaoke* bar filled, of course, with Japanese tourists! When sober, there is a limit as to how much punishment one can take in the form of shrill, tuneless voices. We parted company quite early and it was back to the

Peter Westbury

hotel for a relaxing bedtime massage. Though prettier, Agnes was not as adept as Tuesday's Gina.

14th February 1997

Samal Island. Between scanning my book and sipping my San Miguel, I've been watching, from my bamboo-roofed, plaited-walled villa on stilts over the water's edge, the to-ing and fro-ing of the small boats as they tie up at and, in turn, slip free from the Pearl Farm Beach jetty on Samal Island. One of them ferried me here the hour's ride from the mainland early this morning, so now I'm a temporary 'day-resident' in this blissful retreat, a haven of havens, a favourite with honey-mooners. While the temperature is a tad oppressive, the clouds are taking the glare off the sea and I'm sprawled in my shorts in the shade really very relaxed. Two lizards have come to visit, too, approaching from opposite ends of the bench cum balustrade built into this balcony. They were frightened by the unexpected encounter and went hurtling away.

I had thought they'd been attracted by a small puddle of spilled beer and sure enough one of them plucked up the courage to return, clambered over my toes and took alcoholic refreshment. '*Toast!*' (Cheers!) It has just occurred to me what a helluva place this is in which to find yourself, alone, on St Valentine's Day.

Early evening. I'm back in the hotel lobby, checked out and ready to take the shuttle bus out to the airport, when I spot one of the masseuses doubling as a waitress for the Valentine's Party. Was that a wink?!

And so to Davao airport to meet Cenita Corazon and

Westbury Meets East

together to Badian Island off Cebu: first a 45-minute flight, then a two-and-a-half hour taxi drive and finally a ferryboat. Great to see Cenita and we catch up with each other's news. Davao airstrip departure lounge was purgatory, not so much because the air-conditioning had failed, more because there *was* no aircon, end of story. To be fair, the sign only says 'Pre-departure Area' with no hint of comfort. It was dimly lit by virtue of the fact that over half the light-bulbs had blown (we had time to count) and those that worked were of limited effect, shrouded as they were in surprisingly elaborate *capiz* shell chandeliers. While the other passengers busied themselves with their mobile phones we watched small birds flying in and out of the open sides of the building until the girl official, one of three and barely audible above the general commotion, shouted from the desk 'Your flight is boarding now'. As the queue shortened and we drew closer, the other two girls became noticeably better dressed than the announcer and eventually proved to be cardboard cut-outs. (I'm thinking of employing this technique to solve my staff shortage at Bridewell Heath). But nothing ran late today; possibly because, it is fair to presume, the captains and their crews had Valentine's Day dates.

Even so, it was 1 a.m. and pitch dark when we arrived at the Badian Island jetty and the driver radioed across for the hotel's ferryman to collect us.

He navigated us back by torchlight in an open boat across a calm sea through fine rain but nothing could detract from the romantic welcome at Reception even though the advertised musicians had long since been sent home! We had been booked in in our own names but Joy, the very smart manageress, enquired if we had been married long and were we on our honeymoon? All I said was 'You guessed!' and smiled.

15th February 1997

Described as a romantic paradise, Badian Island is not far short, though, if there is a next time, I'll use the helicopter service. Last night's journey in the dark was tedious; Cenita slept most of the time, head on my chest. In fact she sleeps quite a lot and we had a very lazy start to today with one of those civilized all-day breakfasts via Room Service. Designed to look from its exterior like a *kubo* (native hut), our single-storeyed, 'honeymooners' villa has a large living/

Peter Westbury

bedroom/dressing room and a luxurious bathroom almost the same size. Each evening, two fresh garlands are laid on the pillows. The balcony with its *duyan* (hammock) faces out over the lagoon so we have a view of the jungle-clad mountains on the mainland, the rocky upper edge to their silhouette resembling the long jagged spinal incline of a giant pre-historic reptile. You can read about Badian's coral reefs, the scuba diving and its culinary delights from the guide-books. What you really want to know, like the happy fact of a sewage disposal system that does not go into the sea, is only learned with relief after your arrival! In the afternoon we took a stroll through the tamed wilderness of the gardens and along the beach to give us an appetite for dinner in one of the three restaurants. *Calacouchi* (a magnolia-like white-flowering tree) was in full bloom. There was ripe fruit for the picking: *lanzones* (similar to lichees, about the size and colour of a baby potato) and *ramputan* with very pretty variegated red spiky skin which you peel back to reveal sweet flesh but almost all stone. Later we chose the beach barbecue and retired early.

16th February 1997

By ferry boat to Cebu mainland and then by bone-jarring, teeth-rattling Jeepney along the coast and jungle track to Kawasan Falls. These Jeepneys are not designed for passenger comfort. The driver has the best view out and thank goodness he does.

With automatic transmission he has both hands free to grip the wheel as he steers what he considers the best course between the potholes. There are many options and he is entitled to his opinion. Not exclusively for passenger use, Jeepneys are the most versatile method of transport. You see them serve as builders trucks, goods lorries and even hearses. Come to think of it, in this last context, 'bone-jarring' conjures up an

unfortunate image or perhaps, for funerals, the drivers do go more carefully! The last 50 minutes of our adventure was on foot, crossing and re-crossing the river over flimsy bamboo bridges, the jungle path winding through tiny hutted, infant-strewn communities leaving a lasting impression of washing-lines, cooking smells and smiling faces. I wondered how differently I would have been greeted had I been trekking alone . . .

At the falls, Cenita was content to watch while I swam. The guide and porter served lunch during which there was a heavy downpour. Grins all round – after all, it is God's will. Yes, but there must be days when it seems they'll never get the washing dry.

It is late afternoon back in the *kubo* – time for some diary-writing while Cenita takes a nap in the *duyan*. Let me tell you a little about her. We met in Japan and I like her a lot. Here it has been assumed that we are man and wife; we've tried to fool no-one – we're neither of us wearing rings – but the staff are playing it straight, perhaps it's easier that way. She hails from Mindanao, in the provinces where her family were farmers. She has amazing eyes, intelligent but shy. Sometimes I feel that we are very close and at others that she is very far away. Her father died in an accident three years ago when she was 19. She has now returned to help her mother and two brothers run the store. At school they taught her about birth control and she trusts me but the most effective contraceptive has been the Gideons' Holy Bible which she reads each night at bedtime! She looks adorable in the hammock. Time for a rest.

Dusk. I hope that the real Paradise is not as boring as this. Mind you, that's making a huge assumption! Perhaps it's that I'm not calm within myself, too much going on in my head. I could learn a lot from Cenita about that; she has very little

Peter Westbury

ambition, being very content with her lot.

A shower before supper, her *utong* like marbles.

17th February 1997

This, our last day on Badian Island, was all I could have hoped.
As 'honeymooners', we qualified for the tree-planting ceremony! A lazy afternoon by the pool was rounded off by our
farewell dinner, romantically accompanied by the blind
left-handed mandolin player and his singer-guitarist minder.
The whole staff sang to us and we each received traditional
shell necklaces. We promised to come back one day...

I've still not met the Corazon family and it has not been in
our conversation since leaving Japan. Perhaps we both feel it
would be a *snafu* (mistake) to pursue our relationship though
I think the age difference bothers me more than it does Cenita.

'*Mabuhay*, my dear.'

18th February 1997

Mactan-Cebu International Airport. Three-and-a-half hours'
drive after a 5 a.m. starlit ferry crossing and I am taking
breakfast alone following check-in. I have kissed a temporary
(?) farewell to Cenita and I'm Manila bound. She went off
back to her village wearing my stripey fisherman's top – it
looked much better on her, anyway. She had snuggled up close
in the taxi, through the townships of Moalboal, Alcantara,
San Fernando and Minglanilla (all unidentifiable in the night
of the 14th) but had not lingered when it was time to say
goodbye.

In terms of area, Cebu City is the second largest in the
Philippines (after Davao) and growing fast. The little I saw of
it as we travelled in the slow-moving peak hour traffic from
south-west to north-east was not inviting and I'm glad of my
decision not to over-night here. The airport is confusing, more
so than might be the case because most of Kawasan Falls
seems to have transferred itself to my left ear rendering me
half-deaf to the announcements! A 60-minute domestic flight
to Manila and the pre-arranged meeting with Venus. This may
sound exciting but actually Venus is a chap. In Tagalog the V
is as B in English so he is pronounced Benus, though he has
already told me on the telephone that he prefers Ben for short;

Westbury Meets East

good job it's not pronounced like P – but then it's unlikely he'd want to shorten it! Ben is, with his cousin, a dealer in realty.

They've booked me into the Westin Philippine Plaza so I hope they deal in reality, too, as I'm expecting them to pay the bill. The plan is to have site meetings over the next two days to look at land for potential resort development. But, for tonight and to begin with, a massage, I think.

✿ ✿ ✿

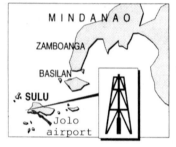

3 foreign firms join oil drilling in Sulu Sea

BY CLARISSA S. BATINO

AMERICAN exploration firm Atlantic Richfield Corp. has brought in two other foreign partners—Prussag of Germany and Malaysian Mining Co.—to initially invest at least $16 million to drill an offshore well in Sulu, fronting the borders of Malaysia.

Local firms Basic Petroleum and Minerals Inc. and Philodrill Corp., leading a consortium of 13 exploration firms, will join the drilling as operators of the zone, which is also referred to as Hippo.

Officials of the Department of Energy said

3 FOREIGN/ p.B4

19th & 20th February 1997

President Ramos is taking credit, probably quite justifiably, for the fact that foreign investment is running at an all-time high. The business pages of the Philippine Daily Inquirer have been full of examples, one being the exploration of oil in the Sulu Sea. At the same time, other articles describe terrorist activity in the same region, with civil war being reported in the northern part of Mindanao, surely enough to deter the faint-hearted. Or is there anything to my theory that this off-putting propaganda is disseminated by those 'in the know' so that they have the (oil) field to themselves?

Anyway, that's a totally different league. I am here somewhat cheekily as I have no fortune,

Peter Westbury

Bishop's plane downed by gunfire, says pilots' group

BY ROCKY NAZARENO

A TOP official of the Aircraft Owners and Pilots Association of the Philippines yesterday corroborated reports that the Super Musketeer plane carrying retired Catholic Bishop Antonino Nepomuceno had been shot at just after taking off from Jolo airport, causing it to crash and kill all those on board.

no funds, no collateral for borrowing even if, as a foreigner, a loan would be agreed to enable me to invest in the President's attractive schemes. Ben collected me from the hotel and conducted me via Makati's Ayala Avenue, the bank-lined concrete canyon that is the business centre of Manila (except that the river of traffic at its bottom is not flowing) to the Ermita district to an office only a block or two from where I was accosted a week ago by Lorenzo el Pimpo. I found myself in a long shabby room over-crowded with mis-matched second-hand desks and green metal filing cabinets (circa 1950) and after an interminable delay and a string of apologetic messages I finally came face to face with Ben's cousin, Jhun, a short round ugly lady with an instantly forgettable aura. But she did have this portfolio of properties, some plans and location maps. Let me describe one island retreat that JAC Realty Corporation had to offer. Towards the northern end of the island of Palawan is Taytay airport, little more than an airstrip in actuality. Incidentally, Palawan has been in the news recently because, by dating treasures found in the wreckage of a 140 metre long vessel in the deeps off this island, experts have been able to confirm Chinese dominance of these waters a century before Magellan. (Not a lot of people know that.) A taxi-drive brings you to El Nido and from there it is 20 minutes by *banca* to San Jose, Tinabian Island.

And what is there on this 41.3 hectares of paradise? A blissful nothing except a freshwater spring and a few fruit-bearing trees. The price-tag of 75 million *pesos* is, I am assured, negotiable. Each of my eye-lids is bat free. 'Have you anything a fraction more challenging?' I enquire. 'My associates are looking for something altogether, um, larger'. And so the pantomime developed over the next two days while they delved in their files and badgered their contacts for promising opportunities that might match my requirements: just the 'right' distance from an international airport yet sufficiently remote for the syndicate I represented to create the irresistible anomaly, the exclusive Five-star Desert Island, for the privilege of staying on which your new-rich punter would be prepared to pay a fortune. With each site visit I solemnly shook my head but promised to discuss it with my 'associates'. Jack, on whose behalf, ostensibly, I'm making these enquiries, will see the funny side. He is absolutely boracic; he's not yet finished paying off Faye's debts.

To recapitulate, Faye is the Filipina *Japayuki* Jack is hoping to marry – pending her divorce from a Japanese husband whose existence she recently revealed. They are up to their armpits in debt, partly due to a complicated domestic situation in both countries involving property but compounded by a madly irresponsible spending spree in Hong Kong last autumn from which it seems possible they may never recover. Anyway, in helpful pursuit of their dream to establish a business here in the Philippines, I have visited a number of small islands, courtesy of Ben and Jhun.

I did insist on paying my hotel bill in the end, by the way, seeing as I was 'unable to take things any further forward at this stage'. It seemed the fairest solution and I do have a bit of a conscience, even with estate agents.

22nd February 1997

I don't know who's likely to be reading this diary stuff but I do hope they're editing out the bits they'd rather not know about before they get to them! I'm taking lunch at the open-air poolside restaurant in the hotel gardens. I'd not seen daylight for the past 36 hours – Aileen and Joy have seen to that. Aileen is a friend of Choco and Joy is a friend of Aileen. Between them they have made an old man very happy. Manila, I am told, has been overcast and dull. It may have been overcast but I can promise you: far from dull.

Cloudy but warm, now, I shall have the afternoon to do a little shopping before returning tomorrow to the snowy mountain top in Fukushima. This evening I'm planning to relax, listening to the 'Take One' jazz quintet with their very dishy singer, Rita Esteves, in the splendid foyer bar which very much reminds me of the *thé dansant* lounge in London's Waldorf Hotel. I wonder if she does requests.

Lunch was grilled *lapu-lapu* (strange to have named a fish after a politician, the fish having been around for so much longer; maybe the politician was named after the fish?) followed by a salad of lettuce, tomatoes, potato, sweet corn, green peas, green and black olives, egg, coleslaw, chopped crispy bacon, croûtons, nuts and sesame dressing. Delicious. Two glasses of Chablis. Perfection. This amazing country that seems to cater so unjudgementally to the hedonistic side of man's nature has worked its duskily beautiful magic for me a second time. At some expense, agreed, but nothing compared with the emo-

Peter Westbury

tional overheads or the actual wear and tear of being married.

At 6.45. pm. my over-running *siesta* is disturbed by sounds of applause and the amplified voice of a lady in mid-oration wafting to my balcony window from a sports arena where a massive rally is assembled. She's really stirring them up – shades of Eva Peron (*Evita* has been showing here). Now hymn-singing is competing with the diesel-roar of the Jeepneys. They seem about evenly matched against each other *and* the dampening blanket of polluted air. But all sound is still struggling to penetrate the deafness in my left ear.

Jeepney

23rd February 1997

Manila to Narita. Examples of Northwest Airlines' Americanisms followed me into 'Business Class' (yes, it worked this time!): printed on the airsickness bag – 'For Motion Discomfort'! In an effort to euphemize, the Americans have made a *canard*. Then, from the flight deck, the reassuring announcement from the captain: 'Welcome aboard Northwest flight no. 6. We'll soon be airborne and bound non-stop for Narita serving Tokyo and then continuing to . . . uh . . . (long pause), uh . . . Boston! Yes, that's where we're headed today, folks!' It didn't affect or bother me but all the destination indicators had shown Chicago! And, finally, from the cabin crew's intercom as we taxied to a standstill upon arrival: 'Please be sure you have all your hand-luggage with you before de-planing.'

So what have I to show for my holiday, apart from the grin? A *bilaan kuwadro* (a traditional hand-painted photo-frame) that I bought while with Bhing in Davao, a polished *capiz* jewellery box for Miyuki and these diary pages. And towards the end of the return flight, a very special bonus: a perfect view of snow-clad Mount Fuji in the sunshine; I got to see it at last, close to!

3rd March 1997

All is not well in the state of Bridewell Heath. From my personal high of the Philippines trip it was distressing to notice the tangible slide in morale back at the ranch. The D-G confided that he's been obliged to accept a drastically reduced salary. His deputy (whom he has nick-named 'The Undertaker') is making himself increasingly unpopular insisting upon time-consuming detailed end-of-shift reports from all foreign staff (only) before they go off duty.

One New Zealander has quit to go and work in Tokyo for twice the money. (Only he, I and one other know, at this stage, that he is going to be a stripper.) Two more have given the required month's notice so that they, too, can go and earn more elsewhere. One of the Japanese office staff has decided she's had enough of the BH style of management and has handed in her resignation. There has been an uprising in the Main Kitchen led by the Japanese sous-chef who has threatened to resign and take some of the key staff with him. The weakening *yen* continues to make our salaries look sicker and sicker.

But the worst is to come: Ben and Amanda, who have been involved in this project from the start, have told me they are just waiting for the right moment to announce their own resignations; they quite simply find the bad decisions and rough-riding by the Japanese junior director no longer excusable after nearly three years of hands-on experience. The same mistakes are being made over and over again and they don't need to take it any more. I have had long talks with them but they have made up their minds which leaves me very sad.

I have compiled a report for direct presentation to the President outlining my anxieties. I have pulled no punches; I hope it loses nothing in translation. All of which has rather taken the edge off my preparations for New Zealand later this month.

Apart from that (!) my social life couldn't be better. I escape to see Miyuki when I can and she is researching a holiday together in April, somewhere warm.

Peter Westbury

New Zealand
One More Time

9th March 1997

THE FIRST THING THE NON-STOP Skyliner express leaving Ueno does, is stop! But then that's right – it would. I mean, sooner or later. Somewhere. But this is a bit sooner than expected and, as for where, I haven't a clue; we're not in a station. This is the first time it has ever happened and, of course, on the very occasion when I'm cutting things fine. The other occupants of the car (carriage) seem unperturbed but then by far the majority are asleep... quite tired myself ... Miyuki has been up for the ski–ing... desperately short of sleep for the last three nights...

A slight tilting of the train brings me back to the present; the delay that seemed like an eternity lasted only four minutes.

Narita. As I board the aircraft I renew my request to be upgraded. The chief steward confirms the check-in clerk's advice that this is not possible but suggests that, in any case, I'd be better off staying put: with three empty seats next to mine, I will be able to sleep full stretch. I must appear unconvinced because he comes back in a few minutes with a 'Business Class' pack by way of compensation: eye mask, toothbrush and paste, bedsocks, earplugs, razor and shaving gel all in a zippered bag with the compliments of Air New Zealand.

10th March 1997

I awake with a start and sit up in the dark. A Kiwi voice is saying 'I can't believe this'. It belongs to a flight attendant. He has just tripped in the aisle and sent his tray of drinks over my head, neck and shirt front. From my point of view, *believing it* is not a problem. He brings absorbent paper towels plus a cotton towel, half wet, half dry. 'Use the wet end first, sir;

Westbury Meets East

you'll be sticky'. It was orange juice. He's done this before. Later, he returns and hands me a 'Business Class' pack by way of compensation. I shall be able to open a shop. I padded in my socks to the lavatory to tidy myself and stepped straight on to a wet floor. The loo had been leaking.

I am joking about it all to the chief steward as we begin our descent to Christchurch. He is very apologetic. 'Is there a lady in your life, Mr Westbury?' 'About five at the moment'. He comes back with five complimentary 'Business Class' packs for ladies.

11th to 14th March 1997

South Island. In view of the worsening staff situation at BH, I have permission to hire any suitable candidates on the spot to bring them out as quickly as possible. Armed with sets of the 7-page invitation and information pack, I have found eight, so far, in Christchurch and Dunedin. Ideally, I need to double that.

There were a few good political one-liners circulating in Christchurch this time, mainly aimed at the Maori deputy Prime Minister who, in common with politicians pretty well world-wide, has come in for some stick from the comedians. Known to have a high opinion of himself, Winston Peters is said to have arrived at the casualty wing of Wellington General Hospital suffering from self-inflicted love-bites. Another quip from another taxi-driver: 'He regularly phones in to Dial-a-Prayer – to check if there are any messages!'

It was while taking breakfast on my last morning at the Millennium that I overheard the following fragment of conversation from a group of American senior citizens:

'I don't regret a dollar overspent on this trip, Martha, but I have to tell ya I'm in one helluva out o' pocket deficit. But then why should I worry as long as I jus' keep takin' the pills. Could I have a little more juice?'

(Pause while she pops the pills.)

'What *are* they?'

'These? It says "chromium capsules" on the packet'.

'Yeah. But what do they do?'

'*I* dunno: he buys 'em; I take 'em.'

'Well, Laura – jus' you mind how you go through that airport metal detector!'

Peter Westbury

As an experiment, I had made a reservation for my second

night in Dunedin at the beautifully situated Larnach Castle out of town on the peninsular. Run as a rather snooty hotel restaurant, the owners, with a detectable air of condescension allow you to stay in the converted stables as long as you are no trouble and conform to the myriad rules meticulously spelled out in an irritatingly idiosyncratic hand for the inconvenience of the guests. The poor 'concierge-cum-maitre d' has a terrible time of it dealing with 'difficult' people like me who don't fit in to the neat category of obeisant, time-no-object traveller with own independent transport. As a consequence we got off to a bad start when he announced I'd given them insufficient notice of my wish to dine (unacceptable in advance by fax at the time of booking) and their realization that I would require a taxi early next morning. To be perfectly fair, I did not go hungry as they produced a cold collation which I ate in my room from a tray on my lap and the *concierge* did spend a considerable time locating a sensibly priced taxi service, offering to drive me to the airport himself if need be. But it is just one more example of a first-rate location carrying second-rate hospitality.

15th March 1997

En route to the airport, I was entertained by Billie, the driver of shuttle bus no. 51, an ex-bulldozer operator with many graphic stories of a career in which hitting power cable seemed to be a favourite pastime. According to the identity photograph displayed in his cab, Billie 'expires' on 6th March 1998. I do hope not. Billie says he'll see how he feels.

Runway 03, Monona airfield. Seat-belted and waiting in the Mount Cook Airlink ATR72, call sign Mike Oscar for the first of two hops to get me to Auckland, North Island. Cleared for take-off from Dunedin. So it's back across the sun-wrinkled mountains of Otago to Christchurch where I change aircraft. At 19,000 feet we encounter a bit of turbulence, this time from the tail end of a sou'wester (Cyclone Gavin has already passed over), to coincide with the serving of tea and coffee. No spillage in my vicinity.

Now, on the second leg, the dusty purple northern end of the Southern Alps gives way to the craggy coastline; turquoise and azure inlets decorate the top right hand corner of South Island. A hammered glass surface effect is all that distinguishes Cook Strait from the identically blue sky, but in no time at all North Island looms, its shape outlined by solid cloud cover that glares back in the sunshine.

It is raining on touchdown but sunny in the city. This country which, it is claimed, can experience all four seasons in any if not every 24 hours, is full of weather experts.

Everybody here recognizes a front when they see it and are familiar with all the meteorological terminology. And humorous with it. To my comment – 'The weather doesn't seem able to make up its mind today', came the taxi-driver's reply: 'Love us no! It's been the same ever since we've had a coalition government!'

16th to 22nd March 1997

Auckland, where, by averaging my hotel expenses, I have included a stay at the highly rated 'Carlton' for my last three nights, looks unlikely to yield the remaining staff needed.

Although March is a difficult time to come recruiting for our mid-May intake anyway, because the bulk of the students are still in mid-course, in the past I've had a reserve list of names on which to draw. Word, however, appears to have got out about the unfavourable exchange rate and my list has all but evaporated. Should I try for an earlier return flight? I convince myself that I'd do better to remain here in the market-place and allow the grapevine time to work. In the meantime, I shall

take this opportunity to see something of the place and I've noticed that *Arcadia*, *West Side Story* and *Romeo & Juliet* are all playing here. I wonder what Suzy's doing this week . . .

Well – I had a ball. I enjoyed the three shows mentioned. Suzy came with me to *West Side Story*. I went on a tour of the vineyards which took care of one full day. Another very full day was spent travelling up to and back from the Bay of Islands. If there's a next time I'll take a friend; Suzy wasn't free. It was the perfect day and if the visitor to Auckland does nothing else he wouldn't be disappointed, as long as the weather is kind. The long drive requires an early morning start. There is a stop at Warkworth to see the old jail and some amazing *kauri* trees, hundreds of years old. You don't see many of these about because the main trunks made good size hulls for Maori war canoes and the other branches were used as weather-boarding for houses. The few that remain do so because of preservation orders but vigilance is still necessary. (Just outside Auckland on the way to the airport, the single tree that gives 'One Tree Hill' its name was very nearly severed recently by a Maori with a grievance and an axe.) The tour continues to Waitangi where the famous Treaty of 1840 was signed; and then back to Paihia.

It is from the jetty here that the most picturesque cruise around the coastal islands commences. For three hours the boat weaves out to the Hole in the Rock and back, attracting schools

The picturesque coast and the 'Hole in the Rock'.

of dolphin that surf on the bow wave. It is the most exhilarating sight.

On my last night I had booked seats for the 'Oba Oba' Brazilian floor show at the Sky City Casino Theatre. Suzy met me at the hotel and we walked the short distance. The spectacle, the colourful costumes, the energetic dancing were great; shame about the sound system.

At dinner, Suzy seemed a little pre-occupied. Then – 'You will have to travel to Hong Kong if you want to see me again.' Her study course is nearly over and she will be returning home. May she stay the night.

23rd March 1997

If all visa applications are successful, I will have scraped together 13 new staff. With only one extending from the existing team, it looks like being another very stretching summer. If only they'd agree to me recruiting some semi-permanent deputy managers from the UK. But, of course, it would cost them more money.

Westbury Meets East

A very amorous hand-delivered letter awaited me on my return from New Zealand. From Sashiko. Expecting to see me, she had made a special journey to tell me she loves me. Golly.

27th and 28th March 1997

Disruption to the normal routine while seven or eight of us modelled wedding gear for a top catalogue. From Father of the Groom, last August, I was promoted to Father of the Bride, a dishy American blonde professional model hired especially. Wise precaution. My ready-made speech was declined (again!) but I did get to dance with the 'bride', which was fun. Damned if I can remember her name . . .

2nd April 1997

It is entirely my own fault that I have a day to kill in Tokyo. I arrived at the hotel yesterday (April Fool's Day, sure enough) to make the overnight stay for the early morning departure flight to Sabah (North Borneo) today but either through over-work and a determination to get away from the office or, more probably, sheer miscalculation, it is costing me two nights now in this ludicrously expensive city as my flight does not in fact leave until tomorrow. So this morning I strolled from Ueno the length of Asakusa *dori* and, bearing left before the river, enjoyed, once more, the bustle of the shrine environs, bought another *o-mamori* and partook of a really quite tasty *okonomiyaki* with an Asahi Dry for lunch. I then retraced my steps past the shops full of temple accessories and religious paraphernalia, past the edge of Kappabashi, the district for kitchenware and appliances, to find myself a park bench to rest and light up a cigarette. The approach path to the central lake and fountain was lined, literally, with blue tarpaulins and the picnic impedimenta of groups of Japanese on *bakeshon*. For this is the season of *Hanami* and a dull day has not prevented swarms of cherry blossom pilgrims from descending on Ueno Park to eat, drink and sing under the trees. Rows of fake pink decorations almost obscure the real thing. Only a few yards from these holiday-makers, other blue tarpaulins form the semi-permanent homes of scores of homeless who will later ransack the *gomi* bags for a supper of leftovers. At last a back-less wooden bench is free and I can sit down. Families and

Peter Westbury

couples stream past: thin people, stout people, tall people and little people, the only clear fashion trend being the 70s flares worn by the young. A tramp wants to sell me a card. At first I take it to be a phone card but when he holds it closer I can see it is a playing card but with the photograph of a famous baseball player. I indicate that I have no interest in baseball so then he demonstrates what he has been trying to tell me: by heating the back of the card with a lighter, the player's genitals are exposed! More technology for which we are to thank the space programme? It is getting cold and I walk away. When I look back the tramp is foraging for my fag-end in the metal ash-can. I made my way through the noisy but well-behaved crowds – I noticed only one uniformed *keikan*, though there would most certainly have been others out of sight on alert – and back to the hotel where I slept for three hours. In the evening I returned to the park hoping to see the cherry trees illuminated and the throng dispersed. On both counts I was disappointed and so I tracked down the French-style restaurant first introduced to me by Harumi when I passed this way in January. I called her up on her mobile but only to keep in touch as I must have an early night. Pretty little waitress in this place, though. She brings me some beef, pumpkin, mangetout and cabbage all served on a sizzling plate

Peter Westbury

with bread and salad on the side instead of rice. Just right.

Back in the hotel a 1990 exhibition poster reveals that Bernard Cathelin, two of whose lithographs now hang in my *apato*, also produced tapestries.

By the drinks vending-machine on the landing, a notice states that the refreshing health drink 'Pocari Sweat' (a permanently mis-spelled 'sweet' since its original launch) contains 'the following positively charged ions – sodium, potassium, calcium and magnesium and the following negatively charged ions – chlorine, citrate and lactate.' I settle for a 300ml can of Suntory Black & Pilsner and am charged Y450 (about £2.30).

Westbury Meets East

Cherry blossom – no sweat

To Sabah with Love

3rd April 1997

HAVING BONED UP on a few suitable phrases so that we can at least convey 'please' (*silakan*), 'thank you' (*terimahkasi*) and 'delicious' (*enak*) in the hotel as well as enter into the spirit of things by wishing each other 'good morning' (*slamat pagi*) and 'good night, sweet dreams' (*slamat tidur mimpi manis*), Miyuki and I are now aboard our Malaysian Airlines flight to Kota Kinabalu. Over the headphones comes the predictable mixture of classical and pop music or equally predictable American jokes from stand-up comics (example: 'I just returned from a pleasure trip' – pause – 'I drove my mother-in-law to the airport'.). Kota Kinabalu ('KK' to the local ex-pats just as Kuala Lumpur is 'KL' and Bridewell Heath is 'BH'), is now the capital of Sabah, Sandakan having been devastated by allied bombing during the Japanese occupation at the end of World War II. 'Sabah' was popularized as such from its old seafarers' name meaning 'Land Below the Wind' referring to its location just below the typhoon belt. There would be a justification for re-naming the country after last year's rogue typhoon flouted tradition and intruded this far south, snatching off tin roofs and causing serious flood damage. No longer can it claim to be free from climatic disturbances but we should be well clear of the rainy season, which is normally from November to February. Sabah had been British North Borneo since 1881 when some British businessmen bought rights to the northern tip of Borneo from the sultans of Brunei and Sulu. Today, Malaysia is made up of Peninsular Malaysia plus the two separate states of Sarawak and Sabah.

It produces rubber, tin, palm oil, timber, pepper and petroleum. In Sabah it was the success of the timber industry that gave rise to its claim of having the greatest concentration of millionaires anywhere in the world. As mere tourists we are still promised access to all sorts of delights from sea cucumbers and edible birds nests (made in caves by swiftlets out of

Peter Westbury

pure saliva) to orang-utan and the amazing proboscis monkey. This latter is extraordinary looking with a pendulous red nose, certain other red thingies, webbed feet, grey tights, white knickers and an orange jacket. This evening an open-air buffet has been set up for supper in the poolside gardens. At twilight, a fire 'ceremony' takes place in the hotel grounds; all this means is that a torch-bearer, to the accompaniment of drums, goes round the paths lighting small braziers on poles. Now we've seen it we won't need to see it again but the flames last for most of the evening and contribute to the magical and romantic atmosphere of the place especially when we look out later from our balcony overlooking the South China Sea. I could get used to this.

4th April 1997

Our bedroom is bordering on the luxurious, the bathroom palatial. I sense the location may be too quiet for Miyuki but she agrees to a 'lazy' day while we research the options and sample the hotel amenities. By lunchtime she is fidgeting to wind-surf so in the afternoon we hit the beach. She struggles very gamely with a sail that is too large for her; they have nothing in her size but she cheers up when, at my suggestion, they telephone their 'sister' hotel in the next bay and find they have exactly what she needs and we arrange a trip there for another day. We also spend some time in the foyer planning other treats and then flop by the pool until it's time to change for dinner – one of the best meals we've enjoyed together in what may seem a strange choice of eating-place: the hotel's Italian *ristorante*. But as Miyuki is a vegetarian, the menu was not restricting for either of us and there was a good wine list, too.

5th April 1997

Mengkabong Water Village. This is reached by a flat-hulled craft, fitted with an outboard engine, after several deviations from the main estuary channel and up minor creeks which gives the guide the opportunity to spook you with her tales of superstitions and spirits long dead. Here you learn of the significance of the different coloured rags tied to the bushes beneath the island graves and other gruesome aspects of the

Mengkabong Water Village.

life of the villagers which includes very primitive sanitation.

Between the sea and the village is mangrove swamp and our boatman steered into the trees to cut short branches from the tangle of fast-growing self-propagating vegetation. The guide made much of the dangers of the tides and currents, the likelihood of running into difficulty, of being stranded unheeded out on the water. How would we alert anyone of our predicament? Nature has provided the answer in the mangrove plant itself. By pulling the stem away from the fruit in a certain way you are left, if you have been skilful or lucky, with a hollow piece that can be used as a whistle. It takes knowing the knack to make it work but I imagine it's a knack you would master quickly if you were in a dire situation. We putt-putted along the edge of the village itself – shanties on stilts linked by plank

'Between the sea and the village…'

walkways over the water littered with the debris of nets and fishing tackle. It would be easy to dismiss this as a tourist attraction but it is hard to see how the villagers themselves benefit from being stared at by strangers, the only money being spent with the boatman and that not a great amount. The villagers were friendly enough, though, the children returning our waves and grinning broadly for the amateur cameramen.

It was on this trip that we first heard the legend attached to Mount Kinabalu (13,455 feet). Centuries ago, a prince visiting from China met and fell in love with a beautiful local girl and made her his princess. Instead of returning to his country, he was persuaded by his wife to stay and they soon produced a child. However, the prince's father was furious at his son's continued absence from the Chinese court and demanded his return. The prince succumbed, promising his wife and child that he'd be back. They never saw each other again for, so the story goes, the prince died on the open sea. His widow took herself and the child up to the higher mountain slopes which are still believed by the hill tribes to be the resting place of the spirits of the departed. They, too, were never seen again but, on a clear day (and if you squint a bit) you can see the princess' profile on the mountain skyline; she appears to be calling out to her prince. Well we heard this legend, with variations, about ten times in six days, sometimes from other tourists. And some say that the name Kinabalu itself translates as 'Chinese widow'!

At no stage during our stay did we muster the energy to climb the mountain even with the lure of cooler temperatures at the summit. White-water rafting was out due to the lack of recent rainfall. So we did a little local jungle-trekking, saw the free range orang-utan at feeding time, took a romantic horse-back ride along the beach at sunset – clichés all but no less enjoyable for that. The water in the swimming pools was still gloriously warm and inviting at midnight. It was a

Westbury Meets East

shangri-la and would serve as the ideal location for a honeymoon: pleasant climate, excellent food, very friendly service, evening musical entertainment if you wished. And so the days passed, sometimes lazily, sometimes actively, always pleasurably. The Borneo Mail reported the visit yesterday of the French spiderman, Alain Robert, to take a preliminary look at the Yayasan Sabah, a cylindrical 28-storey glass-panelled building that he is planning to scale for charity. At the airport on our arrival, the immigration officer mistook me for him (we Europeans all look alike) and I was flattered to be taken for a 34-year old; less so now that I have seen his photograph!

6th April 1997

The Sunday market at Kota Belud. We have taken the hour and a half bus journey along not particularly inspiring roads (described as scenic) running north-east out of the capital. Miyuki has the enviable Japanese knack of being able to fall asleep almost anywhere and did so now. [She even dozed on the uncomfortable seat of the *Bâteau Mouche* later in July, and so missed the exhibitionists making love on the floodlit banks of the Seine]. Spread on the ground beneath woven split-bamboo rectangles providing essential shade are the wares of the marketeers. There is a huge variety of colourful merchandise here, from weird cures and aphrodisiacs to strange fruit and vegetables as well as the expected basketry and fabrics and trinkets. Colourful, too, are the elaborate costumes of the local horsemen, known as 'Cowboys of the East', in the adjacent paddock where sedate rides are arranged for even the most overweight of visitors with every sufferance though I sensed that, in these instances, they shorten the course. Is it fanciful to think that, from this angle, the expression of anguish on the upturned face of the distant mountain has changed to a smile bestowed on this scene? Yes, it is.

A young man is still required to stump up payment of a water buffalo to the parents of his bride and if his own family does not have one going spare then it is to this market that he comes. Photography is seriously discouraged here, especially of the elderly for whom superstition dies hard.

I am no devotee of oriental markets but I came away with a *sepak takraw* (triangular fruit tray constructed from bamboo and coconut shell) and several photo-frames made from cane.

Peter Westbury

7th April 1997

Our last full day in Sabah and we have migrated to Rasa Ria, the 'sister' hotel nearer to the city, an altogether busier location but still very luxurious. Miyuki is wind-surfing.

She is not the only distracting sight from where I'm sitting at the pool's edge. Overheard: 'I'm out of my depth.' (Thinks: 'You're not alone, Madam!')

After lunch a lightning decision to take the ferryboat over to the island of Sapi. A primitive map painted on a board near the jetty shows us on arrival that it is possible to walk completely round this 25-acre island and to climb the path to the highest point. I'm not sure that's wise in this heat; there's hardly a soul around in the event of an emergency...

But we do it; and what a romantic experience, no-one to see us, posing on the white sand, scrambling over rocks and climbing trees like a pair of younger lovers might.

Yes, I'd come back here again.

9th April 1997

I hope I'm sitting in the right surgery waiting-room. I am almost glad to be temporarily deaf in one ear. Through the other one comes a cacophony sufficient to deafen it too. If I have correctly interpreted the little map, annotated decoratively but not very practically in *kanji* (and I religiously counted off the doorways from the Post Office and then from the basket shop at the traffic lights), this has to be the ENT clinic. Patients are divided into two categories: those below school age who are twittering loudly and their accompanying adults who are either mouthing at each other or playing with various gadgetry. One has an egg-timer attached to her device which is like a miniature loud-hailer which she applies directly to alternate ears. Eventually, after everybody has had a good laugh at my height and the size of my feet (I forgot to bring my own slippers) the surgery gets under way and I am invited through the curtain, to the treatment area beyond. Those ahead of me were sat at an array of apparatus, variously sucking, inhaling or listening through tubes, mouthpieces and earpieces while steam and hissing sounds filled the room. I imagined it to be like a sanitized latter-day opium den from the closed eyes and blissful expressions of the participants.

Westbury Meets East

The important thing was that the *isha* did have the appropriate instrument for the removal of the obstruction in my left ear and the difference had to be heard to be believed. I had been blaming some imagined foreign body from a jungle pool but it was simply and unromantically a build-up of earwax! For boring old wax I think the health insurance company can foot the bill.

17th April 1997

It was posing time again this morning when a production group arrived to take still shots for a kimono catalogue, the rolled umbrella/bowler hat ensemble to be a foil along with the village buildings, contrasting with the exquisite embroidered silks worn by the equally exquisite fine-boned models. What is it about these Asian girls?

19th April 1997

Tokyo. Today's schedule ran later and later. Typically, Japanese never run on time and film crews are even less well organized than any other group with whom I have to deal. The plan, today, is to make a CD Rom or, at least, to record those sound and vision parts that are mine in a scenario that has me cast imaginatively as the Butler in a Manor House, initially a villainous character but transformed, by the story's end, into the good guy.

Due to start rehearsals and shooting from 8.30 a.m., for which reason I have travelled up and stayed in an hotel the night before, we eventually commence at 11 a.m. but with some dodgy audio recording equipment which is not fixed until 1.15 p.m. The director is not happy with the early results.

My memory is not co-operating either and the director (who, as luck would have it, is also the writer) is not happy with my improvisation, insisting that I stick, word for word, to the original (contrary to his brief when he first approached me a few weeks ago). The 'Blue Room' (the studio is lined with blue paper, which makes it easier for the image to be lifted separately and placed on the pre-filmed backdrop) is tiny; everyone and everything, especially the lighting, is at close quarters. After every ten minutes or so a break is called to ventilate and cool down the room and spoil the 'actor's' concentration. Each

Peter Westbury

of my costume changes involves a three-piece suit! Yuko, the make-up girl, makes sure that I have plenty of iced tea and that I don't glow too much. As the afternoon shortens and the number of takes lengthens, I am fully convinced that they are making a false saving in not paying for a professional actor to play what they are telling me is the key role in the story. At 4 p.m. the pressure is really on to complete fifteen more scenes plus cameos plus sound-bites before 6 p.m. which is when I have a date with Miyuki. But the technicians are very kind and encouraging, even apologetic when the progress is slow through my fault not theirs. Well, I must say it was a tough assignment. The heat was the least of the problems. The confined space, the restrictions on movement and the fact that the other characters with whom I was supposed to interact were absent . . . these, plus my own inexperience made it a long day. I telephoned Miyuki at 7 p.m. to ask her to revise the time for our table at 'Mr Stamp's Garden' (an intimate little French restaurant in Roppongi I can highly recommend), and told the director and crew that I would be happy to come back when convenient to them for another crack at it, better rehearsed. (As it happens, I had a very gracious letter from the director a week later which included the dubious compliments: 'it turned out better than expected, *everybody* tells me so' and that 'there is at least one take in every scene that we can use *for now*' and, the final accolade 'we love the costumes, they photographed *very* well'!)

So. If you're a game-player and you see 'Manor House' on the shelves in your CD Rom shop, please let me know; there'll be some royalties due!

Production is planned in four languages but, frankly, with no sex or violence, it's not going to make it. A pity. I wouldn't have minded rehearsing a bit of that.

6th May 1997

The hottest spring day so far. Gave a small farewell supper party for 'Lady Amanda Watt', 'Viscount Symons' and 'Dame Dorothea Vickers' (colleagues all). Amanda and Ben have now officially resigned from the staff of Bridewell Heath after having been involved with the planning and running of this village for four years. We have shared each others' highs and lows and I shall miss them a lot. Ben has been a treasure, and to Amanda his wife, who kept the use of her maiden name to save confusion in the office, I will always be grateful for providing me with the opening to use, in reply to one of her committee meeting questions, the immortal line 'Elementary, my dear Watt *san*!' It is a very sad end to our association brought on by their bitter disillusionment with the Japanese inability to manage. Canada is to be their first stop to make a fresh beginning. Of course, it suits the Japanese to think that they are leaving to make babies.

Dorothea, whose contract expires in August, will be returning to Cambridgeshire. She's been a useful ally, too (and I needed her help with the Stroganoff!). I think it was a measure of the evening's success and not of the slow service that they didn't leave until 2.15 a.m. The cramped kitchen and my own inexpertise created some fun of their own accord but I also contributed two anecdotes by way of amusement. The first was part of a conversation I had up a mountain at the weekend with Lady Wright, wife of the British Ambassador to Japan and here to give a lecture. Both she and Sir David had spotted independently of each other and eventually once when out together, a Japanese tramp in the smart district of the Ginza. Bearded and wearing long robes, they both agreed he bore a strong resemblance to pictures of St John the Baptist and was more often than not outside Mitsukoshi, Tokyo's top department store. I commented that he'd hardly want to be found anywhere near Her(r)ods!

The second was told me by the director between the many takes of my scenes in his CD Rom brainchild last month, and goes like this: God summons Bill Clinton, Boris Yeltsin and Bill Gates to heaven to tell them he's not in the least impressed with the way they're running the world, that enough is enough and the end is nigh, two weeks maximum. 'Go back and tell your people; do what you have to do'.

Clinton calls his aides to the Oval Room. 'There's some good news and there's some ba-a-ad news. The good news is – we were right: there IS a God. The ba-a-ad news is He reckons the Russians are screwin' up so bad He's fixin' to end the World in two weeks'. Yeltsin calls his meeting in the Kremlin. 'Comrades. Dere iss bed newse ent dere iss vurse newse. Der bed newse iss – ve vurr wrongk: dere ISS a Gott. Der vurse newse iss, der Yanks have screwed things up so bed He plens to end der Vurldt in two veeks!' Bill Gates gathers his executive team together at Microsoft and announces: 'Guys. I have some great nooze and some even better nooze. First, ah've jus' got back from a summit meeting with God: there's Bill Clinton,

Peter Westbury

Yeltsin and me. Fellers, *I'm* in the top three! The even greater nooze is He's gonna end the World in two weeks – we don't have to waste no more time tryin' to solve '95 Windows!'

7th May 1997

Popped out at lunchtime for a vasectomy. Dr Yonezumi performed his snip-snip and then, after a picnic in Nanko Park, I drove back. The operation cost me Y60,000 if you include the Y10,000 speeding fine on the way down. None of this is recoverable from my health insurance. Phoned Miyuki this evening to say all went smoothly.

11 p.m.: Sashiko rang to say she wants to have my children! How's that for timing!? She tried to tell me last night but I'd taken the phone off the hook during the dinner party. I could really do with a drink but Yonezumi *san* said strictly no alcohol. Oh, bugger it!

12th May 1997

A force 4 earthquake tremor (temblor) threw me slightly off balance as I was dressing this morning. He's not pleased, is He?

14th May 1997

Vasectomy stitches removal day. A day much as usual, really, except for feeling a bit short of sleep owing to the 6.30 a.m. start coming just three hours after Sashiko's call to say she loves me and couldn't sleep. Which is nice. Unfortunately a training session with the new staff arrivals from New Zealand was scheduled for this morning. I had the slight advantage that they were severely jet-lagged and may not have noticed that *I* was not all that sharp. I slipped down unobtrusively at lunchtime to Dr Yonezumi's surgery.

'Yes, *slightly* inflamed', was his riposte to my complaint of suppuration. Well, they can tell us anything they like, these Japanese: they know we haven't the language skills to argue. So, back up the hill as quietly as I had left, to continue with the staff orientation, my face inscrutable, my testicles in cling-wrap.

Westbury Meets East

Later, on closer inspection, it is clear that the urologist has left some of the stitches behind. Botheration – that means another clandestine descent to parade my tackle for the *kangofu* who is beginning to get quite chummy. I can't really do with it.

17th and 18th May 1997

New supplies arrive from England: replacement brown shoe-laces, exactly the right length and hue; two packs of Imodium – the expiry date of November 2001 should present no problem; and triangular chocolate from Switzerland which invokes fond memories of Sachseln near Luzern where, as a boy of 11, I 'discovered' Toblerone, walking-stick badges and a sticky sweet red drink to rival Tizer.

Eleven would have been the age of the oldest child in the Nishigo Village Sports Day I was invited to attend and speak at today – at short notice, of course. An outing for the straw boater and pleased for it in the strong afternoon sun. It was one of those pat-the-baby and grin-at-grandma days, of such stuff as election campaigns are made – and political kudos is what all this is about: the old points system; I wonder what they score for nailing the single *gaijin*? Anyway, it was the children in the musical parade who were the real stars. They were adorable.

When it came to the races, the teams in the relay were cleverly handicapped, each having been fairly allocated amongst their ranks the long, the short and the tall, an 'excused boots', a 'fat boy', etc., but staggered so that the handicaps occurred at random as each lap was run. Fortunes (or misfortunes) were thereby suddenly reversed and the spectators were left guessing until the very end as to which team would win.

Kiko has been to stay the weekend. She has video-recorded me reading aloud the script of her lecture on asthma research that she is to deliver in Seoul next month. This is the revised version after the corrections I made in a late-night proof-reading session with her in my Narita hotel at the end of last week. 'Better than BBC World Service!' she declared; so I threw in an American paragraph and a Welsh and an Irish and a Scots for good measure. She is easily pleased. She has gone back to Chiba leaving behind her shiny new Nissan Urban R *Terrano* for me to use!

Peter Westbury

22nd May 1997

Found myself in the old part of Kuroiso today, the town in neighbouring Tochigi prefecture I hadn't visited since Meriam left. I have never, in almost three years in Japan, attended a *chanoyu* (tea ceremony). When I eventually do, I very much hope that it will be held in this place – just so that I can refer to The Olde Kuroiso Tea Shoppe!

24th & 25th May 1997

The 3rd 'Ambassador's Cup' Golf Tournament and Dinner. I collected His Excellency's party from the station in the *Cima*, driving back up to the village through drizzle and low cloud. 'By George, you've had some heavy rain!' 'Actually, Sir, those large rectangular puddles are the rice fields!' Laughter all round. How to win friends; oh dear! He seemed to have forgiven me, however, by the time he arrived for the drinks reception. A dripping wet escort of two bagpipers plus Jack

Another opening… another show. The 3rd 'Ambassador's Cup' Golf Tournament and Dinner.

with his sabre and kilt flanked the VIP group as it approached the courtyard and the crenellated outline of the Manor House eerily manifested itself in the mist.

The majority of the staff kept going for the next 24 hours without sleep to make sure that we 'papered over any cracks', due to our unprecedentedly low manning level. The guests were extremely jolly, especially the crowd from the Embassy and the Ambassador's wife was kind enough to say that she thought the service and the food were even better than the previous year. But by 6 p.m. on the Sunday with the 164 guests departed and the Refectory re-set for the 80 students arriving next day, everyone had collapsed into bed. The golfers had had a very mixed time of it, much of the course having been water-logged and the Ambassador having a particularly uncomfortable round. One of the Embassy ladies was seated immediately under the recurring leak in the Dining Room bel-fry, rainwater spattering on to the right hand side of her place-setting. I had no space to seat her elsewhere – we were at absolute capacity. Fortunately she took it in good part and I made a game of arriving with a flourish with dry cutlery at the exact moment she was served with each course.

Apart from that, everything went smoothly though I have a bit of a suspicion that I may have crunched His Excellency's foot as I closed the car door when he left. There was a look of pain but the *Cima* is pretty soundproof.

Peter Westbury

Health Check

26th May 1997

TODAY'S LIGHT RELIEF came from the Annual Staff Health Check. If I explain that I was third in line at the outset this morning, between the head dish-washer and the under-gardener but that at the finish I was sandwiched between the chauffeur and one of the chambermaids, it's easy to guess at the likelihood of a mix-up especially as we had been examined, weighed, measured, prodded, poked, tested and processed by a team of Japanese medics playing doctors and nurses with little or no English! Not exactly reassuring. So when, at the end, the notes in my hand listed an operation I'd never had and mentioned that in 1993 I'd suffered from Crohn's disease, I was not entirely surprised. At one stage, a male examiner pointed to Question 4 – 'Is it your period at moment?' I thought this is enough to bring on the Crohn's (which I found myself whistling later... isn't it rich?!).

Today's light relief, though, proved short-lived when I was called to a meeting at 3 p.m. to be told that my contract will *not* be renewed!

And just when, *only this week*, after nearly 3 years of deprivation I've discovered the place to buy McVitie's Ginger Nuts to enjoy with my early morning cup of Earl Grey!

In all seriousness, I'm disgusted at this shabby treatment. 'The Board of Directors cannot accept the conditions you request for the extension of your contract and assume you will be happier in a different employment situation. As employment was only for the contract period to June 30, 1997, there is no obligation to renew the contract. The Board of Directors thank you for your service to Bridewell Heath and wish you success in furthering your career.'

The 'conditions requested' related to the erosion of my salary due to the weakening *yen* and the fact that the salary had

Westbury Meets East

remained frozen for three years whereas deductions at source had increased. But: *no* negotiation! Remove the butler and that'll stop the others from whingeing? Maybe that's the ploy.

The other thing is that my Management Agreement, signed, ironically, by 'The Undertaker' as well as myself, provides for two months notice to be served by either party. I am now being asked to leave by June 15th because they will not otherwise credit me with the accumulated untaken National Holidays that I am owed. This still leaves virtually the whole of July, which would be useful for putting out feelers for my next position. It is very clear that they waited until after the Ambassador's Cup weekend before they dropped the bombshell. Oh – and they asked me at the same meeting to be available to take a key role in a Bridewell Heath promotion going out live next week on national breakfast-time TV! I was fuming over the whole cavalier behaviour until I realized that I might use this broadcast to advantage and turn it into a personal situation-wanted commercial! Transmitting live, they wouldn't be able to do much about it!

[Subsequent unsolicited correspondence from other *gaijin* workers of my acquaintance, confirms this behaviour by Japanese employers to be typical – see example in Appendix A. Other letters from appreciative guests who identified me with the place indicated their amazement and confusion at my departure, kindly stating that the place won't be the same without me. Those that watched the Breakfast TV piece found the news even more difficult to believe because, of course, taking the professional line I played it right down the middle (while they still owed me money!)]

So, if this cautionary tale is to be of any value to others, where did I go wrong? I can only conjecture but here are some possibilities:

1. I communicated *directly* with the President instead of via the Directors and they didn't like my frankness.

2. I witnessed too many of their bad decisions that had led to loss of face.

3. They were jealous of my popularity with the guests.

4. I had supported the cause of the foreign employees too strenuously *vis à vis* salaries and the weak *yen*.

I wonder what will turn up next? Should I try to find work in Japan or head for Europe or even the States where I ought to be a very marketable commodity? Should I try to find a publisher for the memoirs?! Jacket blurb: 'Peter Westbury is the

Peter Westbury

nom de guerre of a twice-divorced fifty-something no-hoper who, at another of life's crossroads and with little excitement in prospect, invests in a course at the foremost International School for Butler Administrators. Within weeks of graduating he finds himself on the other side of the world, assuming a literally new identity and running a fake 60-acre English village, perched at the top of a Japanese mountain and complete with manor house, hotel, pub and sports centre, a staff of fifty, eleven vehicles including a snow plough, a smelly St Bernard called Pepe and butlering for, among other notables, the Emperor's brother, fourth in line to the throne of Japan. This is the diary account of the life and loves of a British butler in almost permanent culture shock as he copes with a turnover of guests, colleagues, staff and girlfriends in this unique environment.'

What do you think?

1st June 1997

Meeting with Jack and all the New Zealand staff to make an announcement.

'This is what the newspapers call a prepared statement,' I said, reading from this script. 'Thank you for coming.

'I understand that, over the past few weeks, rumours have been echoing around BH with regard to contracts. The reason that I have asked you to give me a few minutes from your duties is for the purpose of removing speculation in respect of my own contract. When we all first met in New Zealand, I recall describing my job to you as the best on the planet! It was confirmed by the directors this week that my job continues... (pause)... but only for another two weeks when I shall be leaving the... I was going to say 'organization' but that word, you may agree, seems somehow inappropriate! From then on I shall have to be content with the second best job on the planet – wherever that second best job may be! I'd like to go on to say two things: please give your continued energies to the success of this place. The concept is an inspired one; it's just a shame about the ineptitude of some of the key people here. I will be leaving with more than a measure of regret.' (By this point some of the girls were crying and I lost my composure. I handed the paper to Jack and he continued to read it out for me.) 'The good parts have been working with you Kiwis; getting to visit your country twice

Westbury Meets East

a year has been a tremendous bonus.

'And that's the second thing: thank you for the support you have given me. As they used to say in the music-halls of my youth – I will always wear it! I'm sorry I failed to get you a better salary deal – the President is adamant that he will not link salary scales to the exchange rate even though the value of the *yen* has fallen by 25% since they were established. In pushing too hard for a better deal I fancy I have made myself unpopular. That's it.'

6th June 1997

Midnight. Every spare moment over the past few days has been spent sorting out the *apato* and I have only just sat down from closing the last of my boxes which will all be collected tomorrow by the shipper. Their total volume, almost one cubic metre, has rather surprised me as I have been trying not to become a hoarder. Most of the contents are *purezento* (gifts) from appreciative guests but there are also a fair number of paintings and prints that I've been unable to resist and that I have no intention of leaving behind; the walls and shelf are cleared.

The shipping company requires me to assess the consignment for insurance purposes and clearance by Customs & Excise. How do you place a monetary value on what is probably a priceless antique silk *haori*, a carved wooden hawk or a Malaysian cane-woven mini-football?!

Exhausted physically and, I suppose, emotionally, too, from packing up 3 years of memories, I am now drawing on my cigar and sipping the last of the champagne, watching three unwavering flames from the stubs in the polished silver candelabrum. In the half-light, the bared picture hooks on the far wall resemble dark static moths. Not long now before I'll be saying '*sayonara*' to what became my home. And it won't be over then – only farewell to BH and the artificiality of this pretend village. Another week and I take off for Nagano-*ken* and thence to the heart of the Kansai, the Kinki district, to see the old and real Japan.

12th June 1997

Peter Westbury

Gontagura-*yama* and my last conversation with the *uguisu* (the

Japanese nightingale, often called '*hohokekyu*' derived from his song). I've climbed alone so often to this gloriously remote and peaceful mountain location. The name means 'Nature's Warehouse'. I've shared it with two ambassadors' wives, with Ben and Amanda just prior to their departure, a handful of very special Japanese ladies and, on one hilarious afternoon, with three giggling Filipinas in platform shoes! Today there's just me and the nightingale. 'I don't want to leave'. He's gone quiet.

Gontagura-*yama*.
Perfect peace with the occasional song of the *uguisu*.

Westbury Meets East

Talking to my shelf

Towards the 'real' Japan

To Yudanaka

15th June 1997

I AM IN A PLACE CALLED Yudanaka which is, I think, between Nakano and Shigakogen in Nagano prefecture. I say I 'think' because the route here became very confusing after I overshot the intended exit from the expressway and tried another approach using the mountain roads. Kiko was more interested in chatting than in navigating but I shouldn't be ungracious – it is, after all, her car that I'll be driving and her *apato* that she has generously placed at my disposal while I recuperate for a while and try to get inside the 'real' Japan. She had to return to Chiba this evening.

Having missed her last train from the local station due to fruitless frantic last-minute efforts to purchase a fridge, we had to find the JR station in Nagano City in a bit of a hurry. The 30 kilometres were a nightmare experience owing to so many road works and diversions as Nagano prepares to host the Winter Olympics due to be held here just seven months from now. Luckily, I made the right decisions re-routing my way

Yudanaka, Nagano *ken*

Westbury Meets East

back to this apartment block and then got lost in the building! Flat no. 609 – easy enough to remember, I had thought to myself – should have found it standing on my head.

600 kilometres ago the staff at BH had assembled on the Manor House steps as has been the custom with departing human resources (dreadful American expression) of which there have been many over the past 3 years, resignation upon resignation. I was grateful to be independent of the shuttle bus timetable and was able to cut the farewells short as the lump grew in my throat and I jumped into the car and accelerated away to meet Kiko off the *shinkansen*.

The Nissan *Terrano* was loaded to the gunwales with everything I should need for the next few days from clothes, food and wine supplies to my trusty iron – every butler should carry one even if only for pressing the *shinbun*! And the plan? To use Kiko's place as a base while I 'put out more flags' and to see Kyoto and Nara, at least, before leaving for London and home via Hong Kong and Paris. If the c.v.'s fail to rouse an immediate response then I'll re-occupy the Wiltshire cottage and settle down to writing the old memoirs. For the moment, I'm tired and hungry so it'll be a quick steak, a glass or three of Shiraz and then out with the *futon*.

Before leaving, Kiko had explained to me the plumbing arrangements: because of the abundance of hot springs in this region, there is no shortage of hot water. That is the good news. The bad news is that it is not piped to the flat – you have, as it were, to go and find it. Happily, in the basement under the condominium, there is an *onsen* to which all the residents have access. Open from 6 a.m. to 10 p.m. one simply enters, ablutes and exits. It is locked, however, between 10 p.m. and 6 a.m. so Kiko has left me her key with strict instructions as to the correct procedure – the entrance with the blue *noren* for men; that with the red: ladies only!

It is turned midnight when I descend for my first dip in the communal bath. Try as I might I can't get her key to operate the men's door. Unsurprisingly, it does, with ease, open the door with the red curtains. Nobody about. I strip in the ante-room, take a miniscule towel before entering the spa, collecting a low wooden stool and stubby water tub on my way to the shower area. Thence into the *jacuzzi* from which there are moonlit views of the hillside and a giant *buddha*. The travel-weariness dissolves. Finally the hot spa, deep and

Peter Westbury

penetrating. Sound of voices. Am I to have company? Alas, no – it's only the displacement of water from the bath's edge gurgling down the drain! Never mind.

16th June 1997

My hopes for a lazy start to my first morning in Yudanaka were rudely dashed by a rousing, impossible-to-ignore cacophony very early in the day. I soon deduced that the racket was coming from a temple gong. I looked at my watch but neither the number of strikes nor the timing of them bore any relevance to the actual hour or even the quarter-hour – just spasmodic outbursts from roughly 6 a.m. onwards and presumably perpetrated at random by believers passing en route to work. Is this likely to be the norm for as long as I'm here? (They continued, in unpredictable fashion though less frequently, throughout each and every day and from such a short distance away as to startle me every time.) By 7 a.m. it was clear there would be no settling back to sleep, and by quarter past I had donned my dressing-gown (must try and buy myself a *yukata* if I'm to try to blend in), made a cup of Earl Grey and was inspecting my new surroundings from Kiko's sixth floor condominium window, out of which you have to climb to reach the narrow L-shaped balcony which runs round the two outside walls of the rectangular shaped apartment. Looking out today I recalled my earlier assessment of urban Japan as 'very Slough-like' though this townscape has a very slightly redeeming hilliness. Given my aversion to Japanese towns and cities, it may seem strange that I am making efforts to remain working in this land. But if I edit out of my vision, the ugly flat-topped buildings in the foreground, and all the concrete posts and overhead cables, and then look beyond to the green-grey on grey forested mountain backdrop, there truly is, as there is in Berkshire, a proximity to some of the most lush, tranquil and inviting countryside where it is possible to walk for miles and hardly encounter a soul or see a building.

It was earlier than anticipated, then, that I took the elevator down to the *onsen* for a pre-breakfast shower. To my surprise, for I know how very conformist they are in these matters, I discovered two Japanese, one male the other female, using the communal bath for exercise of a very intimate and rhythmic nature. To spare them embarrassment I maintained only eye contact while endeavouring to communicate that I was an *isha* and that I was perfectly accustomed to seeing naked bodies. But they retreated hastily. There had been a hand-written notice hanging from the entrance door handle as I entered but, of course, in *kanji*. I wondered if he was in fact her therapist. I think I'd be happy to do what he was doing for free.

Kiko faxed this evening – full of concern that I had made it back from Nagano and hadn't had to sleep in the Nissan. She also wanted to know if I had found her video-cassettes. Ever since I told her that my first wife resembled the young Audrey Hepburn, Kiko has collected videos of that actress' films. Sweet.

My amateurish efforts at producing supper were blurred by the second half of the Eden Ridge Shiraz and the relaxing ambience provided by the MJQ. And now I shall watch *Roman Holiday*.

17th June 1997

The caretaker, Ikeda *san*, knocked on the door this morning to explain that owing to a problem down in the spa my morning ablutions would have to be delayed until after 10 a.m. and he regretted any inconvenience. This followed by much bowing. My guess is that the synchronized swimmers don't want to be disturbed again!

Gateball games below the balcony.

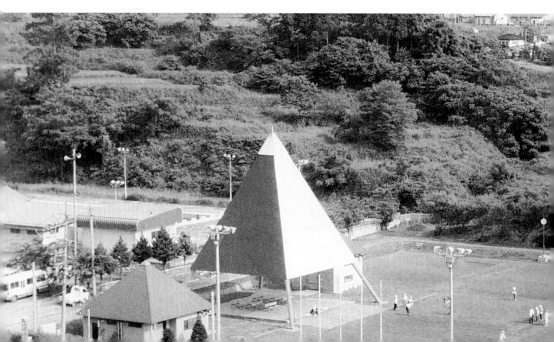

It is 9 a.m. and a heat haze prevails outside. From the balcony I can see a game of gateball in progress (a kind of croquet exclusively, it would seem, for seriously senior citizens) and several of the ancient players take periodic respite from the heat, even at this hour, by sitting under a pyramid shaped modern shelter with the sign 'NAGANO 1998' emblazoned on its roof. Perhaps they have hopes of Olympic recognition.

And now I really must apply my rapidly atrophying brain to this business of job applications. Today's targets are the Managing Directors of the City Club in Tokyo and CCA International in Hong Kong...

When I looked out again the rainy season had got under way. Oh well, perhaps it will keep the crowds to a minimum when I head off to see the tourist attractions in Kyoto next week.

18th June 1997

Today has not been spent entirely at the typewriter. The rain eased off and armed with directions to the local *yubin* (post office), I took my letters to have the postage checked and then went shopping. I needed fresh air as well as fresh vegetables, which I've been missing these last few days. I also purchased a *yukata* (the thin cotton full-length wide-sleeved wrap-over worn by the Japanese *onsen*-goers, men and women, inside their hotels and also out on the street). This one, unexpectedly available in my size, is in a pleasing dark blue and white pattern. I

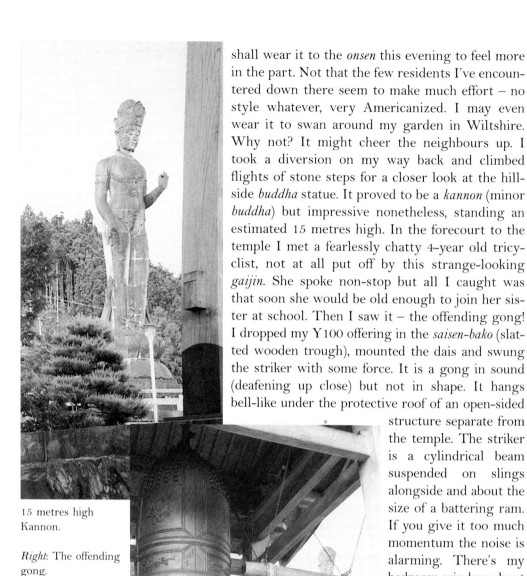

shall wear it to the *onsen* this evening to feel more in the part. Not that the few residents I've encountered down there seem to make much effort – no style whatever, very Americanized. I may even wear it to swan around my garden in Wiltshire. Why not? It might cheer the neighbours up. I took a diversion on my way back and climbed flights of stone steps for a closer look at the hillside *buddha* statue. It proved to be a *kannon* (minor *buddha*) but impressive nonetheless, standing an estimated 15 metres high. In the forecourt to the temple I met a fearlessly chatty 4-year old tricyclist, not at all put off by this strange-looking *gaijin*. She spoke non-stop but all I caught was that soon she would be old enough to join her sister at school. Then I saw it – the offending gong! I dropped my Y100 offering in the *saisen-bako* (slatted wooden trough), mounted the dais and swung the striker with some force. It is a gong in sound (deafening up close) but not in shape. It hangs bell-like under the protective roof of an open-sided structure separate from the temple. The striker is a cylindrical beam suspended on slings alongside and about the size of a battering ram. If you give it too much momentum the noise is alarming. There's my bedroom window about 150 metres away; I do hope they padlock this thing during the night.

15 metres high Kannon.

Right: The offending gong.

＊＊＊

The *onsen* has been closed for cleaning today so the few of us currently occupying this huge building had to bunch up this evening to share the same bath-time. A number of us had not previously met in these circumstances and one sensed a certain awkwardness. Except, that is, in the case of the *concierge*, who arrived in the changing-room just as I was drying myself. Curiosity overcame any shyness that might have existed and

Peter Westbury

he openly exploited this unusual opportunity to give western genitalia a prolonged stare. I will say the shrivelled little fellow (I'm talking about the *concierge*) did look rather wistful but I did not wait for him to climb out of his long johns for a return dekko as I have no doubt at all that it would have put me off my dinner.

19th June 1997

I ploughed on with more correspondence today: letters attempting to explain my departure from BH when, in truth, I cannot explain it to myself; letters to ex-colleagues and past guests; people who became my friends; people whose paths crossed briefly with mine and who kept in touch; people I'll miss; people who'll be surprised when they find I am no longer at BH; people who identified me with the place; people I want to tell personally that I didn't resign and that I wasn't dismissed; people who might care. Now *that* was a note of self-pity – you can cut that out, Westbury. Actually I'm normally testy at this time of the year, ask any of my close family. My birthday is only a few hours away and I know I've never managed to handle graciously the passing of another year. A walk is what I need.

The same little girl was playing alone with her toys up by the temple as I passed; not so chatty today – perhaps she sensed my mood; children are good at that. The weather deteriorated at the same time as the mountain road became a track and I began to realize that a walk had not been such a good idea and turned back, though I had needed the exercise. There was another fax from Kiko in the hall on my return – still concerned about my survival. The *apato* is a compromise between East and West: there is some western style furniture but you sleep on the *tatami* floor. A perfect size for one occupant, plenty big enough for two (if you got on); three, however, would be a crowd. Not a lot of imagination in the layout but really very functional and once I'd bought some extra pans for the kitchen, survival has been a dream.

For the present I'm eating my breakfast cereal out of a saucepan lid – rather surprisingly there are no bowls to be seen. Kiko, it seems, always eats out. For me, washing-up is a hassle with no hot water from the tap and no plug for the sink

Westbury Meets East

but I've developed a system: it's called 'Leave it until the morning'. This is a variation on the system I employed at BH which was 'Leave it until Wednesday morning' which was when the chambermaids came and sorted things out. [Purists (or critics wanting to trip me up) are advised that no items of silverware are or were involved.]

I thought it might be diplomatic to pick out something to admire in the apartment when we first arrived here and I pointed to an attractive table lamp. It was clearly a mistake. Among all the traditional Japanese paraphernalia, this piece happened to be from Korea.

6 p.m. As appears to be the custom, a few bars of Auld Lang Syne have been quaintly broadcast over the town's PA system. From my bedroom window I have just spotted in a garden across the road a pretty short-skirted young woman, pretty at this range at any rate, as she waters her plants. I take my cigarette and drink on to the balcony for a better look but she moves indoors. She is now sitting on the floor and looking back from just inside the *engawa* (verandah) window so I can still see her lovely brown legs.

20th June 1997

Last night's forecast warned of the typhoon and sure enough the deluge started at around 3 a.m. and has not let up all day which I have put to good use writing more letters. The river below, which had been a silvery foaming affair, is now a shade of curry and the gateball rinks are totally water-logged – no sign of the little old ladies but then they *are* rather on the short side!

I spoke to Jack from the basement pay phone and my birthday mail may reach me tomorrow. His other news was that the Directors have terminated the contract with the French firm who supplied BH with all the foreign chefs. The English chef for whom I'd campaigned for so long (after a series of arrogant and unsatisfactory French ones) and who left a position at Claridge's to come to Bridewell Heath, has gone off in high dudgeon, rather justifiably. I had forecast that Japanization was on the cards and reminded Jack to watch his back.

Peter Westbury

On my return from the post office run, I picked up a parcel and letter from Kiko. She will come for the weekend – not just

Towards the 'Real' Japan

Sunday as expected – and enclosed careful directions for me to collect her from yet another station – Echigoyuzawa – some 70 kilometres away. I think she's testing me. The place-names are a challenge even when given in *romaji*, and not just the polysyllabic ones. Nagano, for example, can refer to the *shi* (city) or *ken* (prefecture). Between here and the city of Nagano is a place called Nakano which is not too helpful. Pronunciation becomes critical as directions to places and the meanings of words can change totally according to your inflection. The way you pronounce *seiko*, for instance, will determine whether you finish up with a watch . . . or sex! That example is a bit jokey but it is very frustrating when you imitate a sound in the hope of assistance in translation and they look at you totally mystified, modify it imperceptibly, triumphantly reveal the meaning and then tell you that you've been saying it all wrong. Grrr. Anyway, it is Kiko's plan to show me Lake Nojiri and book us into a nearby hotel. Well this weather will have to perk up overnight if the weekend is to be a scenic success.

At dusk the low cloud was wrapping itself around the folds of the mountains in slow motion. As it descended further it only succeeded in emphasising the pylons and general ugliness of the town.

Bedtime, and the lady with the slender brown legs has been out all day – she must have left very early, slipping out of her house around dawn when I had drifted back to sleep.

21st June 1997

It was probably the same wretched oyster that kept me awake most of last night with stomach pains that I can also blame for the most vivid dream which featured the trendy (and I do hope imaginary) funeral of an old school chum of mine. The innovational aspect of this dream that dominated the plot was the fact that, thanks to some deft handling at the undertaker's prior to *rigor mortis*, 'Grandpa', to the delight of his family, especially the grandchildren with whom he had been a great favourite, had been able to join the mourners for his send-off at the church. Dressed tastefully in a thick overcoat (light oak in colour with brass buttons and purple lining) which provided a certain amount of grip with which to load him into and out of the processional limousine and, later, the pew, propped between his widow and the eldest son, he was only finally transferred to his coffin at the end of the ceremony. If the idea

Westbury Meets East

catches on, the secret is all in the timing and it was clear from the dream that one needs to deliver the cadaver pretty smartly to the dresser with his arms at the right angle so that they can be inserted into the overcoat sleeves in one smooth movement and then the whole thing left to set in the seated position.

I woke up utterly convinced that this was the way forward and that this technique had made all the difference to the success of my friend's funeral, allowing the younger generation, in particular, the pleasure of their grandfather's company right up to the end even though he had been uncharacteristically quiet, having already repeated his renowned and historical repertoire of jokes for the last time. Come to think of it, audio-tapes of his oldest and best could have been played en route to the church for the enjoyment of the *cortège*, though this idea was not tested in the dream. On a practical point, the coffin does need to be Z-shaped because by the time it is needed . . . well, I'm sure I don't have to spell it out. The dream did not dwell on the extra cost or the difficulty of finding a competent bespoke joiner but, if Yellow Pages is half that it's cracked up to be that shouldn't be a hurdle and if there is sufficient demand then prices will obviously come down.

I drove through the drizzle to collect Kiko, arriving half an hour later than arranged. I should have allowed myself longer for the twisting mountain roads and all the road works. Looking back, I seem to have been at the wheel most of the day and my mood was quietening as we checked in to the Tangram Golf Resort Hotel, not the most brilliant choice, I must say.

Following my abortive attempt at phoning England last night using an international telephone card for which I paid ¥3,000 and which registered zero, today I asked the hotel operator to put me through to the Somerset number and, one day late, I was able to congratulate my parents on reaching their Diamond Wedding, an amazing achievement, my own marital record being singularly less of a success story. They remembered that tomorrow would be my birthday and duly sang the traditional verse. Kiko could hardly fail to overhear and recognized the 'Happy Birthday' refrain. My secret was out and she later insisted that dinner should be her treat; I *swear* I had already ordered the Moët before she announced her intention! Something made her change her mind about sharing the room, however, and I volunteered to drive back to Yudanaka alone

Peter Westbury

which proved to be a good move in view of the afore-mentioned gastric upset. Romance was unlikely to be in the air.

22nd June 1997

6 a.m. The weather has cleared and the mountains are back, sharper in outline than on any day since my arrival. The thick-lipped flat-nosed profile of a hermaphrodite on the sky-line is every bit as 'realistic' as the silhouette of Mount Kinabalu in Sabah, though there is a pronounced Adam's apple and as the angle of the sun alters, it slowly becomes clear that she could do with a shave. Who *does* he/she remind me of?

Now its back to the hotel in time for check-out because the reduced rate depends on the two of us sharing and I don't want to embarrass Kiko by my absence. Having said that, I think the hotels recover the discounts they give by bumping up the tele-phone charges. My short call to the UK yesterday came to an amazing Y7,624 (about £39.00) when it came to settling the bill. And worth every penny.

7 p.m. I've just limped back from Nagano after what turned out to be a very punishing weekend with Kiko; but I've deliv-ered her safely to the station and the wine is open – a 1985 Gran Reserva I've been saving for someone who will appreci-ate it. On the CD player, Teresa Teng, a popular Tai-wanese, is singing to me in Japanese anything I choose the words to mean. (Sadly, I learned later from Faye that Teresa Teng died of AIDS passed on, allegedly, from her Italian photographer boyfriend. I'd have preferred not to have been told that).

We did eventually get to see Lake Nojiro this morning and drove round most of its perimeter stopping now and then at the water's edge. With the sweet chestnuts in flower, I couldn't help being reminded of one of the last holidays with D in the

Hermaphrodite silhouette.

Cevennes. The sunshine wore itself out by mid-day so after a lunch of buckwheat noodles insisted upon by Kiko – a bad move, very splashy – we headed indoors to the Tanaka Honke Museum in Suzaka. Dating back to 1733, the middle of the Edo period, these merchant's warehouses are used to display pottery, antique *kimonos*, paintings, furniture, toys and lacquer ware of the times. The store-houses, converted effectively into galleries, form a rectangle round the family home and Japanese-style 'Four Seasons' gardens complete the charming setting. I found the whole place delightful and left feeling I had a better knowledge of the lifestyle and cultural treasure of that era.

Within 30 minutes of closing the door on the world outside, the world outside is in the grip of a giant electric storm, the heaviest rain I've ever heard. And the yellow god forever gazes down . . .

Later. May I confirm that the Montecillo fully lived up to expectations. The rain persists; no lights on in Brown Legs' house. I go down to the lobby to use the pay-phone to get through to Miyuki to tell her I'm really missing her.

At 10 p.m. I'm feeling restless and decide it's time for the *onsen* and then change my mind. I grab an umbrella for a walk in the storm. I've not gone far when I see a woman struggling to unload her car. It's Brown Legs! She doesn't protest too much when I offer to help and, between us, we carry boxes and parcels up the steps to her *genkan*. I've abandoned the umbrella by now. We are soaked to the skin and when we've finished, stand looking at each other in her doorway. It is one of those sexually charged moments. (I remember similar circumstances in Wales when S and I were staying in a rented farmhouse and had been caught while out walking by a sudden downpour). She invites me in for a warm drink and to dry off . . . Whose birthday is it, anyway?!

23rd June 1997

Three years ago today I was met at Tokyo's Narita airport by Ben Symons, a Canadian who had recruited me in London to head up the team that was to front an 'English village in the mountains of Fukushima', a venture which foundered through compromise and became, instead, a shadow of what should have

Peter Westbury

been, the Japanese management proving distrustful of our proposals through ignorance (or was it that they didn't want to admit a lack of funds?) and failure to match the vision of Sako *san*, the lady, alas deceased, whose concept it had been.

I made myself breakfast back in the apartment where I spent much of the day contemplating what might have been. Would fluency in the language have made any difference? I came to the conclusion, not for the first time, that they had not invited us to Bridewell Heath to influence policy-making or to have any degree of control, and that we were merely there as window-dressing which, even in Faringdon High Street, gets changed from time to time!

26th June 1997

It is 8.30 p.m. I am outside on Kiko's balcony. Inside, the Berlin Philharmonic is playing Mozart's Clarinet Concerto in A Major K581 so it was a bit on the crowded side. In my hand is the penultimate glass poured from a bottle of 1989 Marquès de Grinon Cabernet Sauvignon; it is perfection – if you can find any. One of the side effects of my hasty departure from BH is that I have had to bring away with me and consume alone a not inconsiderable quantity of excellent wine that I had planned to share. But I'm forcing it down. The past few days have followed a pattern of sorts: an *onsen* bath or two, sometimes taken in the early morning, around 3 a.m., when I know Sashiko to be awake in Aizu Wakamatsu.

To telephone her, though, would surely disturb her husband in the next room; 'disturb' is right. Her last letter was most explicit. I wonder what the floodlit statue on the hillside makes of it all.

I had an encouraging telephone conversation mid-morning with Etsuko Yamabe who sounds very interested in engaging my services at a new development involving her Company as wedding specialists in Hokkaido – but not until June next year. I have left it that we will meet for further discussion next month in London when our schedules coincide.

The lights have just gone on in Brown Legs' house...

Westbury Meets East

28th June 1997

This looked like being another Saturday spent chauffeuring Kiko around the district in the pouring rain adding hundreds of kilometres on the clock while she practises English conversation. It is all rather pointless from my point of view when the visibility is so poor. This weekend I was determined to put the driving to good purpose and suggested that we tried to locate the site of the new British Country Style complex that is being built or is to be built in Tateshina; they may just require the services of an English butler to lend authenticity. Which is how we found ourselves calling in at the English Garden at Barakura near Chino-shi in the Tateshina resort area. Two gardeners from England, Andy and Mark from Cumbria and Lincolnshire respectively, are on the full-time staff and were more than happy to shelter from the rain and spare the time to chat, the first unstilted conversation I'd had for two weeks, but they had no information on the project we were seeking. This garden is a little gold-mine, swarming with visitors quite prepared, as we were, to stroll around with their umbrellas admiring John Brookes' design. He was invited by Yamada *san*, a highly successful fashion-wear retailer, to realize his dream and the result is a tribute to all those involved. We had proposed such an attraction for BH, prepared and submitted an outline plan for a very similar project – a walled garden in the English style – but, as with most of our ideas, it was nodded at to keep us quiet and then shelved, another disregarded potential earner like the wedding package, the directors only really being interested in golf. Yamada *san* now has garden shops within his other outlets and deserves to be coining it.

29th June 1997

The river has turned to curry again after last night's typhoon. We both slept badly and I slipped down to the *onsen* in the small hours and then back to do some writing. By the time we had got ourselves organized and into Nagano-*shi* with the intention of visiting the *Zenko-ji*, the weather had greatly improved and it was the mountains that beckoned instead, especially as there will be no shortage of shrines and temples on next week's agenda. So we headed out from Nagano Central on route 19 in the direction of Matsumoto but turned right

Peter Westbury

along the toll road to Hakuba which will be the main ski–ing centre for the '98 Winter Olympics. This part of Japan is known as 'Little Switzerland' but I'd say it was somehow more French Pyrenées than Swiss Alps. We ascended by cable-car gondola and ropeway for most of the haul to the top of Tsugaike-*kogen* (*kogen* = heights) and its nature reserve, part of which was above the snow line. The air was so fresh after yesterday's heavy rain and the lilies and marsh plants so colourful that our spirits were in good shape. This mood lasted until I had dropped Kiko at the station when I found myself in the Sunday evening city traffic snarl-up compounded by the massive roadworks and diversions that are part and parcel of Nagano's building and tidying-up programme prior to February. There are some very impressive new edifices – stadia and civic halls of amazing design and scale – but they've a long way to go with the infrastructure and bridges; flyovers and road-widenings are at this stage a woeful tangle of loose ends and temporary connections plus a fair amount of mud. This all makes it easier to be abandoning the car in favour of the railway system on Tuesday when we start our journey westwards to explore the historic cities of Kyoto and Nara.

The Sounds of Japan

30th June 1997

The sounds that will echo in my head long after I have left Japan:

The bedlam of Tokyo Central station.

The lady announcer's recorded message broadcast on the *shinkansen* platform imploring passengers to 'stand behind the yellow line' in American-accented English.

The mechanical high-pitched voice of the elevator attendants reciting the wares in the *Kinokunya* international food store.

The 'Coming through the Rye' jingle at pedestrian crossings.

The senior citizens' *enka* performances in the Sunday lunchtime *karaoke* competitions on TV.

The joyful shouts of the welcoming attendants on the filling-station forecourts, guiding drivers to line up their vehicles with the fuel pumps.

The warning beep of the *Pajero* in reverse gear.

The tinny rattle of rope on bell outside a Shinto shrine.

The melodic strike of hammer on gong outside a Buddhist *jinja*.

Meriam's *ibiki* (gentle snore).

The bloody cock crow at 3 a.m. And 4 a.m. And 5 a.m. And in-between.

Peter Westbury

Towards the 'Real' Japan

The 6 a.m. exercise music from Hamanaka's radio in the *apato* below.

The subtle scuff (and feel) of bare foot on *tatami* mat in a *ryokan* bedroom.

The gurgle of the overflow, like voices, in the *o-furo* (communal bath).

The rush of wide shallow rivers through tall grasses.

The song of the invisible *uguisu* among the evergreens of Gontagura-*yama*.

Faye singing '*Gomene*'.

Westbury Meets East

To Kyoto

1st July 1997.

IT IS A NARROW-GAUGE single-track railway line that links Yudanaka Terminal with Nagano. I found the reason for the chaos in the centre of the town every hour when the train's to-ing and fro-ing activates the level-crossing gates. It is because the three-car train arrives on a curve but the platform is straight; so the front end has to continue beyond the end of the platform (where the road crosses the track) and then, after a points change, reverse partly into a siding. Ingenious. But it doesn't seem to have occurred to them to re-route the road! There *is* the space. It would be amusing to be here in February next year to see how they cope with the influx of

Yudanaka Terminal and level-crossing.

traffic as western participants, spectators and media-men invade this locale for the Olympic snow-boarding events. Perhaps the thoroughfare is protected by some Imperial charter (similar to the Royal charter that preserves till eternity the Spaniards Inn toll-house bottle-neck on Hampstead Heath); but come the winter in Yudanaka and they may be parodying the immortal lines so that they read: 'East is least and West may jest but both the train shall meet!'

The engine-driver finishes his limbering up exercises, dons his peaked cap and white gloves, checks his reflection in the window, lets himself into the cab and turns the handle. We are off on the first leg of my journey to Kyoto. [A tip: it may seem too obvious for special mention but, when you are panicking in the railway station entrance, not knowing whether you have a few minutes or a few hours in which to miss your train, it is worth knowing that you read the time-table board from right to left. The place-names, in *kanji*, won't make any sense but there's a good chance the departure times will be in English numerals and if you know that you are at the end of a branch line then *any* train is going to get you out of here. Your choice is further complicated by variations in the service: slow trains that stop at every station, the ordinary express that stops at a limited number of stations, the rapid express which is the next step up and then the limited express which is the fastest. Departure times for the limited express are usually printed in red. Catching one only ensures you a shorter journey time and

Timetable board at the station entrance.

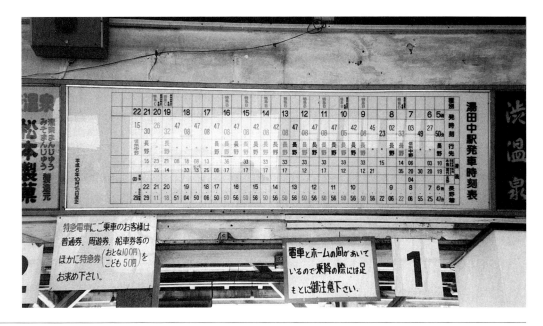

not that you will arrive at your destination any sooner necessarily! For some services you must pay a surcharge in advance;
a conscientious ticket inspector travels on every train.]

The 0908 takes me through the private allotments and apple
orchards that form the back gardens of Yudanaka, Nakano,
Obose and Suzaka, over sideless bridges spanning wide river
beds until we are fairly rocketing along. Now and then a warning sounds as we approach an unmanned crossing. The driver's
response seems to be to increase speed, racing to beat any
pedestrian to the crossing point; it is all very exciting. He
exaggeratedly points at signals showing red or green as if to
convince himself (who else?) that he has noticed them. Forty
minutes of this and we arrive in Nagano (no, not Nakano, close
by) and I find my way to the JR station (a different network)
to meet Kiko and to book the three-hour passage to Nagoya.
Should you ever take this section of the line, sit on the right
side for your better scenic enjoyment. From Nagoya to Kyoto
it's another 30 or 40 minutes, depending on the number of
stops. Now this Kyoto is one of the main reasons for me lin-
gering in Japan. Kiko has been here several times and cancelled
her holiday arrangements in Las Vegas in order to escort me
here and around. If I expected a picturesque city I was in for
a disappointment but it *is* steeped in history, the Tokugawa
shogunate having dominated until 1867 when the Emperor
Meiji took over. The castles, the temples and shrines are
certainly on an impressive scale.

[What follows will not be a meticulously detailed description
of every temple and every shrine visited over the next few days.
To write a definitive treatise on old Japan has not been my aim
– I have neither the inclination nor the qualification for such an
enterprise. There are excellent works already waiting for the
student of Japanese history and architecture – tome upon tome
– and there is a plethora of guidebooks to help the traveller,
many of them well-researched, up-to-date and easy to obtain. All
I hope is that the reader will see beyond my idiosyncratic commentary and accept the selection as *amuses bouches* from a huge
menu to tempt sampling one day at first-hand. By the end of
this one week I had achieved a better understanding of the
Japanese people, their culture and their heritage; they remained
fascinating, their behaviour more explicable and fractionally less
exasperating.]

Peter Westbury

Kiko prefers to eat early in the evening but there was still time,

after booking into the Kokusai Hotel, to scrape into Ninomaru
Palace, within the walled fortress that is Nijo Castle, before it
closed and without rushing. We padded along the corridors in
our stockinged feet, testing the *uguisu-bari* (nightingale floor)
as we went. It seems the Japanese have always had a thing
about intruders (explains a lot!) and contrived
this device. Wherever the floor is trodden
upon, the clamps underneath move up and
down creating friction between the nails and
the clamps which hold the boards in place. This
causes the floor to squeak and it is the bird-like
sound thus produced that gives it the name –
'nightingale floor'. Although only female attendants were allowed into the *Shogun's* living
quarters, treachery not being exclusive to the
male he still wanted to hear them coming. In
case a visitor did reach the audience chambers with evil intent,
concealed behind the seemingly innocuous red-tasselled sliding doors was the bodyguards' room where armed guards
waited in readiness. They were even hidden in the roof above
the earth closets, checking for dangerous weapons concealed
in intimate clothing. This paranoia over knives as instruments
of threat is behind the still traditional and universal use of

**Structure of Uguisu-bari
(Nightingale Floor)**

Foot

(Gravity)

Alcove Slab

Crevice Floor Joints

Clamp

Nail

Nail hole

(Move up and down)

Ninomaru Palace
grounds.

hashi (chopsticks) at the meal table and it is amazing to watch the dexterity with which the Japanese cope daintily with whole fish and larger-than-bite-size portions of much that is served just with these two blunt pieces of wood.

Later, at dinner, I made a reasonable fist of eating with *hashi*. (The next day, at breakfast, I made it much easier for myself by taking the cowardly but strategic measure of choosing only manageable sized items from the self-service buffet.)

I passed comment on the excellence and variety of the vegetables, not just their presentation. Kyoto, being a fair distance from the sea and plentiful supplies of fish, has for centuries specialized in growing vegetables and the local cooks established a reputation for their tasty and imaginative recipes. Sometimes I say the right thing. Kiko, who is an enthusiastic collector of antique *kimonos* (as well as English butlers), was very keen for us to spend the evening in the hotel where *Maiko* was due to perform. *Maiko san* is a phenomenon of Kyoto. (Elsewhere, she has an altogether different role.) By definition under 20 years old, she is a trainee *geisha* and, although in decline, (mainly because their services are really quite expensive even for the Japanese) there are still many of them, known collectively as *Maiko san*. All she does (in Kyoto) is to wear exquisite *kimonos* and elaborate hairdos, dance and play a little music and pour drinks for the guests at a businessman's table. Then she goes home with, no, not the businessman — Y80,000! And the businessmen cough up solely in the interests of preserving the honourable tradition. Admirable. But fortunately tonight we had another option after dark: to go and watch the spectacle of the *ukai* (cormorant fishing) in Arashiyama.

Ukai fishing.

Towards the 'Real' Japan

I didn't mention that I'd already witnessed this 'unique' attraction in Gifu two years ago (as previously described). The price of the taxi was included in the ticket. The price on the meter exceeded the ticket price. Someone had got their sums wrong; perhaps they use the same intuitive method of costing that they use at BH. Anyway, we removed our shoes and clambered aboard the boat, very low in the water, and the boatman poled us along, punt-like, to another mooring on a weir for a close-up view of the fishermen. The other fellow-tourists on board shopped eagerly from a floating supply boat that nudged alongside offering cooked food, novelties and fireworks. One gentleman next to me was ticked off by his wife for tuning in to the sports channel on his pocket radio, 20th century base-ball scores obviously more gripping than 8th century fishing techniques. But we were all suddenly on the alert when a small girl set fire to a giant catherine-wheel and nearly had the canopy alight. Kiko got quite huffy about irresponsible parents but then I suppose she sees a lot of needless accident cases at her hospital. The *u* (cormorants, pronounced 'oo') put on a good show for us, though. Highly recommended.

2nd July 1997

The Japanese calendar is rich with many nationally celebrated festivals and public holidays and in addition each town and village seems to enjoy special events of its own whose pageantry and ritual, music and merry-making, fireworks and dressing-up make them very popular attractions. In number and complexity they more than justify a book in their own right. In fact there are so many of these cultural occasions scattered throughout the year that you would be unlucky if your visit did not overlap with one or two of them. In Kyoto we were unlucky. This was not exactly devastating because we had plenty to occupy us – there are over 1,600 Buddhist temples and 270 Shinto shrines here and we have a day-and-a-half in which to see them. Throw in a distracting festival or two and we'll have no chance! And our timing *had* coincided nicely with the cormorant-fishing season. In any case, I'm not sure, for example, how compelled I would have felt to traipse to the other side of the city to attend what must be one of Kyoto's quaintest ceremonies – the cucumber service – in which people with an ailment write their name, age and type of illness on a form. Temple officials transfer the information to a piece of paper which is then wrapped around a cucumber into which an *o-mamori* (amulet) has been inserted. The cucumber is blessed and handed back to the sufferer who proceeds to rub it over the afflicted part of the body. It is then taken home and buried in the yard. (The cucumber, not the afflicted part.) If you have no yard the temple will bury it for you. When the cucumber rots, the illness goes away! At another temple near to a watering-place and in a variation on this theme, the data is written directly on the cucumber. After the rubbing bit, the vegetable is set in the river, perhaps the least offensive amongst the flotsam you are likely to encounter while bathing.

Another *matsuri* (festival) we missed, just, was the *Tanabata*. This children's festival originated from an ancient Chinese legend concerning two lovers who were turned into stars by the gods (because of their laziness and disrespect – there's usually a moral) and who are re-united but once a year (7th July) when their heavenly paths cross. Children make bamboo decorations around which they dance and sing. Adults buy pairs of paper *ningyo* (dolls); you write your name on one and your partner's name on the other, hang them up together in a bamboo thicket and wish for eternal love. Or three weeks would be good.

Heavy rain altered our original plan to take a walking tour

SANJUSANGENDŌ

and Kiko booked us on to an all-day guided tour by bus covering five or six of her favourite places, the entry tickets for each providing a calligraphic treat in themselves. The holy hall, *Sanjusangendo*, got us off to a most spectacular start. The name means a hall with 33 bays, the number being derived from the belief that *Kannon-Bodhisattva* saves all mankind by disguising himself in 33 images. One thousand and one statues of *Kannon-Basatsu* are ranked in tiers on the vast stepped altar; each is made up of a body composed of many partly hollow blocks of wood, initially only roughly carved; the outside is then carved in detail; in the third stage the statue is coloured or japanned and finally plated with gold leaf. The technique was adopted because it allows several sculptors to work simultaneously on a single figure. It takes 118 metres of hall, 18 metres wide to house this collection in which no two are identical. They take a bit of identifying, too, given the abstract nature of the deification of the majority, Wind and Thunder being easier to nail than Beauty, Wisdom, Devotion, Prosperity, Relief of the Poor, Exorcism or Evil and so on. With 11 faces on each and 20 extra pairs of arms, the arithmetic starts getting out of hand, as it were; and I don't imagine they get dusted very often. Outside and to the rear an historic archery field is still used on special occasions.

The bus brought us to Arashiyama and the Togetsukyo Bridge for a touch of *déjà vu*. It was only a few metres up river from this bridge that we had watched the *ukai* yesterday evening. Without a *bento*, we needed to find a place for lunch so the stop was timely.

The original *Tenryu-ji* had been the Emperor *Kameyama's* villa 650 years ago but it was transformed into a Zen temple after the death of his grandson, the Emperor *Godaigo*, and now ranks foremost among the five great Zen temples in Kyoto. *Tenryu* means dragon, by the way. It seems that a local priest dreamt of a dragon emerging from the river nearby and this was interpreted to mean that the dead Emperor's spirit was restless. To appease the spirit the temple was constructed. After a succession of wars and fires the original chapels or sub-temples, all 150 of them, were wiped out and all that you see today dates from about 1899. What attracts most tourists, though, is the 14th century garden which is exquisite and surrounds a pond shaped like the Chinese hieroglyphic pronounced '*kokuro*' in Japanese which to Zen-Buddhists means 'enlightened heart'. What does take a bit of getting used to is the water-less waterfalls and the empty mini-rivers that are also part of the scheme of things though I can see in practical terms the upkeep is less of a problem. This garden is an excellent example of the Japanese concept of the 'borrowed' landscape where the mountain in the background is incorporated into the overall design inspired, in this case, by a painting of Mount *Horai* (paradise) representing the notion of *nirvana* as held by the Chinese.

What you see on approaching the splendid *Kinkaju-ji* (Golden Pavilion) is entirely reproduction (1955) for it seems that the original building (1397) was burned to the ground (1950) by a monk seeking to 'consummate his obsession with it'. He'd have had difficulty with his matches today in the rain and the wind. The gold-foil exterior is probably even more impressive when the sun shines. By comparison, the *Ginkaku-ji* (Silver Pavilion) looks like a shed. Erected in the 1480s, it never received its intended covering of silver, Shogun *Ashikaga* having died 'before this could be realized'. How it is that the gold pavilion destroyed by the monk in 1950 could be replaced by an exact replica, gold foil and all, by 1955 and yet a pavilion

Peter Westbury

is still called 'silver' after 500 years of waiting for its coating is another of those oriental imponderables. However, this temple does draw the crowds who come in bus loads to see its extraordinarily beautiful raked white sand garden (with its decapitated cone-shaped 'mountain' and meticulously textured 'lake' with parallel waves). Very stylish. Paths lead beyond this area to an extensive moss garden up the hillside which is dissected by brooks. One damp thing after another – especially so today.

Left: The Golden Pavilion and by comparison, *right*: The Silver Pavilion.

Our penultimate stop on this tour was to the *Heian-jingu* shrine, fiercely orange and green. It is another copy, built in 1895 to commemorate the 1,100th anniversary of the founding

Heian-jingu shrine.

of Kyoto. Although on a most impressive scale, the buildings and gateways are actually only two-thirds of the size of the original Imperial Palace of the Heian period. Once again it is the marvellous manicured gardens with their just-so rocks and lakes and bridges that lure the visitor away from the buildings.

Finally to the south-eastern edge of the city and the *Kiyomizu-dera* Temple, up to which we climbed via 'Teapot Lane', so-called because it is lined with many shops selling ceramics. With the sky clearing and a hill-top view of the city,

Kiyomizu-dera
Temple

Peter Westbury

Towards the 'Real' Japan

we could now make out the distinctive candlestick tower near the Central Station. On stepping away from the verandah of the main hall and looking back, you can see that this whole edifice seems perched precariously on the side of the hill, supported by a primitive structure of pegged wooden beams. Cascading into an ornamental basin below is a rivulet of sacred water, held to have medicinal properties. It is possible to bathe there or simply take a scoop and drink. After you, Cecil.

It was convenient for Kiko and me to leave the group at this stage and make our own way to the Hotel Fujita to which our luggage had been transferred. When I opened the opaque-papered sliding inner screens at the 5th floor bedroom window, I found we had an un-interrupted view of a graveyard.

'Well it should be quiet!' said Kiko. A pre-bedtime stroll after dinner found us in an interesting restaurant quarter near the Kamogawa river where, in the summer months, large wooden outdoor platforms called *yuka* are erected to extend over the riverside to form open-air dining areas. Taxis were flitting in all directions, bearing *Maiko san* and her businessmen clients to parties all over the city. The elaborate *kimono* that she wears complete with train takes ages to get into. As, contrary to cynical western belief, no sexual favours are on offer, the speed with which she gets *out* of it is of no real concern – only to her!

3rd July 1997

Before leaving for Nara we have time this morning for some more visual treats that Kiko has in store. Realizing that I am showing more interest in gardens than in religious buildings (that are beginning to merge into one large mental collage of statues, lanterns and gongs), we take a train to see a delightful 'secret' garden, unbelievably well-concealed in the suburbs, that boasts a *suikinkutsu*, a design feature that emerged in

Peter Westbury

Towards the 'Real' Japan

Japan's Edo period. In this type of garden, water drips from a bamboo pipe through a tiny hole in a huge metal vase (sometimes buried), resulting in an incredibly subtle echo. Even gardens, dare I say it, can pall after a time so it was a relief to be seeing something so different; and this was a gem.

However, the setting that really appealed to me, for its remoteness more than anything, was the Zen garden, approached by a 10-minute walk through bamboo groves (traditionally paraded through by brides-to-be for good luck), that had been restored by the movie actor, Okochi Denjiro, famous for his roles in *samurai* epics. We took tea in his villa, which is not as hospitable as it sounds, the actor having died several years ago. The peace and quiet is almost guaranteed, the high entry fee being a deterrent to most, but you get a free postcard as well as the tea and cake and the grounds are tended, well, religiously. Not a great deal of colour in July, but each June and late Autumn should be wonderful; fortunately we found plenty of shade under the acers and acacias on this steaming hot day.

Recovering our bags back at the main station (Tip: a squash rackets sports bag may seem a stylish means of carrying your kit but the left luggage lockers don't come that shape in provincial Japan), we took the Nara line mid-afternoon and eventually checked in to our third hotel in three nights. More expensive and less comfortable than the previous two, it was nevertheless convenient for Nara Park and a romantic wander by the *Sarasawano-ike* (pond) after nightfall. Nara is famous for, among other things, its tame free-ranging deer, revered as divine messengers. You do have to watch out for those messages, though, which are very nearly impossible to see in the dark.

The Great Buddha
Todai-ji.

Westbury Meets East

To Nara

4th July 1997

NARA IS TO Kyoto as Stamford might be to Cambridge or Bath to Bristol. But Kyoto and Nara are bigger. And uglier. For the most part. And actually it's absurd to make the comparisons because they are all very different apart from the shrines and temples which are very much the same except you tend not to get them at all in the Fens or in Avon. Superlatives are a part of any tourist guide's stock-in-trade and today we were to be escorted, rather exclusively as it turned out since there were only Kiko and I in addition to the uniformed guide and driver on the 30-seater bus, to the world's 'largest' wooden hall and 'oldest' wooden structure. I had already seen, back in the spring, a travelling exhibition of Nara temple treasures in the Tokyo National Museum in Ueno Park, with some very impressive sized statues from *Kofugu-ji* on display. However, in no way are they going to be able to shift the huge bronze *buddha* from *Todai-ji*, our first stop today. The Great Buddha stands or rather sits on his lotus throne over 16 metres high in the *Daibutsu-den* (the 'largest wooden hall in

Daibutsu-den.

Towards the 'Real' Japan

the world'), resplendent in his *Yakuza* style perm. The wonder is that he has survived until now. Cast in the year 746, he has been under severe threat ever since from fire, earthquake, riot and civil war, you name it – everything bar theft!

Lest you should think that Kiko and I were alone in this vast temple hall, let me assure you that the team of official photographers was having a hard time coping with bus-load upon bus-load of regimented school-children, each one graded according to his or her height to take their position in the customary group picture. The worst congestion was at the rear of the altar where queues of young girls were waiting to thread themselves through a hole in the leg of a statue, passing through which ensures a life of enlightenment, of no interest to the boys. Perhaps this explains why, among the students who attended courses at BH, it was the girls who seemed noticeably brighter than their well-to-do male contemporaries. Or it may simply be that 'it is easier for a damsel to pass through the knee of an idol than *genki* for Kevin to hint at a rich man!' I had to cheat here. The hole is in fact in the base of a pillar but the spoonerism was struggling to get out.

Just one shrine on today's itinerary: the *Kasuga Taisha* founded in the 8th century. This was the only situation during these days of conducted tours in which I felt an intruder. Whereas other locations seemed 'fair game' as attractions, more museums really than places of worship, this was manifestly a place for private devotion and the atmosphere was very hushed. Some 3,000 stone and bronze lanterns line the paths connecting the various chapels with the main shrine. In Shinto tradition, believers from every social class and occupation pay for prayers or petitions to be attached to these lanterns showing their names and particulars, attesting to the deep foundations of Shintoism among the common people, while historical records show numerous visits by members of the Imperial Court. At festivals held twice a year, in February and August, every single lantern is lit which must be awesome to say the least. They do have a museum here and in it can be seen a collection of armour and masks used in ritual dances. Pride of place is given to The Drum which, it will be no surprise, is claimed to be 'the largest drum in the world'. In the grounds, too, are more of the sacred deer, the description endorsed by one English-speaking visitor who was overheard referring to them as 'blessed deer'; they can be a nuisance.

And so it's onwards to more temples. Next on our agenda are 'the world's oldest surviving wooden structures' in the

Lanterns.

Peter Westbury

grounds of *Horyu-ji* where even the *replacement* buildings (due, *comme d'habitude* to the destruction by fire of the originals) date from the late 7th century. This place is chiefly renowned for giving house-room to some 2,300 of Japan's rarest treasures in some very imposing halls, temples and *pagodas* but at this stage of my initiation they are all beginning to look alike, which is not a criticism; in Europe old churches and cathedrals look pretty much like other old churches and cathedrals and one *can* have a surfeit of *them*. As a form of thanksgiving- prayer *conditional* to his own recovery from illness, the Emperor *Yomei* vowed to build a temple and an image of a *buddha*. This seemed to cut no ice with the Men Upstairs. The quacks were no help either and shortly after making the vow, regrettably he died. But, stout fellow, seemingly unmiffed, he had made it clear on his death bed that his promise was to be fulfilled and further-

Towards the 'Real' Japan

more that the *buddha* statue be dedicated, ironically, to the god of healing.

[Ever since this time doctors have been placed on pedestals regardless – and not just in Japan. Very often the pedestals are of the doctors' own construction . . . and portable.]

In December 1993, as a unique storehouse of world Buddhist culture, *Horyu-ji* became the first Japanese treasure-base to be selected by UNESCO as part of the World Heritage. This has put it fairly and squarely on the tourist trail. Fire walls and other safety mechanisms are to be installed. Everywhere there are triads and individual statues representing all manner of *kannons*, monks, guardians and warriors in bronze or cam-phorwood, sandalwood or clay. I like the idea of a Dream-changing *Kannon* (*Yumechigai*), believed to change omi-nous dreams into auspicious ones. There are a few people that I have encountered recently for whose benefit I would dearly like to set his powers in reverse. The Hall of Dreams (*Yumedono*) is worth a mention. This octagonal pavilion is enclosed within a cloistered gallery in the Eastern Precinct and enshrines the *Kuse Kannon*, a life size statue of Prince *Shotoku*, regent successor to the Emperor whose fatal illness had sparked the whole thing off, a rather misplaced metaphor given the combustible nature of the site. The prince's image has sur-vived in a perfect state of preservation to this day, retaining even its original gilding. We had to take this on trust, how-ever, because it can only be viewed on a very few days, normally being kept hidden and in the dark (to preserve it, of course! Perfectly logical. Imagine applying this thinking to museums all over the world . . .). Novice guides in spick new uniforms were undergoing instruction in this courtyard. The amount of historical detail that they have to memorize must be enor-mously daunting but there seems to be no shortage of willing applicants. To promulgate the city's religious artefacts is esteemed a great honour. Some of them never stop reciting from the minute you join the tour and only in Japanese.

The *Jiko-in* Temple is only 334 years old. The main purpose for calling here seems to be to take a quick circuit round the garden and then to participate in the tea ceremony in which this Temple specializes and which jacks up the entrance fee. I must say a nice cup of tea would have gone down very well indeed. Unfortunately, I have never been able to develop a lik-ing for green tea nor for the green tea flavoured cake which they now proceed to serve. I drink the tea, of course, and eat the cake to be polite. But I never enthuse in case they bring me seconds. It's less unpalatable if you add sugar to the tea but it's certainly not the done thing. I can just see myself shrinking, stage-centre in a Bateman cartoon – 'The Man who Asked for Sugar in his O-cha!' There is much more to the *chanoyu* (tea ceremony) than is apparent to the *gaijin* but then a full appreciation of the 'art' is said to take years of reflection. A highly refined etiquette, mental discipline and devotion are involved and special schools exist to teach the ceremonial skills. It's not just a matter of 'Let's put the kettle on and all have tea'.

To the *Yakushi-ji* Temple. Again various terrible mishaps befell this complex since it was first completed in 698, only to be moved, every hall, storehouse and chapel, to this site twenty years later. It had been planned by the Emperor *Temmu* as a petition for the recovery of his Empress from a serious illness. Sound familiar? Well this time, as so often happens, it was the healthy one who went first and it was left to his widow to creak around and carry out his plan. All but one of the existing buildings are re-constructions, some only completed as recently as 1976 and 1980. '*Yaku*' means drug and '*Yakushi-ji*' translates as 'temple of the drug-god' (god of medicine not god of marijuana) and the drug-god statues are distinguishable from the other *buddhas* by the jar held in the cupped left hand.

Only rather confusingly to the foreigner at any rate, the statue in this temple (actually *named* after the Drug-God) does not hold the jar. Look instead for the medicine chest on which he is sitting in place of the usual sacred lotus.

Pagoda at Yakushi-ji

Peter Westbury

Towards the 'Real' Japan

The East Pagoda ('*pagoda*' just means grave) is the only building to have survived the fires, wars and natural disasters over the centuries, the most damage having been caused to the others during the civil war in 1528. [Many Japanese buildings are embellished with ornamental charms to protect them against fire of which there is a profound and justified fear considering their principally wooden construction. So dolphins can be seen on castle roofs, fish-tails on a temple hall and *suien* (flamey splashing water signs) on finials of a *pagoda*. These water symbols are incorporated into the design to guarantee a plentiful supply of water in the event of fire. They'd do better to spend the money on a few water-butts and a pump or two.] This *pagoda* at *Yakushi-ji* is not your standard three or five-tiered *pagoda*. It is a rare three-storeyed *pagoda* posing as a six-storey *pagoda* because of the *mokoshi* (lean-to!) added to each storey. The Japanese call this style 'Frozen Music' because of the 'fine rhythmic balance of its appearance'. Not a lot of people know that. The steeple-looking bit on the top with the nine rings is the *sorin* and is the symbol for a *buddha*'s grave.

Our last call in Nara today was at the Temple of *Toshadai* to which many pilgrims throng on special days of the year to worship at the tomb of *Ganjin*, the Chinese abbot invited by Emperor *Shomu* to come and teach his precepts to a Japan that was gradually forming herself into a Buddhist country. Having accepted the task, it wasn't until 12 years later that he arrived, having made five unsuccessful tries at crossing the ocean. He must have been pretty determined because by this time he had totally lost his eyesight. He was 67 and was only to live 9 more years, five of them spent in Kyoto based at the *Todai-ji*, and four at this place. He set up training programmes and ordination platforms at both temples. In the fullness of time Japan embraced Buddhism. The *Miedo* Hall contains a magnificent lacquered wooden statue of *Ganjin* (familiar from frequent photographic reproduction); it is on view only once a year, the 6th of June, to coincide

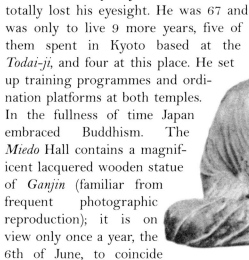

Abbot
Ganjin

Westbury Meets East

with May 6th, the anniversary of his death in the old lunar calendar.

5th July 1997

Our last few hours in Nara and we took a train out to the north-western suburban edge of the city where Kiko wanted to show me her favourite garden with special magnolia trees whose fascination is that the flowers bloom and drop within the span from dawn to dusk on a single day. On the walk from the station we were fortunate in seeing the *hasu* (lotus) in bloom, springing out of muddy pond waters showing large pink and white flowers that last no more than four days in the intense July heat. By mid-afternoon they have closed right up again so our timing was excellent. To the Japanese this short-lived blossom suggests reincarnation, the circular leaves and pointed petals implying the perpetual cycle of existence. The phenomenon of pure flowers rising from the mud is supposed to symbolize enlightenment for all. The roots, well-rinsed, are edible and feature in many Japanese dishes. Later, the seed-pods will have an attractive honeycomb appearance and the seeds themselves will be used as Buddhist rosary beads.

Afterwards we had another, more successful, crack at a tea ceremony charmingly served by a handsome shaven-headed young monk in a delightfully tranquil tea-house in a garden setting designed for meditation. The language barrier was no disadvantage as communication was discouraged with human beings and encouraged with nature so we spent a relaxing hour with an increasing feeling of well-being (if not actual enlight-

enment), gazing from the open-sided *tatami* room at the neatly clipped topiary and the distant borrowed landscape.

Evening found us much further south in Toba on the Pacific coast where we are to stay for two nights in a luxury apartment, courtesy of Kiko's sister except that she doesn't know.

6th July 1997

Toba attracts tourists for its famous *Mikimoto* cultured pearl industry and has all the promotional machinery ticking over ready and waiting to demonstrate (and sell) the product. Divers and demonstrators dive and demonstrate, taking the visitor through every process from seeding to threading but I had had enough of being a tourist and suggested we gave it a miss. Instead we took the sister's car and the coastal toll-road to enjoy the freedom of non-public transport and see the local scenery.

Even with the aircon on maximum, the car was like an oven and after a couple of hours we returned to the town, shopped for some food and I cooked in the flat.

More spacious than the Yudanaka *apato*, the interior of her sister's place gives one the sensation of being on board ship with a magnificent view from the 'bridge' which faces a kilometre wide ocean inlet. Below and to the left is a small sandy cove beyond which there is a cliff path to an hotel that Kiko recommends we use for breakfast tomorrow (she never cooks). With the sun now less fierce we walked down to the beach and jetty, over which crawled scores of, well, crawly things. Not very nice. Then we climbed back to a neighbouring condominium, to the top floor, where I was introduced to an amazing piece of equipment that surely qualifies for an entry in my 'Only In Japan?' list. Called a 'Body Sonic Refresh Capsule', it is an armchair shaped metal structure with comfortably padded leather arms, head, back and leg rests, with a cowl and visor and built-in headphones. The sound selector is lettered A to K

Westbury Meets East

Luxury armchair.

and, at forty channels per letter, the listener has access to 440 international radio stations and audio-tapes. The bass tuner is adjustable so that the intensity of vibration through one's lower back and buttocks may be varied. It is, quite literally, sensational! And when I win the lottery I shall have one.

7th July 1997

By taxi and four trains we returned to our bases, Kiko to Chiba, me back here to Nagano-*ken*. From outside on the balcony I can hear the Yudanaka Town Silver Band practising on the floodlit riverside gateball pitch in competition with the strains of 'The Best of Tim Rice' coming through the open window. The musicians are in full regalia, satin stripe down the outside legs of the trousers, instruments gleaming. What I had taken to be the mace from this distance, turns out to be a flash camera tripod (perhaps it doubles); they are, of course, having their pictures taken. It's not clear what part the orange track-suited figure is playing. My guess is that he's the groundsman. The whole group is being photographed and quite right, too.

[I always think of bad spellers when I think of groundsmen. The groundsman at my prep-school was appointed Spelling Master in addition to his grass-cutting duties and he was absolutely useless. He was the headmistress' brother and slightly manic; whereas she was completely so.]

At one stage, their marching is in perfect unison with 'Salve Regina' which is to say quite brisk. They rehearse their formations over and over, the bandleader toppling exaggeratedly into his forward march to give the others their cue.

Later. All over Japan, *futons* are being pulled from sliding-door cupboards and patiently re-prepared for bed-time. It is to be hoped the band buglers wrap it up soon, particularly as they seem to have got stuck at fanfares!

'Brown Legs" house is in darkness.

Peter Westbury

Towards the 'Real' Japan

The Door Marked
Cactus

8th July 1997

WITH ALL MY JOB LEADS in Japan leading nowhere, plan B, the flight back to the UK on the 12th seems inevitable. I now have to think of a way of delivering Kiko's Nissan back to Chiba without her knowledge as to when. I don't imagine she'd appreciate seeing me and Miyuki off together at Narita Aiport! I do feel badly about deceiving her over my departure date – I've told her the 15th – because she's dead keen to put me up the night before and to make her last farewell. Far kinder, I think, that she should not encounter Miyuki; nor Miyuki her!

Tomorrow I have an interview with the pleasant-sounding head of a language school in Nagano-*shi* but it's not really what I'm after. The lady wanted to engage me over the telephone there and then but I demurred as I also want to check out the nearby Hotel Phenix (*sic*) in case there's an opportunity there. The Norwegian Olympic Ski Team are to be housed from November in this resort hotel prior to their training and in theory they will need someone to help them over the language hurdle.

9th July 1997

Masako *san*, who turned out to own not one but five language schools in and around Nagano, was a chic diminutive lady in a very fetching hat and a delight to meet. By contrast, her overweight pot-bellied American associate was tricked out in a mesh tee-shirt, more a vest really, hideous horror-comic tattoos covering the exposed areas of his arms and only slightly less conspicuous under the fabric, the see-through nature of his sartorial turn-out revealing that these pictorial treats continued over the rest of his torso and who knows how far beyond. It was hate at first sight.

My overtures to the Hotel Phenix were a similar non-event – the manager would be away for a few days. A few days and I'll be out of here.

Westbury Meets East

10th July 1997

Au revoir, 'Brown Legs'.

11th July 1997

All I have to do is stay close to the Toyota in front (licence no. 58–53 which, ironically, states both what I am and what I claim to be) and I should end up at Sakura for my last night in Japan. Teresa Teng has sung 'So long' on the in-car CD player. Outside it's throwing it down, making it that much easier to be leaving. The rainy season took hold this week with a vengeance that claimed many lives in the Kyushu mudslide. In the pilot car, whose spray is keeping my wipers on double time, is Tanaka *san*, a colleague from the early days at BH, dedicated to its success but who lost his popularity with the directors and was discarded. And he's not a *gaijin*. They didn't dismiss him; just moved him sideways to the university on a fraction of the pay; but he is much happier. His task at this minute is to find the way (from my description!) to the hospital car park where I can safely and conveniently leave Kiko's car, mailing her the key with an explanatory note. She is normally on duty at this time on a Friday...

I transferred to the Toyota without being spotted and was soon being welcomed by Tanaka *san's* wife in their Sakura home. Aware of my churned up feelings on the eve of my departure, they showed every kindness and consideration, not expecting me to be falsely jolly and understood when I opted for an early night. But I've been kept awake by a book, a farewell gift from Tanaka *san*; a book that I should have read three years ago: 'The *Kata* Factor'. Had I done so, I might have coped better with the cultural pitfalls that beset the *gaijin* working in Japan instead of finding myself, hurt and bewildered and poised at the door marked cactus.

12th July 1997

Nihon Sayonara. Airborne, now, on the Cathay Pacific flight that will take us via Hong Kong to Europe where Miyuki and I will spend a few days together in Paris and London. We each have a return ticket; will both of us use it? Would I want to return to such a frustrating country? But for the shabby treatment at

Peter Westbury

the end, the answer would have been 'Yes'. I really hoped that my experience, the disgraceful breach of a signed agreement, the insultingly peremptory manner of the serving of notice, the unprofessional handling of many situations, the deceptions and my consequent distrust, were all abnormal. But subsequent correspondence that has reached me from other foreign contract workers has only confirmed the widely held view that the *gaijin* is dispensable, an entertainer at best, a mercenary at worst, to be discarded and paid off at will. What is hard to acknowledge is that while senior colleagues act in friendly fashion, that is all that it is – an act. But their discomfort was real enough when they broke the news and witnessed my disbelief at their duplicity. They knew they were morally in the wrong. They knew they had no quarrel with my work, that I enjoyed the respect of my staff, that I had made tireless efforts working all God's hours to make every guest feel special. The whole episode has puzzled me. Had I, in their eyes, become too popular? Had I, in my push for higher salaries, been unrealistically hopeful of their co-operation? Had I expected too much from their nods that signify only that you have been heard and not that they will be taking any positive action? Or had I simply not taken on board their *kata*, the time-honoured way of doing (or should that be NOT doing) things. They are world-renowned as imitators, not innovators. They hate to be first; they prefer to play it safe; they are in no hurry. They are as uncomprehending of 'western' impatience with delaying procedures and interminable meetings as we are of their reluctance to confront incompetents among their number and their acceptance of prolonged indecisiveness. Was there, perhaps, resentment at our proposals for doing things in the British style? That was, after all, what I believed we had been invited to contribute. Our ideas were very largely ignored (or at any rate unadopted) and I now predict a rapid Japanization of the venture. Many of my Japanese friends were kind enough to write expressing their surprise and dismay at my departure. They may also be surprised and dismayed at my conclusions. Miyuki, sat next to me now, Sashiko, Kiko and the rest have been so genuine, warm and responsive. Let it be clear that I have only happy memories of good times shared; socially I could not have hoped for better. It is exclusively the men folk on the work front that have soured the experience and as this account has been written in part as a cautionary tale so that others might be forewarned, I have to conclude that I would not want to be obliged to do business in Japan. But, should you

Westbury Meets East

have no choice, then read, absorb and implement 'The *Kata* Factor' in advance, be prepared for your negotiations to take forever and be sure you never try to bend their logic.

Better still, though: forget business. Time your visit for a prolonged recreational stay – Japan is a wonderful country in which to keep middle age at bay!

Now then; where to next?

Peter Westbury

O kiotsukete

Appendices

Appendix A

E XTRACTS FROM PERSONAL CORRESPONDENCE.

Letter from a *gaijin* acquaintance working as a teacher in Japan.

Dated July 1997

Dear Peter,

Thank you very much for bothering to write to me after all that has happened to you in your last few weeks in Japan. They really can be quite despicable people at times and yours is a familiar story. It has happened to me and to several people I know. One man I knew, with an MA and a PhD, was given two weeks notice to leave his university, simply because the administration had decided they didn't need so many foreign teachers after all.

We have no rights, you see, and are not considered part of the essential scheme of things; just background decoration – or furniture, as you pointed out. The only way to deal with this is to accept it. It is simply a fact and nothing personal. It's not that they don't like you or me. They don't even think of you and me. They think simply: how can I use this *gaijin?* Do I need it or not?

If you realize this and play by the rules, you can make a certain amount of money. You must be an entertainer and then leave the country regularly for rest and recreation. I would advise you to come back to Japan; you should easily find a job with companies that send foreigners to drill the salarymen in basic English. With your dramatic flair and self-possession you would be a knockout. Just don't expect to make friends with them.

Westbury Meets East

Please let me know what you decide to do . . . remember they just want to be entertained.

Be of good heart and assured of a remembrance in my prayers.

Every best wish,
B.R. (Saitama-*ken.*)

Letter from a Japanese guest.
Dated 1st July 1997

Dear Westbury *san*,

I was flabbergasted to hear that you were leaving Bridewell Heath. I honestly cannot think of the place without you.

You must be feeling rather sad and tired.

I told Madame Reika about this at once. She was also shocked. I know she was thinking of inviting you to Aurora Pavilion so that we can welcome you with the same warmth we received at Bridewell Heath.

I hereby pass you her message:

'Please visit us at Aurora Pavilion. Stay as long as you like – a few days, a week, a month, it doesn't matter. We wish to do our best to help you regaining peace of mind. You would certainly like the tranquil air here. It will be our joy if you could just relax and enjoy yourself.'

I would not like to press you, but it would be too much of a shame if we cannot see you again.

Please contact me whenever convenient. In the meantime, please take care of yourself. Our members all send you the best regards.

I look forward to hearing from you.

Cordially yours,
E.S. (Chiba-*ken*).

Peter Westbury

Appendix B
Newspaper cuttings

LETTER TO THE EDITOR, Daily Yomiuri. Dated 13th September 1997.

Sir,

I have lived and worked in Japan for nine years for a large national company. I speak fluent Japanese and have no problems securing a guarantee for renting my apartment.

I recently decided I needed to change and set out with a few colleagues to find a new place. To my surprise and regret most real estate agents refused to help me because I am a *gaijin*.

The biggest shock came from seeing signs that read 'No pets/No foreigners!' on many of the agents' doors.

Does this mean that animals and foreigners should be treated equally?

The government, I read, is planning measures to increase the number of foreigners coming to Japan to study. How will they be housed? In the Hotel Okura?!

Yours,
T.K. (Tokyo)

Letter to the Editor, Daily Yomiuri.
Dated 15th September 1997.

I read a criticism recently from one of your correspondents concerning the lack of opportunity for conversation practice with native English speakers. There are not, he wrote, enough to

Westbury Meets East

meet the demand.

As an employer and sponsor of native English speakers, I can testify that Japan's immigration policies are always difficult and sometimes ludicrous. I am reluctant to bring any more teachers into the country myself because I am fed up with jumping through the bureau's ridiculous hoops.

I have had teachers wrongfully deported – after they had carefully followed the explicit instructions of the Immigration Bureau (who later allowed them to return after much expense and inconvenience). When I, as their sponsor, called Immigration to resolve the issues, I had the phone slammed in my ear with hardly a word exchanged. This was not an isolated incident. It has happened on several occasions.

I don't know of any native English speakers (long- or short-term residents) who find dealing with our Immigration Authorities anything but a sorry ordeal. If the Immigration Bureau were a business with a shred of accountability, it would have gone out of business a long time ago.

Yours,
Name with-held. (Osaka-*ken*)

Letter to the Editor, Daily Yomiuri.
Dated 22nd September 1997.
(The Japanese government refuses to allow mention of the Nanjing massacre to appear in school text-books).

Sir,

The recent ruling by the Supreme Court clearly supports continuing censorship of all textbooks.

The whole concept of distorting history textbooks is considered repulsive in the modern world. When the truth concerns atrocities committed over 50 years ago during World War II, this censorship exposes a flaw in the Japanese culture. The fact that it is still condoned by the highest court in Japan is frankly deplorable.

Peter Westbury

Because Japanese culture *discourages complaint, questioning or protest.*(my italics) the extent of censorship is quite probably far-reaching. For example, the government's mis-management of nuclear fuel is widely acknowledged but criticism is denied.

Japan is looking for a more senior position in the United Nations but how could Japan participate in a UN Security Council hearing on war atrocities while it censors its own? If Japan seeks fuller recognition as a world power then it *needs to overcome its culture*, become critical of itself and show the world that it *can* learn from its mistakes and not ignore them.

Only then will Japan be a true democracy living with its past as well as its present, both good and bad.

Yours,

S.W. (Tokyo)

Appendix C

H ANDOVER LETTER to the replacement butler, Bridewell Heath. Dated 12th June 1997.

To Whom It May Concern:

At today's date, the senior Japanese staff are still telling me that they do not know your name (!) so I am unable to afford you the courtesy. You should come to expect their strange ways quite quickly. Communications are difficult enough because of the language problem but Japanese also have this thing about not telling you anything that, in their opinion, you don't need to know. Don't be discouraged. Just grasp, as soon as you can, that decisions that you would take five minutes to make in England, will take five months or more at Bridewell Heath. And many, many meetings.

Good people have resigned here out of disillusionment. Most of us were ill-prepared for the dilatory and sheer incompetent qualities of the decision-makers and those who 'run' the place. I did not resign. My contract was simply not renewed. My resentment at the way it was handled and the timing (which is how we came not to meet, which is crazy!) has subsided, so please don't make the mistake of interpreting any of my comments here as bitter; I am trying to be helpful. The change of butler came out of the blue and without any negotiation. I mention this in case you find yourself treated in the same way. Watch out for yourself.

My 'crime' was to campaign too strenuously for better working conditions and, in particular, salaries for the work-holiday service staff. I wrote two proposals – well reasoned arguments for increases – and only succeeded in making myself unpopular. So beware. The Japanese directors have little or no experience in the hospitality industry. This wouldn't be so ter-

Peter Westbury

Appendices

rible if they'd only learn as they go but they keep repeating the same mistakes. Of course, it will help matters if you are fluent in Japanese! I have become increasingly intolerant and critical, I'm afraid. At the beginning I could tell myself (and them) that they were paying me a lot of money to ignore; latterly, however, with a salary reduced by 25% with the drop in the value of the *yen*, that is no longer true!

Naturally, I am professional enough to want to help you with a smooth handover. This is made more difficult by the capricious Japanese decision to ask me to vacate by June 15th and you, I gather, do not move in until later. There is something grievously deficient with their mentality. Take care who you befriend and who you make your enemy.

In spite of all this I shall miss the place terribly, having been instrumental in generating many happy evenings and successful events for appreciative guests. It has only been the dynamic inertia of the hand-me-down staff from Tokyo that has spoiled the experience.

You will have much to read and absorb upon your arrival so I will keep my directions to the point:

Firstly, . . ./recruitment . . ./training . . ./purchasing . . ./imigration procedures . . ./staff welfare . . ./emergencies . . . etc.

All of this would have been infinitely easier if you had arrived before my departure.

One of your pleasant duties (though actually voluntary) is to arrange staff outings to cultural centres. Favourites have been Aizu Wakamatsu and Nikko, both of historical interest. In addition, when I've had the free time I've taken staff on informal outings in the Ura Bandai, Nasu Highland Park and on hikes many and various. All part of keeping your crew happy.

Have you ever addressed the haggis, appeared on television, acted as a male model? You are about to learn! For the more usual butler pursuits, like re-stocking the wine cellar, for example, you'll be taking a back seat. In the matter of wine you'd be over-ridden by the D-G, anyway; which is a pity as he really knows very little about it. Lines of supply for most products have nothing to do with obtaining the best deal. Everything

Westbury Meets East

hinges on what is called the *konnei* (connection). Better that you, the *gaijin*, do not become involved.

They have given me an insultingly short amount of time to pack, perform my usual duties, orientate the new staff arrivals, write your brief and leave the place tidy! And all because they won't pay me for eleven untaken National Holidays owing to me. If ever there was a case of cutting off one's nose!

I wish you good luck in your endeavours. I'm certain there will be some more changes here soon; hopefully they may find the right targets next time.

I cannot supply you with a contact address while I remain in Japan as I shall be on the move, trying to see some of the 'real' Japan I've been too busy to visit. If I think of any other vitally useful information before I leave I will place it with this letter on what used to be my desk.

Yours sincerely,
Peter Westbury,
Butler of Bridewell Heath, 1994–1997.

Peter Westbury

Appendix D

G UIDED TOUR OF THE MANOR HOUSE (requested in English). Abridged.

14th June 1997.

'Good morning, my name is Westbury. As the butler, it is my privilege to welcome you to Bridewell Heath.

'We are standing in the Main Hall of the Manor House. In England a manor house is usually the family home of a wealthy landowner. Increasingly, these houses fall into ownership by the nation as they become too expensive for individuals to afford;

Peter Westbury The circular silk rug and crystal chandelier.

they become what are known as "Stately Homes" and are open to view by the public much as you are doing today. The designers of this Manor House were asked to create a Victorian atmosphere through their choice of furniture and interior decoration. Queen Victoria was on the throne for an amazing span of sixty years during which time furniture and furnishings had time to undergo great changes. The Victorians also travelled widely, visiting not only Europe but the other continents of the world, returning from Africa, America and Asia with ideas and artefacts borrowed from many countries, sometimes even stolen. So the designers working on this project were drawing on an era rich in variety. This could have resulted in an inglorious mish-mash of styles all fighting against each other. Fortunately, the designers used the trick of lining the public spaces with mahogany panels to give it all not just a richness but a unity. So, against this wonderful warm background is set a collection of allsorts: Mediterranean columns, ecclesiastical screens, Gothic arches, linenfold carvings, William Morris botanical prints, Pembroke tables, Ottoman settees, oriental carpets and a miscellany of paintings and ceramics...

'It is a beautiful day so I suggest, before we move upstairs and while the sun is shining, we step outside to take a look at the façade and especially at the Bridewell Heath coat of arms above the portals. The shield is divided into quarters. At the top left hand corner you can see the letters RS, the initials of our President, Mr Sako. To their right you will see, not the logo of the Toyota Motor Corporation, but that of the Sako Foundation that administers this place which was the brainchild of Mrs Sako, the President's late mother who unfortunately did not live to see her dream come true. At the bottom left of the shield is the oak tree – a symbol of strength; it is also a reminder of the number of trees that were felled to provide the half-timbered method of construction of ten of the village buildings. Finally, in the lower right hand quarter is seen an open book – symbol of a place of learning...

'As we return to the Main Entrance Hall, please look up and notice the ceiling. A name you may recognize is that of Sir Josiah Wedgwood. Born in 1730, he lived and worked one hundred years before the Victorian age but he was extremely popular and influenced their design thinking. His designs were created for bone china not for ceilings, it being generally felt a lot easier to eat off plates, but the BH designers drew on his

Westbury Meets East

patterns for their inspiration. He is still much admired in Japan today and if you should be passing through Mitsukoshi's Tokyo store basement you will see many examples from the Wedgwood factory... The stained glass window was made in six sections and shipped all the way to the top of this mountain in Fukushima from the workshops of Salisbury Cathedral in Wiltshire...

'... The five carved panels displayed in the Upper Hall came from Indonesia. Unfortunately, historical accuracy was not the sculptors' strong point. When first unveiled, the panel showing the Elizabethan galleons bore the legend 'Admiral Nelson Rules The Waves'. It has been easier to change the lettering than re-carve the ships so now it is 'Sir Francis Drake...' who 'Rules The Waves'!! Sorry, Your Lordship...

'... The circular hand-woven silk rug on which we are all standing came from Pakistan. At today's exchange rate, this is valued at (gingerly stepping backwards and off it) £80,000... This Bohemian crystal chandelier is the largest in the Manor House. We have two problems with this chandelier: firstly, it has to be cleaned; secondly, it swings about a lot during an earthquake. Actually, these buildings stand on foundations that incorporate a secret formula that will withstand up to force 6 on the Richter scale. This formula is known only to the construction company and myself. I am honour-bound not to divulge the details to anyone, unless they can come up with a suitable amount of cash... The Upper Hall has been used for a number of successful functions, from receptions to fashion shows. Also, by rolling back the carpet and playing appropriate music, it makes an ideal venue for social dancing classes. That is the good news. The bad news is that *I* am the teacher!...

'... Please follow me into what is my own favourite room. Our Library has been designed to resemble the Reading Room in a gentlemen's club in St James', London, a feature of which would be exclusively male membership. *No* ladies! On these shelves you will find upwards of 1,600 antique books imported from Hay-on-Wye on the borders of England and Wales...

'... We have two chess sets on display. This one depicts figures from Tudor times. Henry VIII, that's him here, had six wives. You see there's always someone worse off than yourself.

Peter Westbury

Appendices

Caterina of Aragon, a Spanish lady, was King Henry's brother's widow and after years of not producing the male heir that Henry desired, Henry sought to have the marriage nullified, believing God to be dis-pleased. However, the Pope was not disposed to upset relations with the Emperor Charles V, Caterina's nephew, by co-operating with Henry and managed to prevaricate for seven whole years. In the meantime Henry had met the promiscuous Anne Boleyn whose eventual pregnancy, in spite of Henry's impotence (contrary to his popular image of manliness), speeded up the need for a divorce and made a secret marriage necessary especially as the soothsayers were predicting a son. Anne gave birth to Elizabeth who, three monarchs later, became Elizabeth I. The bishop, here, is Cranmer; appointed by Henry, he, of course, engineered the divorce from Caterina. Anne took lovers and was beheaded (action and sound of chopping). Wife number three was Jane Seymour. She was lucky – she died! Cromwell persuaded Henry to accept an arranged marriage to Anne of Cleves which may have been politically correct but Henry found her singularly unattractive, dubbing her the 'Mare of Flanders'. Another divorce later and Henry was married to wife number five, Catherine Howard. Upon her adultery, she, too, was beheaded (chopping pantomime again). So Catherine Parr became the sixth wife of Henry the Eighth. And *she* was lucky – Henry died! . . .

'. . . The other chess set shows figures from the Sherlock Holmes stories . . .

'. . . Have we any married ladies here today? . . . Single ladies? . . . Really?! Me, too . . . Actually, I've been single many times. Can anyone tell me what this piece of furniture here might be? No? Well it's a kissing couch (Demonstrate with single lady, stopping short of embarrassing her). Please do not ask me what a kissing couch is doing in a gentlemen's club! . . .

'. . . Here, Sir George Hayter's splendid portrait of Queen Victoria at the age of 19, taking the Sovereign's Oath on the altar steps of Westminster Abbey, leaves you in no doubt, thanks to his skilful draughtsmanship as to the silk, velvet, lace and brocade of the clothes and vestments. He has even made the young Queen realistically pretty – which she never was . . .

Westbury Meets East

'. . . (Pantomime of knocking on the door of 'Her Majesty's

'The most dangerous room in the whole prefecture.'

Bedchamber before entering). This room has been furnished to resemble one of the private rooms at Buckingham Palace or Windsor Castle. It is as though one family has collected the pieces over a period of time, this time a justifiable mish-mash: the French *chaise longue* and *chiffonier*, the Regency dining suite and striped satin chairs, the Irish marble-topped consol, the German wardrobes and the colonial half-tester with its painted decoration piled on top of the early Victorian ornately carved original. In the bathroom, too, a mixture of styles: French Empire, art deco, English porcelain, American gold filigree accessories and – *Toto* [leading Japanese manufacturer of sanitary ware and heated loo-seats!] . . .

' . . . In the King's Room – a magnificent Tudor post and panel tester bed. I am frequently asked whether it is possible for guests to book into these royal bedrooms and the answer is: 'Most certainly!' – if you can afford ¥80,000 a night. Meals are extra but butler service comes free! Actually only two people have slept in this bed. (Pause.) *Me!* To test it out. And Hitachinomiya-*denka!* . . .

'The portraits that line the Gallery show nine British Victorians who were invited to Japan by the Emperor *Meiji* to take part in his programme of westernization. They came to set up universities, hospitals, libraries, newspapers, build lighthouses, make maps and so on and so forth. Probably the best known is Sir Thomas Glover who introduced and developed ship building and coal mining and whose house in Nagasaki is open to the public. He is credited with inspiring the character of Pinkerton in 'Madam Butterfly'. He dealt in gold and silver and also imported guns at the time of the Satsuma Rebellion. Unfortunately for him, he over-estimated the volume of arms needed and went bankrupt. However, in recognition of his services to Japan, the Emperor bestowed on him the Award of the Rising Sun, *second* class! That showed him. A bit like losing a shilling and finding sixpence . . .

Peter Westbury

Appendices

'The Snooker Room is popular with students, of course, though they do complain that the pocket jaws are not as wide as those on a pool table. Ladies are very welcome to play as well as the gentlemen and tuition is available free from our good-looking young male staff of all ages! . . .

'I'm now going to show you the most dangerous room in the whole prefecture. Here we are in The Chapel. People *get married* here! As a matter of fact we have only had the one wedding here so far. In May 1995, Miss Suzuki came to Bridewell Heath to marry Mr Honda – and they drove away in a *Mazda*! This is a true story! May I draw your attention to two antiques in our chapel: firstly, the pulpit dated about 1875 and imported from Yorkshire; and secondly, me! – undated and about to be *de*ported!

'Thank you for listening if you have been. If you have any questions my staff and I are here to assist in any way we can and to do our best to make your stay memorable'.

And so it's 'Goodbye' from him to all of that and them.

Westbury Meets East

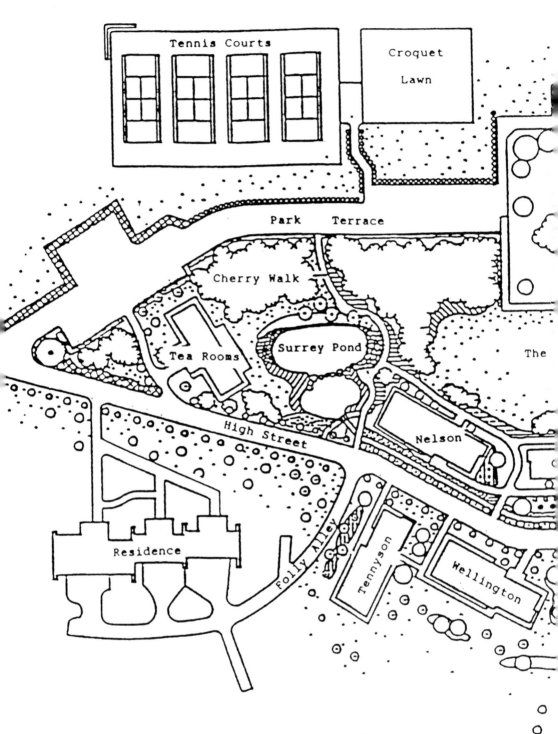

Tennis Courts

Croquet Lawn

Park Terrace

Cherry Walk

Tea Rooms

Surrey Pond

The

High Street

Nelson

Residence

Folly Alley

Tennyson

Wellington

Bridewell Heath

Fukushima-ken, JAPAN